Contemporary Irish Filmmakers

Contemporary Irish Writers and Filmmakers

General Series Editor:
Eugene O'Brien, Head of English Department, Mary Immaculate College, University of Limerick.

Titles in the series:

Forthcoming:

Contemporary Irish Filmmakers

Neil Jordan

Exploring Boundaries

Emer Rockett and Kevin Rockett

The Liffey Press

Published by The Liffey Press
Ashbrook House, 10 Main Street,
Raheny, Dublin 5, Ireland.
www.theliffeypress.com

A catalogue record of this book is
available from the British Library.

ISBN 1-904148-18-2 paperback
1-904148-28-X hardback

*This book has been published with the assistance of grant-aid from
An Chomhairle Ealaíon, The Arts Council of Ireland*

Printed in the Republic of Ireland by Colour Books Ltd.

Contents

About the Authors

Emer Williams Rockett has taught film studies at University College Dublin, National College of Art and Design, Dún Laoghaire Institute of Art, Design and Technology, and on New York University's Dublin film programme. She has written on or presented papers on Irish cinema, the body and technology, and on the visual arts, while her research interests include cultural theory and early cinema.

Kevin Rockett is a Lecturer in Film Studies, Trinity College Dublin. He is co-author of *Cinema and Ireland* (1987), *Still Irish: A Century of the Irish in Film* (1995), *The Companion to British and Irish Cinema* (1996), and *Irish Film Board 1993–2003* (2003), and is the editor/compiler of *The Irish Filmography: Fiction Films 1896–1996* (1996). His study of Irish film censorship, *The Los Angelesation of Ireland*, is forthcoming.

Series Introduction

Given the amount of study that the topic of Irish writing, and increasingly Irish film, has generated, perhaps the first task of a series entitled *Contemporary Irish Writers and Filmmakers* is to justify its existence in a time of diminishing rainforests. As Declan Kiberd's *Irish Classics* has shown, Ireland has produced a great variety of writers who have influenced indigenous, and indeed, world culture, and there are innumerable books devoted to the study of the works of Yeats, Joyce and Beckett. These writers spoke out of a particular Irish culture, and also transcended that culture to speak to the Anglophone world, and beyond.

However, Ireland is now a very different place from that which figures in the works of Yeats, Joyce and Beckett, and it seems timely that the representations of this more secular, more European, and more cosmopolitan Ireland should be investigated and it is with this in mind that *Contemporary Irish Writers and Filmmakers* has been launched.

This series will examine the work of writers and filmmakers who have engaged with the contemporary cultural issues that are important in Ireland today. Irish literature and film has often been viewed as obsessed with the past, but contemporary writers and filmmakers seem to be involved in a process of negotiation between the Ireland of the past and the Ireland of the coming times. It is on this process of negotiation that much of our current imaginative literature and film is focused, and this series hopes to investigate this process through the chosen *auteurs*.

Indeed, it is a sign of the maturity of these *auteurs* that many of them base their narratives not only in the setting of this "new Ireland", but often beyond these shores. Writers and filmmakers such as Seamus Heaney, John Banville, William Trevor and Neil Jordan have the confidence to write and work as *artists* without the necessary addendum of the qualifying "Irish". Their concerns, themes and settings take them outside Ireland to a global stage. Yet, as this series attests, their "Irishness", however that is defined, remains intact and is often imprinted even in their most "international" works.

Politically and culturally, contemporary Ireland is in something of a values deficit as the previous certainties of party political and religious allegiance as hegemonic forms have been lost in a plethora of scandals involving church and state. The role of art and culture in redefining the value-ethic for our culture has never been more important, and these studies will focus on the notions of Irishness and identity that prevail in the late twentieth and early twenty-first centuries.

The role of the aesthetic in the shaping of attitudes and opinions cannot be understated and these books will attempt to understand the transformative potential of the work of the artist in the context of the ongoing redefinition of society and culture. The current proliferation of writers and filmmakers of the highest quality can be taken as an index of the growing confidence of this society, and of the desire to enunciate that confidence. However, as Luke Gibbons has put it: "a people has not found its voice until it has expressed itself, not only in a body of creative works, but also in a body of critical works", and *Contemporary Irish Writers and Filmmakers* is part of such an attempt to find that voice.

Aimed at the student and general reader alike, it is hoped that the series will play its part in enabling our continuing participation in the great humanistic project of understanding ourselves and others.

Eugene O'Brien
Department of English
Mary Immaculate College
University of Limerick

Acknowledgements

Thanks to Neil Jordan; Sarah Jordan; the Film Institute of Ireland; National Library of Ireland; Anil Kokoram and Hugh Denman, Trinity College Dublin; Liam Wylie; our engaged and conscientious editor, Brian Langan; and the series editor, Eugene O'Brien. Thanks to copyright owners listed in the filmography for the use of film image quotations. Special thanks to Willie and Pat Williams for their generosity, time and support, most particularly with our son Matthew during the writing process.

For Matthew

Introduction

relationships + fantasy

Donal, the central character in Neil Jordan's novel *Sunrise with Sea Monster*, warns when discussing Irish culture not "to believe things are as they seem" (1994: 75), while elsewhere he celebrates a storm, describing it thus: "There was exhilaration in the chaos, in the loss of all reference to boundaries of land, sea or air" (1994: 118). Central to the novel, which explores the triangular relationship of father, son and stepmother/lover, and issues around desire, jealousy and betrayal, is a discourse on appearance and perception, most humorous and poignant perhaps in the plot to attack Madame Tussaud's Waxworks and hit the British Empire "where it hurts most": at the level of the symbolic (1994: 126).

It is these notions around appearance, reality and "unreality", or the irrational; the psycho-sexual dynamics of the family, but most especially around the young male and the oedipal triangulation of desire; the interrelationship of private and public; the (im)possibility of transformation and the blurring of categories other than in negative terms; an enjoyment of the sensual, of fantasy and the impossible made possible, that inform Jordan's work. Indeed, for a writer/director to have worked successfully not just in and across so many genres, but within the local and international markets of Ireland, Europe and the USA, it is unsurprising that the trope of mutability should figure.

This book is not intended to be exhaustive or, more importantly, definitive, nor could it be given the sheer volume of Jordan's work, which sadly has not received the critical engagement or analysis that it deserves. It simply lays down through individual textual studies avenues of exploration and seeks to suggest some of the varied and multiple readings available. It is testament to the richness and depth of his work that such an approach is conceivable. In that sense, clearly this is not an auteurist-driven attempt to locate intentionality and timeless interpretation, though as Jordan himself noted, "No particular culture or experience is interesting in and of itself. It's made interesting by the perspective of an author or a filmmaker" (Linehan, 2000).

The book is framed by a first chapter focused on his early career, and a final chapter discussing the production and exhibition contexts of his films; the latter is essential to understanding Jordan's position within the Irish film industry. The central part of the volume concentrates on individual films. His fiction writing will be treated only in so far as it crosses over, complements or enhances ideas expressed within his cinema. For our part, our favourite films are those where his voice is most clear, those films that are largely free from external aesthetics and interference, and which display his sumptuous delight in the visual as well as the acoustic.

Jordan is never simply an Irish film director but one who transcends, yet epitomises, nationality. It is such a paradox which provides a way into Jordan; everything is never, yet always, what it seems. It is only by refusing to accept closed categories that one can truly engage with Jordan. This is especially pertinent in seeing his films not as two distinct strands of creative output in which one is focused on Ireland or politics and the other on fantasy and allegory. If many have unwittingly fallen into this misapprehension with such films as *Angel* or *Michael Collins* in relation to Ireland, a film like *The Butcher Boy* clearly refuses and makes a mockery of such a simple and disabling dichotomy. Indeed, it is this appreciation of how Jordan is always drawn to the "in between" — the confusion, richness and complexity at the site of boundaries, whether these borders are social, political, psychic, sexual or cultural; or are physical or abstract; or, in terms of film, are generic, national or industrial — that give this book its title. Neil Jordan's work is nothing if it is not a challenge to the fixity of categories and rationality.

Chapter One

Early Career

Neil Jordan, born on 25 February 1950 at Rosses Point, County Sligo, a seaside area near Sligo town, was the second child of Michael and Angela Jordan. His father was a teacher, a researcher of popular children's literature, an amateur violinist, and occasional choirmaster, while his mother was a painter, a profession followed by Neil's sister Eithne. The family moved to Dublin when Neil was two, eventually settling in Clontarf, a middle-class area on the north side of Dublin bay. His strongest childhood memories are of summertime on the north Dublin and Meath beaches of Howth, Portmarnock and Bettystown — experiences which have coloured his writings — while his adult homes have overlooked the sea, at Bray, County Wicklow and, at present, Dalkey, County Dublin, and his holiday home in west Cork overlooks the Atlantic. As a child, television was unavailable at home, while visits to the cinema were confined to once every two weeks (which contrasted with the weekly or biweekly trips that his friends enjoyed).

He was educated at the local primary school, Belgrove, where one of his teachers was the writer John McGahern, and at a nearby secondary school, St Paul's College, Raheny, where he won the school president's prize for a short story entitled "Sunday". Subsequently, he went to University College Dublin where he studied English and History (his minor thesis was on the lives of the saints), graduating with a Bachelor of Arts degree in 1971. That year, he married Vivienne Shields, a law student with whom he later had two daughters, Sarah and Anna. Due to the severe economic recession in Ireland at the time, the couple migrated to London where he worked at manual labouring jobs while writing short stories. Returning to Ireland in 1973 for the funeral of Vivienne's aunt, they decided to stay, and he took jobs as a teacher and nightwatchman. While his wife worked as a lawyer, he stayed at home, looking after the children and writing.[1] His first published story, "On Coming Home", appeared in the New Irish Writing page in the *Irish Press* in September 1974. Other stories from this period include "Last Rite", which was published in the prestigious British literary magazine, *Stand*, in 1975. (It later became the first story in the *Night in Tunisia* collection.) The story depicted the bleak life of a labourer in London who commits suicide.

At university, he had met brothers Jim and Peter Sheridan (both later playwrights, theatre and film directors), and they collaborated, along with actors Vinnie McCabe and Garrett Keogh, writer Des Hogan, and David McKenna, on theatre and music projects. They worked in two groups: the Children's T Company, a somewhat anarchic outfit putting on shows for children, and the SLOT (St Lawrence O'Toole) Players, based in Sherrif St, in Dublin's inner city. Though a writer for these collectives, Jordan also recalls being dressed as a fish for one of their productions in "a skin-tight leotard with a fish's head on St Stephen's Green playing the saxophone" (Toibin, 1982: 17), a sight which must have frightened passers-by, if not the children! Later, a more subtle form of surrealism and the fantastic informed his work. At the Project Arts Centre's Abbey Street premises they also performed a prescient play, *Journal of a Hole*, about the experience of youngsters sent to the brutal Artane Industrial School,[2] a theme which was later developed in *The Butcher Boy*; they performed a version of Yeats's "The Cat and the Mouse" on Dollymount Strand, Dublin; and Jordan played Tiresias in a production of *Oedipus Rex* at the Aula Max, University College Dublin, the narrative of which is central to understanding Jordan's work, but explicitly so in *The Miracle*. One of the group's most memorable experiences was a trip to Chicago funded by an Irish-American. Jordan recollects putting on

Sean O'Casey and Samuel Beckett plays for Irish-Americans, who found it all "terribly sad" (Toibin, 1982: 16).

In addition to his writing and theatrical work, Jordan also played guitar, banjo and the saxophone — which he learned around 1974 after listening to Charlie Parker records — in a showband. Ironically, considering his future career,[3] the band's name was *Eyeless*, while one of their experiences would feature in his first film, *Angel*. According to the founder of the group, Niall Stokes, later editor of *Hot Press*, he once arranged a gig in a lunatic asylum in Portlaoisé, a town about 50 miles from Dublin. While they were doing the soundcheck, the patients filtered into the hall, watching them tune up. "It was a strange experience," recalls Stokes, "and one that ended up directly in the film" (O'Mahony, 2000: 6–7). However, Jim Sheridan relates a similar experience during their theatrical American tour. In both instances, the connection is made to a scene in *Angel*.

As early as 1972, Jordan wrote a radio play, *Miracles and Miss Langan*, which was later broadcast on RTE and the BBC. In 1979, this play was filmed as a television drama by RTE. It was directed by the future film director Pat O'Connor from Jordan's script, a collaboration which continued with O'Connor's version in 1983 of the short story "Night in Tunisia". Other television work by Jordan includes writing four of the thirteen episodes of the RTE production *Sean* (1980), based on Sean O'Casey's autobiographies.

Nevertheless, it was as a writer of short stories that Jordan first came to national and international prominence, with his work translated into several languages, including French, Spanish, Italian, Dutch, Swedish and Japanese. The short story collection *Night in Tunisia and other stories* was first published in 1976 by the Irish Writers' Co-operative, a collective of writers founded in 1974/75 of which Jordan was a member, the others including Ronan Sheehan, Steve McDonagh, Des Hogan, Leland Bardwell, Lucille Redmond, and Jimmy Brennan. In 1979, when the book was reissued by the Readers' and Writers' Co-operative, it was joint winner of the *Guardian* Fiction prize.

Of all his written fiction, this collection is the one which continues to be singled out for praise, and indeed includes many themes and images that inform his later film work, most obviously *The Miracle*. The stories often deal with the recurring theme of the slippage between one state or identity and another, as in, for example, "A Love", which clearly is central to such films as *Company of Wolves*, *The Crying Game*, *The Butcher Boy* and *In Dreams*, while the adult world of the boy in that story finds an echo in *The Crying Game*. Additionally, Jordan's exploration of the gulf between self and others, often figured as men and women, can be found in *Mona Lisa*, while the desire for the miraculous is explored in *We're No Angels*, *The Butcher Boy* and *The End of the Affair*. The list goes on.

The set of ten stories, of which the title story is the best known, comprise, as already noted, a tale of suicide, but also a search for meaning in the material ("Last Rites"); a teenage homosexual encounter by the sea which also explores the mystery of woman ("Seduction"); a brother trading his sister with a tinker boy for a ride on the tinker's pony ("Sand"); a father–son relationship and an absent wife/mother who left them and whose "death" is understood as an effect of the holiday town ("Mr Solomon Wept"); another father–son/absent mother relationship, explored through the rites of passage of music and sex ("Night in Tunisia"); a woman breaking free of the mundane but finding nothing — no miracle or meaning — within the various skins of the onion, or in her visit to the sea where she hopes to find release and desire ("Skin"); an encounter between a man and woman who has just realised that her soul has left her ("Her Soul"); a story of a woman's alienation from the world and her middle-class earthbound partner who prays for the "miraculous plus" ("Outpatient"); the desire to see the impossible in the landscape and the "miracle" of a tree in bloom, which turns out to be a wishing tree, something that is invoked in both *Angel* and *High Spirits* ("Tree"); and a love affair between a boy and an older woman to whom his father is also attracted, and their subsequent meeting years later during the time of Eamon de Valera's funeral ("A Love").

The *Night in Tunisia* collection brought Jordan to the attention of film director John Boorman, who, like many others, highlighted the visual quality of Jordan's writing. He subsequently invited him to collaborate on a script, *Broken Dream*, an adaptation of a futuristic French novel about a man who learns how to make things vanish. Though the script went through a number of drafts, it was never made into a film because, according to Boorman, it "never matured into a film".[4] Nevertheless, impressed by his ability, Boorman engaged Jordan to work on his long-cherished film project *Excalibur* (1979), a tale of Arthurian England and the search for the Holy Grail. This collaboration earned Jordan a credit as Creative Associate on *Excalibur*, and the allocation by Boorman of £25,000 from the film's budget for a documentary about the film. *The Making of Excalibur: Myth into Film* (1981) gave Jordan his first experience as a director. Finding it a "baptism of fire", he said that he could not have attempted *Angel* without this experience (Toibin, 1982: 18). Notwithstanding the fact that Boorman's cinema is very different to that of Jordan, their shared interest in the "supernatural" or the non-realistic, while at the same time making films grounded in historical and contemporary political realities, allows for, at least, a superficial parallel to be drawn between the careers of the two directors.

Always a prolific worker, Jordan had by this time completed two major pieces of writing: his first novel, *The Past* (1980), and a film script treatment, "Travellers". *The Past* is an exploration of family memory, an attempt by the narrator to discover from his mother's elderly friend Lili the truth about his parents and his own origins. He gradually pieces together, from Lili's recollection, the state of his family from 1915, when an actress, Una O'Shaughnessy, and her husband Michael return to Dublin from an extended honeymoon in Cornwall with a baby daughter Rene, through to the 1930s, when the narrator is born illegitimate. His Republican grandfather is killed in Dublin's Booterstown and Rene, seeking to become an actress, goes to live in Bray, County Wicklow. There she meets the Vances, a Protestant family of photographers in financial decline. Recalling the short story "A Love", both Vance senior and junior fall in love with her. It is the narrator's mission to discover which of them is his father. As part of his exploration of the past, the narrator meets Father Beausang (a name, if not

the same character, who, like Rene(e) appears in *The Miracle*),
who had known the three of them, but is unable to give him
the information he needs. Lili suggests it is the elderly James
Vance. In County Clare, Rene, by now pregnant, continues performing with a touring repertory company, a route followed by
the narrator in the company of Lili and Fr Beausang.

In *The Past*, Jordan sought to explore whether "human beings
lose their memory of the past, whatever the significance it has
for them", and so lose their ability to criticise and to understand themselves. Stylistically, he sought to start from "an ahistorical, observed reality, go into a personalised reality, go into a
family relationship, into a love relationship and end up with
something as universal or intangible as landscape" (Toibin,
1982: 16–17). Jordan intersperses his fictional characters with
"real" historical events, such as the Booterstown assassination,
which echoes the killing in 1927 of Kevin O'Higgins, the Free
State's Minister for Home Affairs, while Eamon de Valera
makes an explicit appearance, as he would, in a more villainous
mode, in *Michael Collins*. As the trio conclude their journey at
Lisdoonvarna, County Clare (also the destination of the lovers
in "A Love" and *Sunrise with Sea Monster*), de Valera arrives in
his motorcar, "his face abstract and expressionless, though
somewhat kindly, eternally fixed in that gaze with which it met
photographers, as if it is anticipating a photograph" (Jordan,
1980: 217). The discourse of photography, the Vances' profession, permeates the book, whether through the memory of
Edward Muybridge's visit to Dublin (Jordan, 1980: 75), or
through James Vance's preparation for a photo session. Indeed,
meditation on the photographic image is a recurring feature of
Jordan's films.

On numerous occasions Jordan himself (and reviewers of
his literary fiction) have laid stress not so much on the narrative drive of his writing, but on its visual power. In fact, *The Past*
is largely devoid of dialogue. Commenting in 1997, Jordan described *The Past* as being "entirely composed of visual description", adding that he felt he was "writing himself out of this
form entirely". He regarded it as "pointless to continue writing
just to describe what things look like" (Dwyer, 1997: 1).

Two years earlier, he had said that once he had become involved with film-making "it was hard to concentrate on anything else . . . It was like an attempt to make the novel do
something it wasn't meant to do. I seemed to be struggling with
two completely different forms."[5]

While Jordan did not abandon prose fiction — two further
novels, *The Dream of a Beast* (1983) and *Sunrise with Sea Monster* (1994), were subsequently published — nevertheless, it is
as a filmmaker that he is best known. Some critics and reviewers regarded this as a great loss to literature: "fiction's loss",
the *Irish Times* literary critic Eileen Battersby wrote in 1994,
"was filmmaking's gain".[6] However, a "literary style", or a determined focus on narrative and meaning, periodically hovers
over even his most visual films, and, indeed, for a filmmaker
concerned with the visual, ironically, unlike his early prose writings, his films are sometimes surprisingly "wordy".

Jordan has commented that one of the reasons he shifted
from literature to film was that Irish writing had gone over the
same territory time and again. Yet, Jordan himself, at least in his
early film work, revisited aspects of that dominant literary tradition. Predating his involvement with *Excalibur* or the publication of *The Past*, Jordan had won the Arts Council Film Script
Award for 1979 for his script of *Traveller*, which was directed
by Joe Comerford and released in 1981, the only feature film
script he has written which was made by another director.

Filmed in the West of Ireland (Galway City and County,
and County Clare, especially), the film concerns the relationship between travellers Angela Devine (Judy Donovan) and Michael Connors (Davy Spillane), whose marriage is arranged by
their respective fathers, Devine (Johnny Choil Mhadhc) and
Connors (Paddy Donovan). (Interestingly, Angela and Michael
are also the names of Neil Jordan's parents.) After their wedding, the young couple are sent with £1,500 to Northern Ireland to buy televisions and radios to smuggle south of the
Border. (In *The Butcher Boy*, it is partially through these media
that an alternative non-Irish culture is "smuggled" in.) During
their journey they come into contact with the British army and
meet up with a renegade republican, Clicky (Alan Devlin).

While on their way south, Michael crashes the van and they are injured.

During the subsequent sojourn, Angela reveals in voiceover to Clicky that she had been jailed for hitting her father with a bottle when he tried to rape her. Michael robs a post office, and the couple stay at an abandoned Big House, but when the gardaí arrive, they escape and make their way to Galway city, and eventually move to a traveller encampment at the Cliffs of Moher. Meanwhile, Clicky goes to see Angela's father and challenges him over his incestuous attack on his daughter. In a seaside resort, one of Jordan's many familiar settings, Michael and Angela visit an amusement arcade and, in an alternative version of the Bradys in *The Butcher Boy*, stay overnight in a small hotel where Angela tells him that she doesn't want either him or children. When she says she will go off on her own, he responds that he didn't want her either. Finally, she reveals her father's sexual assault on her.

They meet up again with Clicky, and Michael goes with him to see Angela's father. Borrowing Clicky's gun, Michael shoots Devine as he watches a documentary about the Northern Ireland Civil Rights movement. (Such ironic juxtapositions are a hallmark of Jordan's work.) Michael then seeks to comfort Devine and gives him the money he is owed. Afterwards, Michael rejoins Angela, Clicky declares he'll be back after the civil war, and a map suggests that they will emigrate to Australia and the American West coast, though it seems it is Clicky and Angela who will go to America and Michael to Australia.

Confusion has surrounded the relationship between the finished film and Jordan's script, and while the writer has declared himself satisfied with Comerford's film, calling it "very interesting", he nonetheless adds that "it wasn't the film I'd written" (Toibin, 1982: 18). While Comerford's film often eschews direct politics in favour of the incestuous attack (which he regarded as metaphorically reflecting a breakdown in Irish society leading to civil war),[7] Jordan, by contrast, declared that he tended to be "very brutal" about his concerns, adding that when he made a moral statement he expected it to be reflected in the work. Already indicating the influence American cinema held over him, he saw his script as a road movie within the tradition of Nicholas Ray's *They Live By Night* (1949), an extract from which was later included in *Mona Lisa* (1985), and Arthur Penn's post-classical *Bonnie and Clyde* (1967). Unlike Comerford, where indirectness and obfuscation are often central features of his filmmaking vision, Jordan wanted to tell "a coherent story". As a result, he decided not to accept the situation and when the opportunity arose with his first commercial feature, *Angel*, he argued successfully (with Boorman's backing) to be allowed direct it.

There are substantial differences between Comerford's film *Traveller* and Jordan's five-page outline of the story, "Travellers", which is included amongst Jordan's film scripts held at The National Library of Ireland.[8] Most especially, there is evidence of a conscious reworking of John M. Synge's *The Playboy of the Western World* (1907), one of the most influential plays of the Irish Literary Revival. In the play, Christy Mahon arrives at a shebeen and declares that he has killed his oppressive father, Old Mahon, with a single blow of a loy. Impressed, two village women, sensuous Widow Quin and the publican's daughter, Pegeen Mike, compete for his affections. As Christy is basking in popularity, his father appears with a bandaged head, and the villagers, especially Pegeen Mike, ridicule Christy. Seeking to restore his lost status, he hits his father again, apparently killing him. Realising he is now a real murderer, the villagers plan to hang him, but Old Mahon revives again. After a trial of strength between father and son, Old Mahon accepts his son's superiority and the pair depart for home, leaving Pegeen Mike to grieve for her loss.[9]

In his script treatment, Jordan includes a scene, replicated near the end of the film, where Michael apparently kills his father-in-law, Devine, with a brick (a gun in the film) because of the incestuous abuse of his daughter, Angela. (The mother is absent from Synge's play, Jordan's script, and Comerford's film.) In a significant departure from what is depicted in the film, the script shows an "incredulous" Angela: "You killed my da, she says, laughing hysterically. That's what I did, he replies, suddenly

very proud. If my mother only knew, she says, laughing on . . .
The car fills with laughter as they drive towards the west."

The killing in the script provides the release required for the
consummation of their marriage, making explicit a theme which
recurs throughout many of Jordan's films, especially his Irish
ones, the connection between sex and violence, although these
are also, of course, the central themes of most cinema. However, in the film, the couple separate and emigrate to different
continents. In Jordan's script outline, the couple go on a honeymoon, to the Puck Fair at Kilorglin, County Kerry, a pagan harvest festival associated with fertility (and with travellers).
En route, having robbed a second post office (this time in Port-
laoise), which causes local republicans to get unwelcome attention from the police (ironic in the sense that the town's prison
housed most republican prisoners during "The Troubles"), they
go swimming in a river between Limerick and Killorglin. Following this, they "begin to make love, naturally this time, and . . .
are overtaken by feelings they know nothing about".

It is at this point that Jordan's love of Italian cinema rever-
berates in the script. In interviews, he has often cited Italian
cinema, especially neo-realism, not so much its more political
and socially committed immediate post-war cycle, but the later
extension of the boundaries of neo-realism into what Amédée
Ayfre has called "phenomenological realism". One such film is
Federico Fellini's *La Strada* (1954), which broke with the formal
constraints of the earlier films, and "which keeps the mystery
intact without reducing it to cheap mysticism".[10] For example,
in a 1982 interview, Jordan commented that he became "obsessed" with *La Strada* because it could tell a story "without the
burden of history on its shoulders", unlike, of course, the earlier neo-realist films, or, of course, the Irish cinema in waiting
(Toibin, 1982: 15).[11] More than that, it epitomises Jordan's own
interest in phenomenology and magical materiality, or the secular miracle.

In *La Strada*, a travelling strongman, Zampanò (Anthony
Quinn), "buys" a simple girl, Gelsomina (Giulietta Masina), (an
arranged "marriage", like in *Traveller*) from her impoverished
mother who lives near the sea, a locational motif which is asso-

ciated throughout with Gelsomina and would recur in Jordan's films. While the crude Zampanò fails to appreciate Gelsomina until after her disappearance and death (and even then, his "remorse" is questionable), she travels a path of enlightenment and self-knowledge, like Angela in *Traveller*. Whereas Gelsomina leaves Zampanò out of love, in Comerford's film, Angela leaves Michael out of disinterest, or at least a rejection of the arranged marriage. In Jordan's treatment, the couple transcend their estrangement after her husband has apparently committed the oedipal slaying, thus occupying the patriarchal role in relation to his wife.

Even in the script's most direct resonance of *Playboy of the Western World*, there is a direct allusion to *La Strada* and the world of performance and circus. The scene in which Devine reappears with a group of travellers, with "his head bound by an immense bandage", like Old Mahon, is set during a performance by a travelling showman, fire-eater Roz. This "magic creature, part of the new emotion they have found together" is a clear parallel to Fellini's friendly clown (played by Richard Basehart), whose ill-treatment at the hands of Zampanò leads to Gelsomina separating from her "husband". At this point, Jordan's treatment descends into farce, with Roz setting fire to Devine's bandage during his act in a pub, and the young couple retreating to a travellers' encampment, to where they are followed by Devine who starts to whip Michael until Clicky (a republican clown?), shoots him in the leg. Clicky then rescues the couple, and along with Roz they escape to the sea. As he does so, he tells Michael and Angela that he had been sent to kneecap them for carrying out the robberies: "Only certain people are allowed that luxury," he tells them, a comment which ends the treatment. If the introduction of Roz and the world of the showman, as well as the fairground, echo *La Strada*, they are features that recur elsewhere in Jordan, including in *Angel*, *The Miracle*, *The Crying Game*, *The Butcher Boy* and *The End of the Affair*. Of course, the escape (or return?) to the sea appears in almost all of Jordan's films.

In a commentary on Jordan's dual career path as writer and filmmaker, Fintan O'Toole notes that his work "represents not just one man's pursuit of ideas and ambitions, but a significant shift in a nation's culture". By starting out as a writer of literary fiction and then "re-inventing" himself as a filmmaker, "he symbolises a much bigger change in the way the country sees itself" (O'Toole, 1996: 21). Though Jordan has given numerous interviews, many of them formal and extended, he has only very occasionally engaged in discussions about Irish film culture and, specifically, the perceived limitations of Irish visual culture. One revealing early example is the appropriately entitled "Word and Image", written in 1978. This rare example of film "criticism", Jordan's first piece of writing about the cinema, presents a review of Irish film director Cathal Black's first film, an adaptation of a John McGahern short story, *Wheels*. The context in which Jordan was writing about *Wheels* was that only a handful of films were being made, but these were initiating what would become within little over a decade an internationally acclaimed cinema, by which time Jordan was to the forefront of that Irish cinema.

In his article, Jordan noted that, while the most prominent screen images about Ireland had concerned the Northern Ireland troubles, other images of Irish experience had found expression only in the written word. In common with many Irish commentators, he suggested that "if one were to anticipate what form these images will take, when they eventually are filmed, one would have to examine the literary medium, through which the shapes of Irish experience have been most thoroughly and brilliantly drawn". Acknowledging that comparisons and marriages between the written word and visual images were unfashionable in the 1970s, he added, nevertheless, that it was in Irish areas of visual achievements, especially the decorative calligraphy and monumental sculpture of Early Irish Christianity, an area he investigated as an undergraduate, that "the visual image performs a function that is uncannily close to the verbal concept". Indeed, he noted that the "best achievements" of indigenous Irish cinema to date, Bob Quinn's *Caoineadh Airt Uí Laoire* (1976) and *Wheels* both took their impetus from literary works.

This endorsement of a cinema informed, on the one hand, by a modernist engagement with the past and, on the other, by the literary "realist" tradition highlights the raw tension which is at the core of Jordan's film work. Be that as it may, it was the Irish modernist (as well as the "surreal" and gothic) literary traditions which he chose to endorse in 1978. Thus, while *Wheels* explored "the tacts and contours" portrayed in the Irish short story, similar, as he put it, to "the landscape from which the masterpieces of Italian cinema emerged", nevertheless, there is another Irish "imaginative" landscape, mapped out by James Joyce, W.B. Yeats, Jonathan Swift and Samuel Beckett. He noted that the work of these writers is not as easily analysed as those of the short story, "but its myths, its obsessions and its metaphysics are as much part of our heritage as is the concrete landscape" of the short story. He added that "the attempt by film to depict that world would be infinitely more difficult", but also "infinitely more rewarding" (Jordan, 1978).

This also proved to be Jordan's approach to cinema, which would happen four years later, that he would seek to explore both the "realism" and "fantasy" of the Irish literary tradition, while opening up a series of cinematic spaces for Irish cinema previously unexplored. As he put it following the release of *The Crying Game* (1992),

> I like to take stories that have a realistic beginning, that start from the point of realism and go to some other place that is surrealistic. I suppose there is a certain impatience with reality. That sort of thing, that's Irish. (Burke, 1993: 20)

He added that he thought Irish people were impatient with the "real world", pointing to the strength of the fantastic rather than the realistic in Irish literature. In the following chapters, as each of his films are explored in chronological sequence, "realist" and "non-realist" modes, and "rational" and "irrational" worlds, are all parts of a process in Jordan's stretching of boundaries, not only of the family and of the "nation", but of humanity itself.

Notes

---

[1] By the 1980s, Neil Jordan had separated from his wife, but later that decade he met his current partner, Canadian Brenda Rawn, with whom he has two sons, Dashiel and Daniel. She had been post-production co-ordinator on *We're No Angels* (1989) — the film was shot in British Columbia, Canada — as well as his personal assistant on *The Miracle* (1991). Between these two long-term relationships, he also has a son, Ben, by Dublin architect Mary Donohoe.

[2] The play was first performed at the Project Arts Centre, Dublin, in 1971. It later transferred to University College Dublin's Little Theatre.

[3] A strand of Jordan's work is concerned with challenging sight as the primary sense of understanding and knowledge. Indeed, throughout he is interested in appearances and visual surfaces, something most explicit in his latest film, *The Good Thief.*

[4] Interview in *Neil Jordan: A Profile* (1988). A copy of the script dated 1991 is at the Irish Film Archive.

[5] *Books Ireland*, February 1995: 5.

[6] Eileen Battersby, "Strike the Father Dead", *Irish Times*, 31 December 1994: Weekend, 8.

[7] See Kevin Rockett, "'Like an Expedition . . .'", *IFT News*, Vol. 5, No. 2, February 1982: 4–6.

[8] Neil Jordan papers, Manuscripts Accessions 4761, National Library of Ireland. There are seven boxes of scripts; box two contains the outline of "Travellers".

[9] A feature film adaptation of the play was made by Brian Desmond Hurst in 1962. Of course, the reviving of the corpse even more famously originated in Dion Boucicault's *The Shaughraun* (1874).

[10] Millicent Marcus (1986), *Italian Film in the Light of Neorealism*, Princeton, New Jersey: Princeton University Press, 162–3.

[11] Another favourite film from his college days was Ingmar Bergman's *The Seventh Seal* (1957), in which a disillusioned Crusader plays chess with Death.

Chapter Two

Angel (1982)

Neil Jordan's first feature film, *Angel*, is, unfortunately perhaps, best known for two negatives: one, the controversy surrounding the manner of its financing; and, two, its refusal to engage directly with questions of paramilitary (political) violence in the context of a divided Northern Ireland. While both of these issues are important in themselves, the result has been that *Angel* has not been treated cinematically either in terms of its own aesthetic or vision, or its significance within Irish cinema. In this latter regard, Jordan draws on the rich modernist or art film vein of European cinema and culture as the *visual* means of exploring Irish "life", in a manner, ironically, not too dissimilar from some other contemporary Irish filmmakers.

While later, Jordan moved away from this formal European modernism in favour of hybrid commercial cinema genres, so that it appears in retrospect to be atypical of his work, *Angel* also hints at the predominant direction that Jordan followed, namely, a sumptuous and engaging world more fully embracing the fantastic and the supernatural, or what can be seen as the non-rational place of the imagination and art, beyond, yet linked to, reality. Notwithstanding the detachment of the camera, the gritty realism and the bleak barren landscapes, particularly the image on which the film closes, there are moments when Jordan lapses into the beauty and the tropes which characterise his later work. These can be seen in the lush "forest" where Deirdre and Danny exchange a kiss; the seaside (Bray) backdrop to the band's publicity shot; their pink shiny costumes, which find a counterpart in, and explicitly comment on, the boy oracle's electric blue suit; religion and its relationship to the body, repression, hypocrisy and superstition; and the film's interest in miracles or the mystical. Typical also is Jordan's exploration of the effect an environment has on the inner life of a person. As Bonner says to Danny after he has been shot by Bloom, he "grew up around here", a comment which elicits Danny's response encapsulating the film's (and the North's) sense of tragedy: so, too, did Annie.

One of the charges levelled against the film is that it is not concerned with the "real" world, but that it is interested in exploring the roots of "psychic" violence, yet, the film is anchored in a very real and traumatic event, the sectarian killings on 31 July 1975 by loyalist paramilitaries of three members of the Miami Showband, whose bus was ambushed on their way south from a gig in the North. At the time, as noted in the previous chapter, Jordan himself played in a dance band. An early treatment of the film had as its starting point the massacre of all but two members of a showband by a group of unknown assassins.[1]

It is this apparent juxtaposition of reality and unreality which defines Jordan. As he has commented, he has an "impatience with basic realism" (Glicksman, 1990: 71). Recalling "Night in Tunisia", *Angel* opens in the world of the dancehall band, and the film's protagonist, Danny, played by Stephen Rea in the first of eight appearances in Jordan's films, is an Irish showband saxophonist playing with the band at a country dancehall in Northern Ireland. Like the world of the fairytale which generally begins rooted in reality, the film starts out as anchored in the everyday before Danny descends into a primal and terrifying mythological space removed from reality. Before the gig, he meets Annie (Veronica Quilligan), a young deaf mute girl, and after the dance is with her when he witnesses the band's manager Ray (Peter Caffrey) (who had earlier argued over protection payments) being shot dead by three gunmen, one of whom wears an orthopaedic shoe. Annie, too, is shot dead as she wanders bewildered towards the scene, while Danny looks on horrified. He remains hiding in a concrete pipe until the killers leave, and then runs to her body. As he bends down to her the ballroom explodes in flames. Later, in a reverse of the "Pieta", he rests her body on his lap.

Questioned by detectives Bloom (Ray McAnally) and Bonner (Donal McCann) as he recovers in hospital, Danny offers them no clues. After recuperating with his Aunt Mae, he rejoins the band at rehearsals, and resumes his tentative relationship with singer Deirdre (Honor Heffernan) who is increasingly drawn to this "charmed" man. He asks her why she was not there for him that night: he tells her he had wanted to touch her, so instead he went with Annie. For Danny, bodies become interchangeable, or put another way, identity is not fixed. He describes himself, as Renée does Sam in *The Miracle*, as being the same as all the other musicians. Similarly, by using the non-specific pronoun "they" to refer to those connected with (legal and illegal) violence, the film registers that all killers are the same. Indeed, Danny (sexually) compares himself to one of the killers who in answer to Danny's question of how he could have killed Annie, points out that Danny already knows, having also killed. Danny goes to stay with his Aunt Mae (Marie Kean) who can read cards, but when she deals the ominous Ace of Spades, which means death, she puts them away, telling him that she has lost the knack. He then goes to bed where he finds his dead uncle's soprano saxophone and, looking outside at a uniformed soldier, remembers Annie. As the cards foretold, Danny has fallen into a hypnotic trance with death and becomes obsessed with finding the killers.

The first person he tracks down is the man who owns the specialised medical shoe shop whom he had seen (and heard) at the hospital. He breaks into his house, and in a scene that recalls *Performance* (Donald Cammell, Nicolas Roeg, 1970), finds amidst the chaos and floating aerofoam a machine gun which he fetishistically pieces together, as he did his uncle's sax, to the soundtrack's accompaniment of choral music — the same as that heard when he and Annie were together. (Later, in another pairing of violence and the saxophone, he places the gun in the saxophone's case.)[2] He then waits for his victim, whom he shoots through the door, on which ironically hangs a picture of a "cool" male, a symbol of American (and cinematic) masculinity. Returning later to the scene of the crime to recover the gun, Danny hides as two of the dead man's associates discover the corpse and leave the scene without emotion.

Danny is questioned again by Bloom, but he doesn't comment on a file photograph he recognises. He then visits the suspect and shoots him on the beach. Danny traces the third killer, almost accidentally, through the killer's estranged wife, who had briefly flirted with Danny on that fatal night — her wedding night, a clear linking of political violence and domestic neglect and abuse. She tells him that he meets his Catholic girlfriend in the forest every lunchtime. He follows him there and hides in the back seat of the loyalist's car, from where he surprises both of them. They argue, hell and religion are mentioned, and though the killer offers to name "the big man", he continues to goad Danny until he shoots him.

Danny returns to his other life to join up with the band, but the twilight images of the water, and the magically lit white marquee which is their venue, outlined with soft glowing lights (of entertainment or religious ritual) suggest that he is locked out of reality, in the same way that the lighting, the cinematography and Danny's costume had in the previous forest scene. Inside the tent, he witnesses the band's drummer Billy (Alan Devlin) paying protection money. Danny angrily shouts at him, saying that's what they did to Ray, and he shoots the collector. Deirdre approaches, her red hair contrasted against a sumptuous blue background with a single glowing bulb which echoes the white-yellow orbs behind Annie. She is disgusted at Danny's brutality, which ends the possibility of their dream of being together. After wriggling free from his desperate embrace, she tells him in a comment that rejects all violence, that the police — "them like you only in uniform" — have been looking for him, to which he responds by going on the run.

At an isolated farmhouse, Danny demands clothes and a haircut from widowed Mary (Sorcha Cusack) who, halfway through cutting his hair so that it will be short like her dead husband's, attacks him with a knife. Danny is simply annoyed that she hasn't finished her job, but treats her with kindness. Subsequently, she bandages him. After he confesses to Mary (and himself) that he does not know anymore why he wants to kill, she warns him, in what is the film's central message, that hating has its own waste, that she hated her husband and asked God to take him, and in a miracle He did. Yet this leaves her with guilt and an empty void that eventually sucks her in. Everywhere she stands, His eyes look down on her. The screen fills with the picture of the Sacred Heart, and off screen, to the horror of Danny, and in a mirror of his reaction to Annie's death, no longer wearing her blue house coat (itself resonant of the Virgin Mary), but a black cardigan, she kills herself with his gun.

Back at the site of the burnt-out dancehall, Danny comes across a young commercial faith-healer (Macrea Clarke), who, in another Jordan reference to the mystical, is the seventh son of a seventh son. (Such a boy also makes an appearance in *Sunrise with Sea Monster*, 1994.) As the boy holds his hand against a backdrop of holy pictures and cheap gold tinsel — a direct comment on the church and its reliance on the spectacle — Danny collapses. He is dragged from the caravan by Bonner, who admits to heading the protection racket and is about to shoot Danny as the boy, who can be read as a reincarnation of Annie, looks on. Mockingly, he tells Danny that only a miracle can save him. On cue, there is a gun-shot, but it is Bonner that has been shot in the back by an off-screen Bloom.

The spell which Deirdre perceives that Danny is under can be interpreted not only in the negative representational terms of John Hill, which will be discussed below, who sees it like the curse that befalls those characters who stray from the path and choose paramilitary violence which only leads to death — as the poster in the beginning of *Cal* reads, "The wages of sin is death" — but as Annie's wish at the wishing tree. She does not just wish to make love to him, but to protect him.

In his review of *Wheels*, Jordan (1978) noted that the most prominent screen "landscape" of Ireland was that of the Northern Ireland "troubles", with its bombed-out streets, gutted hotels, barricades and burnt-out buses. While these images had circulated around the world, other images of Irish experience were largely ignored by cinema and only found "expression in the written word". Clearly, it was Jordan's intention to redress this.

By the time *Angel* was made, a group of Irish fiction film-makers, mostly working on 16mm, had made a small but important corpus of films. Besides *Wheels*, Cathal Black had made *Our Boys* (1981), a powerful exploration of Christian Brothers education; Bob Quinn had made the breakthrough *Caoineadh Airt Ui Laoire* (1975) as well as *Poitín* (1978); Joe Comerford, before making *Traveller*, had made a number of shorts and a feature study of working class Dublin teenagers in *Down the Corner* (1978); Kieran Hickey had directed two dramas exploring middle-class sexuality, *Exposure* (1978) and *Criminal Conversation* (1980); Thaddeus O'Sullivan had made the formally challenging feature about Irish emigration, *On a Paving Stone Mounted* (1978); and Pat Murphy and John Davies had collaborated on *Maeve* (1981) which examined the relationship of feminism to republicanism in contemporary Northern Ireland.

Largely due to these, and the efforts of other filmmakers and film activists, the Irish Film Board was established in 1981, the first statutory agency with a remit to develop filmmaking in Ireland. The Film Board had emerged out of a long period of struggle, during which Irish filmmakers successfully had fought off the attempts by the nationalised National Film Studios of Ireland (better known as Ardmore Studios) to gain control of the production finance being promised by the government, which turned out to be a fund of £4.1 million (€5.2 million). That campaign had often been bitter and when the Chairman of the studios, British director John Boorman, an Irish resident since the early 1970s, was appointed a member of the Film Board, many filmmakers were dismayed, not least because initially they were given no representation on it.

When the first allocation of funding from the Film Board went to *Angel*, whose writer/director had limited film experience, the fears of Irish filmmakers seemed justified. Jordan became entangled in what would become a long-lasting recriminatory public row, which was not helped when it became known that Boorman was the project's executive producer. The issue was made worse when, at the end of the first period of the Board's activities, money was returned to the government rather than committed to other film projects. Unsurprisingly, many filmmakers felt alienated and betrayed.

The animosity continued even after the film was made. Its premiere at the Celtic Film Festival in Wexford in April 1982 was boycotted by the filmmakers' organisation in protest at the manner of its funding. (See Rockett, 1987, and Chapter Fifteen below.) As a result of the furore, a clear rift emerged between Jordan and Boorman on the one hand, and many of the Irish filmmakers, a schism which was played out endlessly in the media to the detriment of all concerned. Despite his subsequent success, which vindicated the Board's decision, arguably it was not until Jordan became a member of the (reconstituted) Film Board in 1993 that the issue was put behind him.

Consequently, discussion of the film has been overshadowed by these events. However, much of the more text-based and cultural commentary that was generated about the film displeased Jordan, who resented critics reading the film politically rather than as a tale of how reality and events impinge on the personal and cause one to become an apparently irrational beast. For Jordan, the film was ultimately about the terror and waste of all violence and how "individuals kill people they don't know" (Glicksman, 1990: 71). From this perspective, it was not concerned in any specific way with Northern Irish violence or in taking sides in that conflict. Nonetheless, the film is clearly about the paramilitary landscape, even if this has less to do with the real politics of Irish nationhood or Ireland's relation to Britain.

In the most influential piece of writing on the representation of Irish history and politics in British commercial cinema, John Hill traces the manner in which a cycle of British films — including *Odd Man Out* (1947), *The Gentle Gunman* (1952), *Shake Hands with the Devil* (1959), *The Violent Enemy* (1968), *Hennessy* (1975) and *The Long Good Friday* (1979) — represent the Irish as having an insatiable appetite for violence while not offering any historical or political contextual framework against which the violent events may be rationally understood (see Hill, 1987: 147–93). As a result, he suggests there is a bias against understanding (Hill, 1987: 184).

Hill's controversial argument is that *Angel*, and Pat O'Connor's 1984 adaptation of Bernard McLaverty's novel *Cal*, even though they are Irish films, continue this ahistorical and depoliticised representation of the Northern Ireland conflict. Drawing the parallel, noted also by *The Observer*'s film critic Philip French, to *Odd Man Out*, Hill argues that *Angel* is "concerned with the destructive power of violence". In *Odd Man Out* and the other films cited, those characters involved with political violence, usually as members of the Irish Republican Army (IRA), are doomed unless they accept the "rational", non-violent, parliamentary road and reject the "armed struggle". In the case of *Odd Man Out*, not only does the "odd man" Johnny (James Mason) die in a hail of bullets at the film's end, but so, too, does his sweetheart, Kathleen (Kathleen Ryan). Similarly, in the War of Independence feature *Shake Hands with the Devil*, the IRA leader Sean Lenihan (James Cagney) refuses to accept the Anglo-Irish Treaty and, as his behaviour becomes more pathological, he is killed by one of his comrades.

This representation of the asocial psychotic can be discerned (in a somewhat diluted form) as early as 1926 in *Irish Destiny* (George Dewhurst), where the local IRA leader shows no emotion at the news of the hero's death. Only for those who turn their back on the organisation, such as brothers John Mills and Dirk Bogarde in *The Gentle Gunman,* or even women such as Granny in *Odd Man Out*, can there be any hope of "normality", if not sexual promise, at least in the domestic sphere.

Hill argues that Danny in *Angel* is within this tradition as he sets out on "a trail of violent revenge, only to arrive at 'the heart of darkness'" (Hill, 1987: 178). Unlike in Hollywood cinema where positive action, including violence, solves problems, in *Angel*, as in much British cinema, the "use of the revenge structure is entirely negative in its implications", with Danny's actions leading only to his own brutalisation, and inevitable return to where he started, the burnt-out dancehall, and with Mary's hate leading to her own suicide.

Hill also draws a parallel to John Boorman's *Point Blank* (1967), where, as in *Angel*, the central character who believes he is in control of events discovers he has been manipulated all

along by others, in Danny's case by Bloom as he tries to identify the (loyalist) sectarian killers. (Boorman himself, in his introduction to the published screenplay of *Angel*, also notes the
film's debt to his film, Jordan, 1989a: *viii.*) Nevertheless, in the
scene in the morgue, Bloom in effect gives Danny permission to
kill the assassins, telling him that because of his "poetic licence"
he (Danny) can go places where he (Bloom) cannot go. Considering, of course, that Bloom is Jewish (and notwithstanding
Danny's laconic query as to whether he is a Protestant Jew or a
Catholic Jew), this is ironic, not just in that he is not a wan-
derer, like Danny, but that he carries the name of the most
famous walker in Irish literature, James Joyce's Bloom.

The film also, of course, raises the prescient spectre of collusion between the North's police force, through the character
of Bonner, and loyalist paramilitaries, which would become
such a significant feature in the investigations of the deaths of
republican activists, as well as of solicitors Pat Finucane and
Rosemary Nelson. In short, though the off-screen shooting by
Bloom implies for Hill a sanitising effect, where, as in crime
films generally, the state's guilt is absolved because it is deemed
necessary in order to protect society, it remains the case that
Bloom is the real killer or, at least, is complicit in Danny's acts
of vengeance. In effect, Danny becomes Bloom's "weapon".

In that sense, even if the price that all the characters pay is
the emptying of the self, registered in the film's final "post-
apocalyptic" image accompanied by the sound of a helicopter
which sums up the oppressive political situation, there is at
least for Danny a release from the spell (of violence). His walk
away from the scene with Bloom and the boy can be reinter-
preted in a similar way to the walking away of the brothers at
the end of *The Gentle Gunman*. As Jordan himself put it in a
commentary on an early treatment of the script, the hero's
"search becomes one for the heart of evil, his final killing is
done with the sense of having finally vanquished that evil, of
having to assume many of its attributes to do so".[3]

As noted, and as is clear in the context of his later work,
Jordan is ultimately less concerned with the "real" world of
politics and violence than with a "metaphysics of violence".

With regard to *Angel*, this has been argued by one of Jordan's champions, philosopher Richard Kearney (1982), who sympathetically draws out authorial intention and Jordan's explanation of the film as "about the effects of violence . . . in a *pure* way", because when you "pull out a gun . . . things cease to be in your control" (Peachment, 1982) (emphasis added). Clearly, such a metaphysical notion necessarily eschews social and political specifics. Nevertheless, Kearney endorses the film as exploring the "psychic roots" of violence in terms of a "metaphysics of the unconscious" as well as highlighting "the fundamental nexus between aesthetic creativity and violence". This allows the film to highlight "the dark, hidden atavism of the psyche", which, Hill points out, "are the shared source of 'both poetic mystery and violent mystification'".

For Hill, Kearney's contention that *Angel* represents a "highly original and perceptive" exploration of Northern Ireland, is necessarily problematic, for by stripping "violence to this common psychic foundation, all violence . . . is fundamentally the same". Accordingly, contextualisation through political explanation is not possible and so "the most commonplace perceptions of the 'troubles' as both futile and intractable" are confirmed. In support of this, Hill quotes one Irish reviewer as saying that "seldom has the hopelessness of the Irish situation been so well captured on film" (Hill, 1987: 180).

While these two divergent perspectives cannot easily, if at all, be reconciled, but are valid ways to understand the film, there are other, perhaps more rewarding, approaches to the film, namely through art history and visual and cinematic culture. As acknowledged by Jordan, one of the central inspirations for the film came from the painting "The Immaculate Conception of the Virgin" (1619) by the Spaniard Diego Velázquez (1599–1660), which hangs in the National Gallery, London.[4] The painting, whose dark palette informs the film's overall look (consider the bedroom scene after Danny and Deirdre have made love), features the Virgin Mary with a halo of twelve stars. She wears a pinkish-white tunic shadowed by purple tints (which finds an echo in the shimmering pink costumes chosen by Danny and Billy) and navy black mantle as she stands against the sun, which is painted in (a dirty) ochre (rather than as a magic realist bright yellow) within luminous white clouds. The moon is positioned under her feet, and the symbols of the litanies are built into the almost black landscape below. Her face is framed by her golden-brown hair, while her hands are flawless, limpid shapes, washed by the smooth paintwork.

What is remarkable about the painting is how the face of the Virgin so closely resembles that of Veronica Quilligan, the actress who plays the mute and deaf Annie, and who has sex with Danny prior to being killed by the loyalist gunman. Perhaps if this image is taken, metaphorically, or otherwise, as a way into reading the film, a very different "political" interpretation is made possible.[5] Like the Virgin, Annie, too, wears a blue tunic (if not as dark as Velázquez's Virgin). Like her, and indeed, many of Jordan's women characters, she is not real and does not exist beyond her physical engagement with Danny. In other words, this deaf-mute exists only as a visceral hallucination, an earlier, more real version of Our Lady in The Butcher Boy who likewise, if indirectly, causes retributive murder(s). In Ireland, the silent or mute idealised woman is central to nationalist iconography through the persona of Mother Ireland. This figure, which is often represented as an idealised, allegorical, or asexual female figure, but serving/supporting the male realm of violent national(ist) action, has proven to be a central iconic representation of Irish nationhood, which can be seen most potently in W.B. Yeats's play Cathleen ni Houlihan (1902).[6]

Thus, far from having a non-political status, at the religious-cultural level, Angel is firmly anchored within a nationalist/loyalist discourse, with the silent, or silenced, Catholic-nationalist Madonna/Mother Ireland figure Annie killed by loyalists as part of their vendetta against the band's manager because he has been paying protection money (probably to republicans). It is not the only reference Jordan has made to the great painters of the sixteenth and seventeenth centuries, with inspiration coming from, amongst others, Watteau and Poussin (Company of Wolves and Interview with the Vampire), Leonardo Da Vinci (Mona Lisa), and El Greco (The End of the Affair).

Equally as pertinent to *Angel* is its debt to European art cinema. A neglected aspect in discussions of *Angel* has been its visual iconography and formal style. Within the history of Irish cinema (an endlessly interrupted "tradition"), there are few visual stylists. While the indigenous films of the 1910s were important components of the struggle for independence, and occasionally Irish films displayed a European cinema sensibility (such as *Irish Destiny*'s debt to German Expressionism), mostly their form was conventional, and derivative of American and British cinemas, as well as of the Irish historical novel. Similarly, with the coming of sound, the opportunities for films with high production values were limited as much by training as by finance, while non-fiction production until the 1980s was dominated by conservative Griersonian aesthetics, where the emphasis was placed on empirical reality rather than on representational or critical analyses.

Thus, the pioneer 16mm filmmakers of the 1970s such as Quinn, Black, Comerford and O'Sullivan made important breakthroughs, not least in terms of content so that they provided a radical reimagining of Irish cinematic tropes and concerns. Nevertheless, they often failed to overcome the barriers to the distribution of such "non-commercial" films erected by foreign and native commercial exhibition companies, because in terms of their different looks and styles they tended to eschew traditional images of beauty and narration. This owed to a number of factors, including their political, social and cinematic content, their engagement with avant-garde practice, but most especially to their minuscule budgets which clearly militated against the polished look favoured by mainstream cinema audiences. Thus, with the completion of *Angel*, a new commercial cinema stylistic norm was introduced. No previous Irish film had so clearly drawn on the conventions of *film noir*, that all-encompassing style (rather than genre), which has been associated with the Hollywood crime film of the 1940s and 1950s, and which is also evident in *Odd Man Out*. Of course, *noir* was also enjoyed and reworked by the other creative shadow of *Angel*, Jean-Luc Godard.

Godard's influence can be understood not at the level of his signature elliptical narrative, though the logic or cause-and-effect within *Angel*, more akin to post-classical cinema, is not typical of the tight structures of Hollywood, but at the level of the film's visual signs and colour. Throughout the film, but particularly during the scenes when Danny and Annie make love, and when Danny returns — like a "ghost" — to the band and plays "Blood is Thicker than Water", colour is used as a formal device in a similar way to Godard or the distancing practices of modernism. If reference could be made to Godard's masterpiece, *Pierrot Le Fou* (1965), where he uses the (French) national colours (red and blue), it is tempting to continue the quotation and read the scene with Danny and Deirdre in the Morris Minor car as akin (though photographed mostly from behind by Jordan) to the static two-shot of Ferdinand (Jean-Paul Belmondo) and Marianne (Anna Karina) in that film, while Danny, complete with dark glasses, dancing with Deirdre in the dance competition which is filmed in saturated deep reds, blues and yellow could also be read as a reference to Belmondo more generally. Additionally, Godard's interest in advertising "signs" and the commercialisation of leisure is seen in the exterior shots of the Dreamland dancehall where there are two billboard advertisements offering Coca-Cola and Smirnoff Vodka, but also in the fake wishing (palm) tree where Deirdre tells Danny, but by then too late, that they are a pair. Later, this is explored in a more subtle manner through Jordan's continuing interest in surfaces, images and appearance. The use then of advertisements which act as a shorthand to illustrate the contrast between the capitalist fantasy and the (often violent, mundane or poor) environment is the precursor to Jordan's more sophisticated exploration of the gap between fantasy and reality or images and identity or meaning.

Furthermore, and in the same vein, no attention has been paid to the film's *hommage* (through use of a publicity postcard) to Michelangelo Antonioni's *L'avventura* (1960), which marked "the birth of a new, anti-conventional film language and disjointed narrative structure". *L'avventura* is an exploration of "the moral and emotional bankruptcy of the bourgeois condition, the diffi-

culty (if not impossibility) of personal intimacy and the individual's increasing alienation from social and natural contexts".[7] By
contrast, Jordan also includes posters from a number of run-of-
the-mill American films, including *Outlaw Blues* (Richard T. Hef-
fron, 1977), *The Other Side of Midnight* (Charles Jarrot, 1977) and
House Calls (Howard Zieff, 1978), films which are no artistic
match for his preferred cinematic referents.

Another important aspect of all of Jordan's films is their rich
and varied music tracks, and this is especially true of *Angel* which,
after all, was conceived of as a musical. Although he has yet to
make a musical, it is something he has expressed a wish to do
(Glicksman, 1990: 70). Notwithstanding *hommages* to the musical
or his use of music as an expressive narrative device, the nearest
he has come to straight musical is his contribution to the Cole
Porter tribute *Red Hot & Blue* (1990)[8] (see Filmography), which
was released to mark the centenary of Porter's birth and to raise
money for AIDS research. It features seventeen individual performances of various Porter songs filmed by the same number of
directors, who, besides Jordan, included David Byrne, Jim Jar-
musch, Alex Cox, and Wim Wenders. Jordan's sequence, performed by Kirsty McColl and The Pogues, is of "Miss Otis
Regrets" (1934) which is seamlessly followed by Shane
McGowan and The Pogues' "Just One of Those Things" (1935).
"Miss Otis Regrets", a hit for Ethel Waters and included in Michael Curtiz's 1946 Porter bio-pic *Night and Day*, tells of a
woman who, betrayed by her lover, shoots him dead. The two
songs are juxtaposed so that the female personal tragedy and
pathos is relieved or commented on by the more jazzy energetic
and altogether more exuberant, if flippant, male-performed "Just
One of Those Things". In both, Jordan conveys the songs' meaning beautifully, but always is careful to announce their level as
(stage) performance. For example, the camera includes the foot-
lights of the stage while the staging is largely flat and theatrical.
Indeed, two-dimensional backdrops (cut-out/printed) are used to
great effect in "Just One of Those Things" for which he also
employed filters, as he does in *Angel*. In the first, McColl, dressed
in black, stands in front of The Pogues, each suited and placed in
a line behind music stands fronted with a banner typical of the

big band era. As she delivers the song's narrative, the weight anchored in the strong musical beat, four couples dance in ballroom style (and dressed accordingly) and complement/act out the sad events of the song. Jordan's choreography is not limited to the dancers themselves but their relationship to each other as mirrors and to McColl. Contrasting the sadness and formality of "Miss Otis" are the erotic or physical performances, during "Just One of Those Things", of dancers drawn from various cultures, or more correctly, parodying the stereotypes of musical theatre including New York, honky-tonk American, "Broadway's Sailors", French Can-Can, Irish traditional, Russian Cossacks, Spanish Flamenco, French comic-circus tradition and exotic Polynesians. (Or, as another Cole Porter song puts it, "Even in Boston the bees do it".) These various dancers then join each other in the manner of the "final big number" when at the song's end they, one by one, emerge from a subway carriage.

Angel's original title was *Brute Music*, the first treatment of which was completed in June 1980. In an introduction to that outline, Jordan wrote that the film would start from a documentary premise and allow its thriller elements to take over slowly. While the "sectarian/political conflict would not be made an issue", it would be an exploration of human beings "involved in an act of pure death, pure evil". It would be a musical, "since music would be such an integral part of the story and theme — but an ironic musical that always contrasts the freedom of music with the oblivion of murder or acts of violence". Surprisingly, at this stage Jordan thought that the music would be predominantly country and western, but the sax player "would play jazz on his own, as many showband players do". In another commentary, Jordan called the proposed film "a musical with violence", with the scenes of "romance and fantasy associated with musicals always contrasted with the world of murder and death of thrillers".[9]

Though not a musical in the strict generic sense, *Angel* still operates like an integrated musical with the songs never simply performance pieces, though they are that too and are beautifully choreographed and staged, but function to chart the film's narrative. For example, the songs Deirdre sings sum up Danny and her relationship with him. Perhaps no other Irish (or indeed western) filmmaker has made such eclectic use of popular song and modern musical forms as Jordan. This is most clear in his evocative use of jazz, which has drawn more than one critic to explore the (post-colonial) relationship between Jordan's sound-tracks and African-American musical and cultural experience.

Maria Pramaggiore (1998), for instance, explores a central expressive feature of *Angel*, and before it, "Night in Tunisia": the extensive use of jazz. Both the band's manager and singer Deirdre call saxophonist Danny, the "Stan Getz of South Armagh". Whatever about such an incongruous juxtaposition, it neatly encapsulates Danny, as a white musician (like the brilliant Getz who served as a bridge from his black contemporary John Coltrane to the white mainstream) who is "reinterpreting" whiteness for the people of Northern Ireland. The Irish in America, after all, as Pramaggiore notes in drawing on the work of Noel Ignatiev,[10] sided with the WASP establishment to advance their material power and in so doing often opposed the emancipation of African-Americans. Pramaggiore argues that while Jordan "addresses experiences and effects of cultural alienation by invoking the (generally absent) figure of the African-American jazz musician", it allows him "to allegorize what are often perceived as similar, if not shared, histories of cultural theft, enslavement and subjugation". In this way, Jordan uses jazz music to suggest "a shared experience of alienation" (Pramaggiore, 1998: 273).

However, the difficulty in drawing on such a culturally specific form of expression also invokes, indeed appropriates, African-American for particular ends. Thus, as Pramaggiore argues, "Jordan's jazz is a means of expressing male sexuality" — explicit in Annie's touching of Danny's saxophone and him using the string which holds his instrument to pull Deirdre close to him after they have made love — "and violence and, as such, may reinscribe notions of the spontaneity, expressiveness and hypersexuality of the black male performer". As a result, in his homage to Charlie Parker and Louis Armstrong, Jordan is in danger of evoking black stereotypical representations by "re-circulating primitivist assumptions of jazz's spontaneous voicing of the soul and the utopian fantasy of the jazz soloist's ability to assert individualism within a group structure".

Nevertheless, as Pramaggiore acknowledges, Jordan uses jazz "to direct visual style and narrative form, thus translating jazz into film style", which may be seen in the "red" musical numbers ("Blood is Thicker than Water", "Strange Fruit") while his editing "adapts to the rhythm, pace and colour of jazz" and, in this way, undermines "narrative coherence and chronological time". Pramaggiore concludes that "such inter-ventions into narrative form . . . underscore thematic anxieties regarding 'impure' cultural or biological origins and non-linear history". Such visual and auditory "'specularity' defer or short circuit narrative trajectories, reorganizing the film according to repetition and revision around narrative and visual ellipses, which is consistent with the film's thematic concerns with cul-tural and personal loss" (Pramaggiore, 1998: 274), which is summed up in Aunt Mae's comment to Danny that "we've all lost something".

Jordan has made explicit the relationship between Irish and African-American political and psychic experiences. Comment-ing on the use of the Billie Holiday/Lewis Allen song "Strange Fruit", which concerns the "lynchings" (itself an Irish-originating term) of blacks in the American South, he points out that "you could almost transpose the whole lyrics over to Ireland". In the song, killing is motivated by "racial differences" and has "noth-ing to do with any kind of human emotion whatever"; a similar situation obtained in Northern Ireland, though perhaps cultural and religious, even national, might be more accurate terms to use than "racial" (quoted in Kearney, 1982: 302). The second time "Strange Fruit" is sung, it is to a roomful of mentally ill patients in an institution, but unlike the modernist staging of them when earlier they had listened to Danny's "Mountains of Mourne", the camera focuses on the face of Deirdre, which is intercut by a strange dance and free movement of one of the female mental patients. The scene, as noted in the previous chapter, draws on Jordan's own experiences as a performer.

Thus, Jordan is marrying a range of very distinct cultural traditions in *Angel* — from the sumptuous paintings of the Renaissance, to the oblique references to the divided community in Northern Ireland, through to a narrative trajectory which draws on British and American cinematic genres, and African-American jazz, while at the same time acknowledging its debt to European modernism. *Angel* was the first in a long list of 1980s and 1990s films which explored the Northern Ireland conflict within the constraints of mainstream commercial cinema. And while Jordan himself returned to some of the themes of *Angel*, notably in *The Crying Game* and *Michael Collins*, it was less the concern with issues of "pure violence" than with how violent political activity affected the private sphere, especially its debilitating effect on personal relationships, which would mark the later "political" films.

Notes

¹ Neil Jordan Papers, Manuscripts Accessions 4761, Box, 7, National Library of Ireland.

² Music and death are similarly juxtaposed in *Sunrise with Sea Monster* (1994) in the scene describing the executions of the captors during the Spanish Civil War: "Their guards make an untidy half-circle, raise their rifles and create an intermittent staccato like a badly played kettledrum till the line [of men] has become a crumpled heap" (p. 510).

³ Neil Jordan Papers, op. cit.

⁴ Neil Jordan interview, *South Bank Show*, 1988.

⁵ While the belief that the Virgin had conceived Jesus without taint of original sin did not become Catholic dogma until 1854, debate had raged for centuries concerning it, most especially in early seventeenth-century Seville where Velázquez's painting was conceived and executed. By 1619, thirty-eight books were in print in Spain on the subject, and the following year, Velázquez's mentor, Pachero, wrote a paper on the topic, establishing certain iconographic norms for painters to follow. These included the Virgin being twelve or thirteen years old, having twelve stars about her head, and to wear an imperial crown of golden hair. She was to be dressed in a white tunic and blue mantle; her feet were to rest on the moon, and she must be enclosed

in the sun, represented as an oval shape in ochre and white. See José López-Rey (1999), *Velázquez*, Cologne: Taschen/Wildenstein Institute,: 43–5. Adoration of the Virgin Mary has been no less intense in Ireland than in Spain, with the continuing strong hold of the belief that the Virgin appeared at Knock, County Mayo in 1879 at the height of an agrarian crisis.

6 For a discussion of a key film from the 1980s, *Hush-a-Bye-Baby* (Margo Harkin, 1989) which is, in part, a contemporary exploration of these issues, see Butler Cullingford (2001: 234–57).

7 Geoffrey Nowell-Smith, *The Companion to Italian Cinema*, London: Cassell and British Film Institute, 1996: 16.

8 The name of course is taken from a Porter show, the first version of which opened in 1936, although it fell short of his previous hit *Anything Goes* (1934). *Red, Hot and Blue* is also the title of a 1949 musical-comedy featuring Betty Hutton and directed by John Farrow.

9 Neil Jordan Papers, "Brute Music" outlines, op. cit., Box 7.

10 See Noel Ignatiev (1995), *How the Irish Became White*, London: Routledge.

Chapter Three

The Company of Wolves (1984)

A central concern within Jordan's work is that of transformation and the related issue of mutability and non-fixity of borders and identities. In the case of *The Company of Wolves*, this is explored thematically (and graphically) in terms of the werewolf and its metamorphoses, but also in the reimagining of the Little Red Riding Hood narrative.[1] Formally, it achieves this, firstly, through problematising linearity — while the film follows a loose narrative, it is organised as a series of dream (within dream) vignettes, punctuated at various moments by stories and events tangential to the main action — and, secondly, in its eschewal of simple generic classification. This is not a standard horror film; it belongs to the sub-genres of the female gothic, the werewolf and the nightmare, as well as to the genres of (sexual) coming-of-age, fantasy, surrealism, expressionism, and *film noir*. As with his novella, *The Dream of a Beast* (1983), and his later work, most notably *We're No Angels*, *The Butcher Boy* and *The End of The Affair*, and in keeping with the fairytale tradition of which *The Company of Wolves* partakes (as indeed do *We're No Angels* and *In Dreams*),[2] Jordan introduces us to a world that is not explicitly fantastic.

Notwithstanding the music and the cinematography, the opening scenes give us a middle-class England complete with the Volvo-owning nuclear family of the Big House — "a checklist" of Thatcherism[3] — it is only as the action unfolds does a truly magical world emerge which threatens to overwhelm and

engulf both the characters and the audience, and in doing so
buck the trend of British cinema which, at the time, largely favoured small-screen productions, naturalism, and literary texts.
(One could read this in cultural-political terms as an Irish director subverting a British aesthetic.) It is within this second
world, between the real and the other, or what is permitted
and open, and concealed and transgressive, that *The Company of
Wolves* hovers.

It is the sense of borderland and "inbetweenness" which the
film, at its best, explores. After all, despite the apparent differences between democratic suburban England and traditional
feudal culture, as *appearance* suggests, everything from within
the dream belongs to the real world, just as the images in a funhouse mirror are a reflection of three-dimensional reality.

However, the film's ending arguably dilutes, if not altogether
undermines this challenging of the status quo, precisely because
it fails to deliver the disturbing image of the wolf and Little Red
Riding Hood in bed together, both in the dream ending, and the
film's ending proper (also a dream?). (At least in the second
ending, the wolf invades Rosaleen's (Sarah Patterson) bedroom,
even if she remains fearful rather than fearfully excited.)[4]

Company fits neatly into Jordan's oeuvre, in its concern with
appearance, or the surface of things and perception; transformation; its fascination with the dark and surreal aspect of the ordinary; its debt to fantasy, most particularly gothic; its recognition
of the compulsive autonomy of desire and emerging sexuality,
explored here (as in *The Miracle*) through the pleasure-seeking
oedipal child; and in its positive registering of the artistic impulse
figured in this instance as dreaming and storytelling. Yet, for
many critics, the film was seen exclusively in terms of writer
Angela Carter with whom he collaborated, and on whose short
story the film is based. For one reviewer, the film incorporated
"recognizable Carter ingredients: the critique of patriarchy, the
genesis of female sexuality, the fascination with the themes of
children's literature and with the fantastic, [and] the taste for
the grotesque" (cited by Anwell, 1988: 77). While Carter's creative impetus is undeniable and will be considered, the focus
within this discussion will remain on Jordan and *his* use of

Carter, not least because, as Anwell (1988) has argued, if negatively, the film is not just a filmed version of her initial story.

Though the film largely draws on Carter's story, which is a
feminist revision of Little Red Riding Hood, other stories, including "The Werewolf", "Wolf Alice", and "The Tiger's
Bride", from her collection The Bloody Chamber (1995; orig.
1979) of which "Company" is one, inform the narrative, as
does Jordan's The Dream of a Beast. Other sources, or at least
creative shadows, include Jean Cocteau, not just in terms of the
thematically related film, La Belle et la Bête (1946), but in its surreal and poetic treatment, and Charles Laughton's atmospheric
The Night of the Hunter (1955). (The film's script identifies a
song which the central character hums as being from this film.)[5]

Perhaps the closest and most quoted (no doubt because of
the film's producer Stephen Woolley's references to it)[6] cinematic affinity is with the British film industry team of Michael
Powell and Emeric Pressburger, whose richly textured visual
and aural surreal and erotic worlds, such as the one created in
the fairytale-inspired The Red Shoes (1948), find a match in Jordan's sumptuous aesthetic. Furthermore, the duo, prefiguring
Jordan, operated in their time against the dominant British realist mode; transcended genre; played with binaries such as good
and evil, rationalism and irrationalism, the spirit and the flesh,
most especially in Black Narcissus (1946) in which paganism and
Catholicism are brought into conflict; placed an emphasis on
texture, spectacle and synergy, rather than on tight linear narrative; but foremost, they explored issues around love, sex and
desire (both sacred and profane) and the implications this might
have within the public sphere. In The Red Shoes, this is figured in
terms of the woman's career. They also drew inspiration from
the arts such as theatre and ballet in The Red Shoes, and opera in
The Tales Of Hoffman (1951), while also suggesting the "transforming power of imagination through art" (Christie, 1985: 89).
Furthermore, prefiguring Jordan, Powell and Pressburger employed deliberate staging and theatricality, and, in so doing,
called attention to the medium itself. This is most explicit in the
cinematically self-reflexive horror Peeping Tom (1960). Indeed,
metaphors of vision and seeing are frequent within their work.

If this is echoed in *Company* at the formal level, most notably in the dream/sleeping girl punctuation and the cinematography which frequently privileges an unanchored eye — what is
often referred to as the shifting pronoun function which creates tension and unease so common in horror films — it is also
at the thematic centre of the film, which seeks to question the
validity of seeing and thus the project of the Enlightenment and
Western thought since the Renaissance.[7] Seeing, Rosaleen suggests, is not the only access to truth. Is not touching as real or
as valid, if not more so, than seeing? But then, as Carter writes
in "Wolf Alice", "two-legs looks, four-legs sniffs" (Carter, 1995:
119; orig. 1979).

Jordan first met Carter at an event in Dublin in 1982 during
the centenary celebrations of the birth of writer James Joyce.
At that time, "The Company of Wolves" had already been reworked as a radio play, and Carter had been commissioned by
Channel 4 to develop it as a thirty-minute script. However,
Jordan argued that, given the shortness of the original tale, a
richer film might be produced by incorporating other stories
from the collection and weaving them together using a dreaming girl as a portmanteau device. While Jordan's reference was
the structure of *A Thousand and One Nights*, in which a young
woman tells enchanting stories in order to stave off her execution, fortuitously, it recalled Carter's engagement with *The
Hundred and Twenty Days of Sodom*, in *The Sadeian Woman*
(1979) in which four prostitutes are imprisoned and survive by
telling stories. Likewise, in *Company*, storytelling (and dreaming,
which is equated with artistic creativity), is recognised, as it is
in other Jordan narratives, as potentially transformative and
liberating.

While dreaming has the possibility of creating another
space — such as literally in the "Dreamland" ballroom of *Angel*,
or the at times transgressive fantasies of Rosaleen — liberation
is not necessarily synonymous with rejection of traditional or-
ganisational arrangements. Often it is the same. In other words,
the dream world is not necessarily different to reality with all
its restrictions and constraints. The Beast returns to his wife in
The Dream of a Beast, while the young Rosaleen is still terrified

at the sight of the wolf, but what is different is their respective acknowledgement and celebration of their secrets and (repressed) desires. Whether the change of Rosaleen from lamb to wolf (Jordan) is permanent or not, or whether she was better to have stayed a lamb and learnt to run with wolves (Carter) is less important perhaps than the fact that Rosaleen learns to write her own biography (as George, Rose and Bob do in *Mona Lisa*, *The Miracle* and *The Good Thief* respectively): she becomes a storyteller herself rather than simply listening to her granny's stories or retelling them, even if the narrative she chooses to retell and so entertain her mother with is one in which a woman occupies a position of power.

Through Rosaleen (who doubles in her dreams as Red Riding Hood, who is called Rosaleen), the transitional space between childhood innocence, curiosity, and the adult world of desire and eroticism is explored. Wearing red glistening lipstick, rouge on her cheeks, and sleeping restlessly with a teenage magazine on her pillow — *My Weekly*, with feature story, "The Shattered Dream" — we voyeuristically invade her room, filled with toys, yet infected by new objects of womanhood, such as the sleeveless shaped white ball gown that hangs on the back of her door.

While downstairs her parents discuss her moodiness, her father, acknowledging his own inadequacies, refuses to intervene on the subject of her awkward *period*, out of which her sister has already broken, we symbolically "rape" this unconscious Lolita and enter her dream. In so doing, not only do we leave behind the safe reality of contemporary England, but we refuse to accept the non-penetrability of borders on which the symbolic depends, and which is attacked as a matter of course within the subgenre of body horror.[8] Indeed, one of the genre's defining features is its graphic translation of the concept that the postmodern condition erases the "private halo"[9] of protection, leaving the subject open and vulnerable to penetration, or traumatic and (in)voluntary transformation, as is the case with the werewolf who feels "the call of nature". In short, bodies become foregrounded and feminised.

In her first dream, her sister Alice (Georgia Slowe), arguably figured as de Sade's submissive Justine, complete in flowing white dress (which recalls Alice's attire in Lewis Carroll's *Alice's Adventures in Wonderland*), runs through a typically staged eerie forest, but, given the Hammer film tradition, all the more threatening for that, only to be killed by a pack of wolves. During her fatal journey, which is a dark echo in reverse of the film's opening scene, when a similarly dressed Alice runs through the (real) forest so as to be home before her parents' arrival, she encounters Rosaleen's toys. These toys belong to the secret world of the imagination and nighttime. No longer inanimate, they breath, are larger than life — expressed in their magnified scale — and know the secrets of the parents' bedroom. They are not some philosophical agents akin to Pinocchio or the Replicants of *Blade Runner* (Ridley Scott, 1982/1991), to aid the understanding of what it is to be human or real, but expressions of the uncanny, who belong to a "marginal, liminal, potentially carnival world" (Kuznets, 1994: 2). The sailor man, like the giant teddy bear, wants to hug the frightened Alice in an embrace that clearly promises something more, perhaps too much. Yet their threatening aspect is born through her lack of innocence, her adult knowledge and voyeuristic desire to gaze upon the primal scene.

Indeed, when she approaches the oversized dollhouse, which may betray a "longing to be small enough to return to the womb" (Kuznets, 1994: 119), of all the rooms, she is drawn to the master bedroom. There are no dolls to enjoy the model of bourgeois (repressive) organisation, but a large, all-too-real rat peeping out of a four-poster bed. Though she reacts in disgust at the animal invasion and the base physicality of sexuality, it is an image that recalls Beatrix Potter's *The Tale of Two Bad Mice* (1904)[10] in which two subversive and destructive mice invade a dollhouse and, prefiguring the werewolf hunter of *Company* who smashes granny (Angela Lansbury) into porcelain pieces, the pair, frustrated by the artificiality of the dollhouse, throw the food made of nothing but plaster until it breaks into little pieces. Despite their wearing of clothes, and their own version of domesticity, they are presented as a more engaging, warm and natural alternative to the inanimate world of the dolls and middle class over-civilisation.

If Alice refuses this world enjoyed by the rat and Potter's mice, her sister, like Lucie in Potter's *The Tale of Mrs Tiggy-Winkle* (1905), one of the books that lies on her shelf, whole-heartedly enters it. Of course, this particular world belongs to Tiggy Winkle, the hedgehog[11] washer-woman who cleans the skin-coats of the various animals. Rosaleen's werewolf, who can pull off his skin, then is only a darker version of this more benign childhood fantasy, that ultimately remains surreal, just like the enormous turnip of Rosaleen's other book.

By killing off Alice, Rosaleen effectively removes the first obstacle to her own maturation and sexual fulfilment. As in fairytales, the absence created through the death of the (grand)mother or eldest daughter is filled by the next in line. In order to resolve the oedipal journey, the child must necessarily displace the older, more sexually attractive, competition. Arguably, that is the reason why Little Red Riding Hood gives precise directions to the wolf as to where the grandmother lives; it is not to direct the danger to a woman who should know (better) how to deal with it, but to have her destroyed.[12] While such intergenerational conflict is suggested in "Company" through the image of granny's bones rattling as Red Riding Hood and the wolf begin to discover their mutual desire, it becomes explicit in Carter's "The Werewolf" when Red Riding Hood reveals her granny to be the werewolf. Having forced her out of the community, she takes over her home wherein she prospers.

The dreams that follow move away from the intimacies of the childhood bedroom and into a more obviously psychosexual world of Red Riding Hood. Into, in other words, the territory best explored by Bruno Bettelheim in *The Uses of Enchantment* (1978) in which he argues that the function of fairytales is to act as "magic mirrors" into our inner selves, which help in the discovery of the path(s) to adulthood, contentment and independence.

Red Riding Hood is known in many versions (see Zipes, 1993, and Bettelheim, 1978: 166–83, passim): Charles Perrault's (1697)[13] cautionary moralistic, anxiety-producing tale in which both granny and Red are gobbled up; the various sanitised modern retellings where the wolf hides granny in the closet, Red is saved by a hunter (the father), and where even the wolf survives; the feminist readings of either Roald Dahl[14] in which Red whips a pistol from her knickers and shoots the wolf, or Langley[15] where the damsel(s) in distress are saved by the mother/daughter, while the wolf, in a crisis of masculinity, is removed from a position of power and learns never to talk to "strange" girls again; and the revisionist tales of Charles Marelles's[16] Golden Hood in which Red's hood, spun from the rays of the sun by her granny (who is regarded as something of a good witch), burns the wolf's mouth before granny drowns him, and later, Tex Avery's modernist self-reflexive film cartoons (*Red Hot Riding Hood*, 1943, *Swing Shift Cinderella*, 1945, *Little Rural Riding Hood*, 1949) which, steadfastly refusing the sentimentality of Walt Disney's 1922 animation version, present a sexually bubbling and unavailable Red, the granny as a wanton lush and the sexually aroused wolf. However, the most popular version remains that of the Brothers Grimm ("Little Redcap(e)" / "Rotkäppchen", 1812).[17]

In order to understand its reworking by both Carter and Jordan, here is a summary of the Grimms' version. Red is sent by her mother to her ill grandmother. Though she is warned away from over-curiosity and the discovery too early of adult secrets — do not "stare all around the room" when you get to her cottage — and reminded not to stray from the path — "you'll fall and break [your] bottle" (Grimm, 1982: 63) — when she meets the wolf in the forest, not only does she tell him exactly where she is going, but she allows herself to be persuaded by him to experience the pleasures of nature. In this " innocent" way, Red delays and goes deeper and deeper into the forest picking flowers. When at last she could carry no more, she goes to her granny's. There, in her granny's bed wearing a bonnet, is the wolf. (Perrault's wolf remains naked and hiding under the covers, and invites a willing Red to join him in bed.)

Red goes through a series of observations which catalogue all but one of the wolf's senses: "what big ears you have [hearing] . . . eyes [seeing] . . . hands [touching] . . . jaws [mouth/ taste]" (Grimm, 1982: 64).[18] The wolf responds to her interest in him by eating her (the end of Perrault's tale). A huntsman who happens to be passing hears the loud snores of satisfaction and, fearing something the matter with the old lady, goes in. In her place he finds the "old sinner" (Grimm, 1982: 65). As he is about to shoot him, he thinks that she may be inside him, so, refusing his own desire (of vengeful violence), he slits the wolf's "pregnant" belly open and out pop the pair. It is left to Red to punish the wolf, whom she decides they should fill up with stones, the weight of which causes him to fall over and die. Now safe, Red learns her lesson: "As long as I live I'll never again leave the path and run into the forest by myself, when mother has said I mustn't" (Grimm, 1982: 65).

Carter's Red refuses this lesson but, as in Gustave Doré's illustration (described in Bettelheim, 1978: 176; Zipes, 1993), finds liberation with the wolf. She happily burns the "protection" given to her by her over-doting grandmother, which doubles as sexual invitation — her red cloak, the colour of passion and of menses, the blood she must spill to live and become a woman — before she freely kisses him (cf In Dreams, Chapter Twelve).

In many of the tales, Grimms' and Carter's included, we are reminded that Red is too loved and is too spoiled. If this suggests a transferring of fault from the child to the adult, in the film, culture is also implicated. For the bespectacled grandmother is nothing more than a life-size replica of the porcelain doll who sits benignly on Rosaleen's bedroom shelf and who speaks the myths, superstitions and the consolatory fictions of "sweetest tongue" yet "sharpest tooth"[19] which seek to control by reproducing and ensuring subjection to the dominant ruling (patriarchal) ideology. If art or creativity, in the form of her dreaming, gives a possible way out to the sleeping Rosaleen, the social fictions (and narcissistic fantasies of her own beauty and difference from the other villagers, as well as her discovery of the nest) are figured as subtle forms of ideological entrapment, which elsewhere are explored both by Carter (in her non-fiction such as The Passion of New Eve, 1977, and The Sadeian Woman, as well as in her fairytale collection The Bloody Chamber) and by Jordan (Dream of a Beast, The Butcher Boy). Arguably, the film Company makes this point in a much more obvious way than the short story. As the werewolf says to Rosaleen on their first meeting, "for believing in old wives' tales, you deserve to be punished".

Rather than simply play with an uncontextualised Red Riding Hood narrative, Carter opens by placing the wolf within the dangerous economy of natural or non-rational appetite, and relates a series of tales and origin stories about werewolves (all but one appearing in the film in some form). Only then, having drawn the wolf as a sexual flesh-consuming creature with "huge" genitals (Perrault's wolf), does she give her account of Red.

Importantly, the adventure is temporally located within the Christian Calendar, for according to legend (noted in both the short story and the film), anyone born on Christmas Eve is predestined to become a werewolf, all the more certain, if also born feet first and of a wolf father (story) / priest (film). Red's/Rosaleen's walk into the forest begins on Christmas Eve and by the story's end on Christmas morning, the werewolves' birthday, she and he sleep "sweet and sound" in granny's bed.

While such a time-frame is not invoked in the film, other than Rosaleen's comment on the wolves' carol singing, religious imagery and the church in general is given more emphasis, even if, like the pious old granny's bible in "Company", or the convent in "Wolf Alice", it is seen to be largely irrelevant and having little value or use against nature/natural desire. (In the film, the hunter father (David Warner) refuses to wear the silver cross, preferring instead to take only his gun. Through this pact with nature and violence, he shows himself not to be as wise as the Grimms' huntsman or as his no-nonsense wife (Tusse Silberg) who seems to intuitively transcend, though not at a material level, the myths designed to control her sexuality. As she tells Rosaleen, "if there is a beast in men it finds its match in women".)

While in film, Hammer's *Curse of the Werewolf* (Terence Fisher, 1961) was the first to emphasise the werewolf's anti-Christian aspect, it had already been an established part of the mythology.[20] Likewise so, too, was the understanding of the wolf as evil, just as much as the telltale physical characteristics — deep-set eyes, bushy meeting eyebrows and the index finger longer than the middle one — and its relation to cannibalism,[21] sin,[22] and magic.[23] After all, the preeminent Christian text, the bible, regards the wolf in an almost wholly negative light.

Poor granny believes in "the Word" or the patriarchal positioning of women and men. As such she is like Alice, who appears only in the film and not in Carter's story. Both then are lambs to the wolf, and are groomed like de Sade's Justine, just as granny, in turn, grooms or attempts to groom Rosaleen for the slaughterhouse. However, Rosaleen, though barely a woman, knows she is "nobody's meat" and simply laughs "full in the face" (Carter, 1995: 118; orig. 1979) at the wolf. In that one act, she frustrates his power over her, simultaneously "demolishing fear and piety . . . thus clearing the ground for an absolute free investigation".[24] It is only in this way that she repositions herself so that she can be free to seduce him, not as a victim who enjoys her seduction but as an active agent.

The problem with the film as a feminist text, or as a translation of Carter's intention, is that no such act of resistance or subversion happens. Instead, Rosaleen acquiesces when she comes face to face with the handsome werewolf and he demands his kiss. However, when his kiss bites her, she nervously jumps back — no longer a "sealed" system, her own desire has removed her innocence and, in Carter's words, has shown her "how to shiver" (Carter, "The Company of Wolves", 1995: 114; orig. 1979). As she pushes him away she cries, "Jesus, what sharp teeth you have." She then shoots him unconvincingly with his rifle, managing only to wound his shoulder. This sets off a rage-pain induced orgasmic transformation at which she looks on in frozen fascination, after which he is little more than a whimpering, gentle wolf — his masochism satisfied.

A similar connection between the terrific pain occasioned by the metamorphosis, often played out on the soundtrack as much as in the physical contortions required of the subject, and the ultimate exhilaration which it produces is common within post-1960s body-based cinema. If in The Fly (David Cronenberg, 1986), the effect of Seth's first tele-transportation is a heightened sexual appetite, many other films, including The Howling (Joe Dante, 1980) and An American Werewolf in London (John Landis, 1981) which initiated a new cycle of werewolf films[25] of

which *Company*, while more than these, is also one, see bodily
pleasure as occurring in the precise moment of the labour-
birthing process. These werewolf films distinguish themselves
from their earlier counterparts in their high budgets, their focus on physicality and viscerality, and their reliance on often
gross, though spectacular, effects.

While *Company*'s traveller man's transformation neatly fits
this pain-satisfaction model (or masochistic-induced orgasm)
adopting new horror's paradigm of crunching bones and
stretching bloodied ligaments and muscle, the huntsman's re-
birth does so also, but differently. This is because the first is
figured within an economy of property rights and punishment
— she is, after all, legally his wife — while the other is about
sexual union and desire. In this latter case of the huntsman
(Micha Bergese) and Rosaleen, the metamorphosis in part is
fetishistically presented as undulating, thrusting flesh against a
black background. His body is abstracted and eroticised; only
after this does the camera pull back in order to see the "erection" shot of the wolf's head violently emerging out of the
hunter's mouth. This image can be read as a male form of giving
birth (or couvade) and recalls the belief that a werewolf simply
wore his pelt inside out. Like the pre-eighteenth-century one-
sex theory in which the woman was understood to be an inverted or interiorised and therefore inferior male, this celebrates the possibility of slippage between one state and another
(and Jordan's interest in fluidity and in-betweenness).[26]

Rather than dismissing the image which follows of Rosaleen
petting the now quietened huntsman/wolf as she tells him a
story about a she-wolf (who came from the well — the subal-
tern water of the village — and who, like Francie in *The Butcher
Boy* or Vivian in *In Dreams*, though meaning no harm, is feared),
as unproblematically belonging to a tradition of Victorian sentimentality of the child within domesticated nature, it is more
fruitful to understand it as a metaphor of ambiguity. As such,
like the tiger cub who rests on Michael Jackson's knee on the
cover of his *Thriller* album, it plays on the notion of barely contained "menace beneath a cute and cuddly surface".[27]

When the villagers arrive at the scene, the werewolf as wolf escapes, yet inside the cottage another wolf stares at the intruders. Rosaleen's father raises his gun to shoot, just as his wife notices that around the wolf's neck hangs Rosaleen's silver cross. As she restrains him, Rosaleen the she-wolf escapes. Given the film's overriding interest in the male werewolf and the connection made to male sexuality represented through the granny's stories as aggressive and bestial (though this is not validated in either the village boy's courtship of Rosaleen or in her mother's account of the marital bed), the (unseen) metamorphosis of Rosaleen troubles the meaning of what a werewolf signifies. At the Freudian level, it may be interpreted as the ego (Rosaleen) failing to negotiate the id (desire) and, in a dissolution of the subject, becoming the id. As such, this could be seen as her rejection of the symbolic (and its oppressive law and language) and a return to the imaginary; put another way, a realisation of the masochistic fantasy. Alternatively, is her transformation the result of his bite under a reddish full moon; her acknowledgment of sexuality and him having "lick[ed] the skin off" her (Carter, "Tiger's Bride", 1995: 67; orig. 1979); an ironic reversal of fairytales' animal groom — in keeping with the logic of the sympathetic wounding of the wolf/man — in which instead of the beast changing back into a human, the lover sympathetically becomes a beast; or, because she has become monstrously "other" through her monthly bleeding?

At the most basic level, the transformation can be read as a continuing interest in the continuity between man and beast in a culture that seems obsessed with our interrelation and oneness with the technological, most popularly expressed in the figure of the cyborg. Indeed, it is fitting that while the film is not specifically located in history, it invokes the period of the Enlightenment. Even if its faith in reason, logic and seeing is critiqued, in line with postmodern thought, it was through the philosophical work of La Mettrie, Descartes and others, and later, the scientific studies of Darwin, that the pre-eminence of man was challenged and a link made between animal and machine, and animal and man.[28] (A theme the film more subtly explores through the dreaming Rosaleen is the later insight of psychology that man is not even the master of his own mind.)

This periodising is explicit in granny's story, retold by Rosaleen, which is set in the lavish aristocratic world of the eighteenth century and tells of a spurned woman who exacts revenge. One of the film's centrepieces, it suggests the fungibility between man and beast, but within a cultural framework of class and national identity that graphically re-imagines the decline of the "Big House" traced by the Gothic novel in a most abrupt way. It is not industry and the rise of a working/middle class, but the reassertion of the marginal, the primitive and the magical which is the cause of their removal from power. (Jordan returned to this theme in *High Spirits* and *Interview with the Vampire*.) Within a great marquee in the grounds of a big estate (Rosaleen's own twentieth-century home), wigged and powdered ladies and gentlemen greedily enjoy a wedding feast. A pregnant woman (Dawn Archibald), with flowing red hair and natural dress, intrudes. After revealing the groom's (Stephen Rea) carnal relationship with her, she looks into a mirror, which reflects back images of the guests and, causing it to shatter, transforms the entire party into wolves with the exception of the servants and musicians. In this state, every night, they visit to serenade her and her child with their howls which, as Rosaleen understands, though her mother does not, gives the woman power over them. While Carter's story describes the source of their song as "misery", the film is more ambiguous. Interestingly, in the story the woman is simply a witch, yet in the film she is marked as Other in more mundane ways, not least by her Scottish accent, the fantasy of the Celtic oppressed.

The ending proper returns us to the film's beginning; once again we are in Rosaleen's bedroom. The dreaming girl wakes up screaming as her dreams become real. A company of wolves invade her home in a manner that echoes the family dog's attempted intrusion into her bedroom in the opening scene. In short, that which was her repressed fantasy becomes liberated. One after another, the wolves crash through a picture in the hallway, in what conceivably represents an attack on passive femininity and the "lies" and illusions produced by art. While the freeing of the repressed and the film's aperture — central to so much horror — is undeniably positive, her scream also invites negative comment. Despite her dream of assertion over the body and critique of Alice as submissive, because she embraced her role as sacrificial lamb, she, it would seem, is still Little Red Riding Hood, not yet a woman.

Concluding the film with a recitation of Perrault's Poem only seems to confound the problem, even if it can (or should be) read against itself to suggest that it is smug ideological righteousness or those who prescribe to the dominant discourses of control (such as the granny) that ultimately represent the "sharpest tooth" rather than the silky-voiced seducer werewolf, who, after all, only has power in proportion to his attraction.

That said, Jordan too has acknowledged his own misgivings with regard to the film's ending, feeling that he could have done more justice to it. The initial intention was that, after dreaming, she wakes with a start only to die, then dives "into the floor which is like a swimming pool and the floor boards ripple and she vanishes . . . but I just couldn't realise it"[29] (Jordan in Dwyer, 1997: 2). While, as Jordan notes, "it would have been a beautiful thing to see", more than that, it would have highlighted Jordan's (rather the Carter's) interest in the borderland and the bat's philosophy, in *Dream of a Beast*, who tells the beast, "you take your texture from whatever surface you inhabit" (Jordan, 1993: 156; orig. 1983).

Unfortunately, special effects got in the way. Yet, ironically, the film, at one level, is nothing more than its various effects and animatronics, even if like many science fiction films it uses and depends on technology to critique the technological and technocratic culture, and celebrate desire and the irrational. Notwithstanding the film's straddling of many genres and the danger and inappropriateness of seeing *Company* as a horror movie — it was because of this that it failed at the box office in America (see Finney, 1996: 81–2) — nevertheless, as already noted, it belongs to the material world of body horror, and thus to the sub-generic category of special effects.

One of the primary elements of the body horror aesthetic is the unflinching photographic presentation of the physical body which is subjected to violent manipulations to the point where its integrity is no longer apparent. In that sense, it is ultimately a cinema of attractions, whereby cinema's ability to show and transform is celebrated, but the act of showing goes beyond presentation and (self)consciously (through promotional material, fanzines, programmes on special effects and "The Making of . . .") demands to be seen as effects: ones judged not according to anatomical correctness, but cinematic and aesthetic norms. Therefore, the effects are not invisible as technological innovations that enable imaging and meaning, which is how they often function in *Interview with the Vampire* or later in *The Butcher Boy*, but are in themselves crucial to the creation of meaning.

To conclude, Jordan's *Company* is not myopically focused on Carter's feminism, but presents a world that is resolutely physical, ambiguous and fluid. If his Red is also Lolita who is rarely given the privileged cinematic point of view, such as the scene when she climbs the tree and looks below to the forest floor and her lost young suitor, and fits the dominant representation of Red as a female who "asks for it" (Zipes, 1993), she is allowed at least to confront her own desires, and in her dream learns to use art to transform herself. In that, she is a typical Jordan character.

Notes

---

[1] For an in-depth discussion of the different literary versions of the fairytale, complete with the full texts of over 40 of these, see Zipes (1993). The texts range from Charles Perrault's 1697 version to Sally Miller Gearhart's 1990 "Roja and Leopold".

[2] Jordan has described *We're No Angels* as "a little fairytale with a very ironic twist to it" (Glicksman, 1990: 68). It was not until *In Dreams* (1998) that Jordan returned explicitly to fairytales. The latter film is a reworking of "Snow White", though it draws on a number of other fairytales.

3 See Sue Harpur (2000), *Women in British Cinema*, London and New York: Continuum, 149.

4 However, there is also the argument that to have Rosaleen as sexually willing only serves to facilitate the male fantasy whereby the girl enjoys her own rape and submission. See Zipes (1993).

5 *Sight and Sound*, Vol. 53, No 3, Summer 1984: 164–5.

6 Woolley in Finney (1996: 71).

7 See Martin Jay (1993), *Downcast Eyes*, Berkeley, Los Angeles and London: University of California Press.

8 For an overview of Body Horror, see *Screen Special issue on Body Horror*, Vol. 27, No.1, 1986.

9 See Jean Baudrillard "The Ecstasy of Communication" in *The Anti-Aesthetic*, Hal Foster, ed. (1983), Seattle: Bay Press, 126–33, who suggests that the postmodern subject or schizophrenic has "no halo of private protection, not even his own body, to protect him anymore" (p. 132).

10 Originally published by Frederick Warne & Co, it is widely available, separately or as part of the 12-volume *Peter Rabbit* collection.

11 It is the sight of the hedgehog that leads the traveller man on his wedding night to hear the call of nature. Ironically, in the pre-Perrault oral version of the tale as it was probably disseminated in the French countryside during the late Middle Ages, the little girl uses the excuse of needing to relieve herself in order to escape the werewolf at Granny's house. She persuades him to tie a rope to her foot and let her go outside. Once there, she ties the rope to a tree and escapes (Zipes, 1993: 346–8, and 18–25).

12 Zipes (1993) offers an alternative reading of Red's actions. For him, the different versions of the stories are largely sexist, in that they display a male fantasy of rape, whereby the female makes a "pact" with the seducer and is asking for trouble. In this, they prop up notions of male power and rationalise male dominance. Accordingly, Red's directions to the wolf are part of her contract with him: her sacrificing of her granny so that she can share her granny's bed with him.

[13] Included in *The Blue Fairy Book*, Andrew Lang, ed., orig. 1889, London: Longmans, Green and Co.; unabridged 1965, New York: Dover, and in Zipes (1993).

[14] Roald Dahl (1982), "Little Red Riding Hood and the Wolf", in *Revolting Rhymes*, London: Jonathan Cape. Much of the more experienced and recent versions since 1983 have been written by women and are feminist (Zipes, 1993). One such feminist reworking that Zipes includes is the Irish writer Anne Sharpe's "Not So Little Red Riding Hood" which was published as part of a feminist revision of classic fairytales under the title *Rapunzel's Revenge*, Dublin: The Attic Press, 1985. The anthology also includes Carol Lanigan's "All the better to See You".

[15] Langley, Jonathan (1992), *Little Red Riding Hood*, London: Picture Lions (An imprint of Harper Collins).

[16] "The True History of Little Goldenhood", in *The Red Fairy Book*, Andrew Lang, ed., orig. 1890, London: Longmans, Green and Co.; unabridged 1966, New York: Dover. Included in Zipes (1993), dated as 1888.

[17] The Grimms offer two different versions of the story. In one there is a variant ending "in which the girl and her grandmother trick the wolf into falling off the roof and drowning" (Grimm, 1982: 398). Other versions can be found in Bettelheim (1978) and Zipes (1993), who offers almost 40 complete versions of the tale, and titles and bibliographic details of almost 150, as well as including references for further Little Red Riding Hood bibliographies. Additionally, readily available narratives include the sanitised and unfortunately popular version by Maureen Spurgeon, *Fairytale Treasury Book Three*, Leicestershire: Brown Watson, 1995. In Spurgeon, the wolf puts granny into the closet, and just as he is about to kill Red Riding Hood, a hunter arrives and saves her. He goes to shoot the wolf, but the wolf runs away. Another re-telling is the self-conscious "Little Bad Wolf and Red Riding Hood" (by Timothy Tocher in *Newfangled Fairytales, Book #1*, Bruce Lansky, ed.) In this re-working, Red is never in real danger but is exploited by the wolf who dressed as the granny gives her daily grocery lists. The wolf's son in an ironic twist is warned not to stray onto the path because people are dangerous. See also Michael Cole-

man (1999), *Fairy Stories: Top. Ten*, London: Scholastic. Includes "Snow-drop", pp. 73–82; and "Little Red Riding Hood" pp. 128–37.

18 It would seem that Red, unlike Rosaleen, relies primarily on her own vision; in Jonathan Langley's narrative Red is alerted in the first instance by the "funny smell of old dogs" as well as the gruff sound of the wolf's voice.

19 Reference to Charles Perrault's Poem (1697), included at the end of the film.

20 See "The Werewolf" in Daniel Cohen (1971), *A Natural History of Unnatural Things*, New York: McCall, 33–52.

21 Plato recounts a tale of a man who on eating human flesh is transformed into a wolf.

22 Those excommunicated by the church were in danger of becoming a werewolf.

23 It could be brought on through magic or the devil's ointment, various herbs and spells.

24 Mikhail Bakhtin (1981), "Epic and Novel", in *The Dialogical Imagination*, Austin: University of Texas, 23, cited in Robert Stam (1989), *Subversive Pleasures*, Baltimore, London: John Hopkins University Press,: 120, note 36, 248).

25 For a comprehensive listing of werewolf films, see Bryan Senn and John Johnson (1992), *Fantastic Cinema Subject Guide*, Jefferson, North Carolina and London: McFarland, 557–92; and Stephen Jones (1996), *The Illustrated Werewolf Movie Guide*, London: Titan.

26 For a discussion of the one-sex model see Thomas Laqueur (1990), *Making Sex: Body and Gender from the Greeks to Freud*, Cambridge: Harvard University Press. See also Carol Clover (1992), *Men, Women and Chainsaws*, London: British Film Institute.

27 Kobena Mercer (1986), "Monster Metaphors: Notes on Michael Jackson's 'Thriller'", *Screen* (op. cit., note 8).

28 See Bruce Mazlish (1993), *The Fourth Discontinuity*, New Haven and London: Yale University Press.

²⁹ Throughout *The Dream of a Beast*, Jordan uses the image of water. In one dream, for example, the beast/husband dreams of being a boy looking down into a room of women who hold cups glistening with liquid; after they enter a tiny arch, they re-emerge with empty cups. He bends to look closer, but they notice his shadow and look up, the glass on which he is supported melts slowly, as does he and he as a liquid falls into a cup, and "a woman's face with two soft, feathered lips bent towards me to drink" (Jordan, 1993: 97).

The novella's narrative is about the possibility of transformation and finding acceptance and love, even within the constraints of the family. The story follows the inner turmoil and physical change of a man who feels alienated from his wife and child and work. In response, he becomes a beast, an excessive male, with hairy biceps as a way to deal with his environment. He breaks out of the domestic trap and has an affair with a mysterious woman client of his who has employed him to do an advertising campaign on the perfume, "musk". He finds shelter in a boiler house where he strikes up an intimate relationship with a young boy. Soon his lover cannot bear his monstrosity and leaves. He learns to fly with "pure desire" and takes the boy with him. He finds his lover who has been similarly transformed, but it is too late for them. He incorporates the dying boy into himself and sees his wife who has their daughter inside of her. They kiss. His voice become like hers, his lips soft again, and in his visage reflected in her eyes he sees "something as human as surprise" (Jordan, 1993: 175).

The novella, which draws on a number of issues — around the body, the family, alienation, transformation, difference, love — also pre-empts *The Miracle* and Sam's dream forecast of his death, in that the father is seen to fear that he cannot live up to the requirements demanded by his family. At one point, he involuntarily drowns his wife and child because he cannot perform, he loses the liquid beat, and the sweat on the keys, a sign of his failure, washes over them, and turns everything to liquid (Jordan, 1993: 132–3). Parallels, especially the notion of humans flying, can also be drawn to the unrealised project *Broken Dream*.

Chapter Four

Mona Lisa (1985)

Mona Lisa, Mona Lisa, men have named you
You're so like the lady with the mystic smile
Is it only 'cause you're lonely they have blamed you
For that Mona Lisa strangeness in your smile.
Do you smile to tempt a lover, Mona Lisa
Or is this your way to hide a broken heart
Many dreams have been brought to your doorstep
They just lie there, and they die there
Are you warm, are you real, Mona Lisa
Or just a cold and lonely, lovely work of art.

In *Mona Lisa*, Jordan's first sustained foray into contemporary British life and its seedy underside, he explicitly introduced the issue of race. While he had already explored this implicitly in "Night in Tunisia" and *Angel*, where it had been filtered through the culturally expressive African-American jazz music central to both narratives, in *Mona Lisa*, two of the film's central characters are black — Simone (Cathy Tyson), "the tall thin black tart" or "nigger whore" with whom the *film noir* "hero" George (Bob Hoskins) falls in love and whom the film's mystery surrounds, and her aggressive though suave pimp, Anderson (Clarke Peters), also known as Mr Lester Smith. This interest in race has since emerged as one of the most controversial aspects of his cinema, particularly in the wake of *The Crying Game*.

However, it has been mostly bound up with representations of women, who, more generally, have tended to operate in

symbolic rather than real terms. This latter point is clearly acknowledged in the film's title song, where the very enigma that
woman presents is registered. In the song, as in much of Jordan's work, rarely is the woman allowed a voice or life. Instead,
she becomes a work of art, a silent projection of male fantasies
which she unproblematically reflects back. Indeed, when George
at the film's end recounts a summary narrative in the third person of his relationship and infatuation with Simone, the accompanying image that Jordan presents is of her seen as an image in
George's car rear-view mirror. Unsurprisingly, as a result, Jordan has been criticised by feminist writers.

If Jordan tends to favour representations (and the traditional virgin/whore dichotomy) over "real" women, he nevertheless highlights their status as such and in so doing raises
interesting questions concerning reality and art. For example,
the boys in "Night in Tunisia" are seen to be caught in a web of
messy images and classifications which finally cancel out the
woman, while George, it transpires, and he finally accepts,
never really knew Simone. He was just like all her clients who
see in her what they desire and reinvent her identity to suit
their tastes. She becomes George's "lady" only in so far as
teenage prostitute May becomes Cathy so as to fit his desire.

Jordan's interest in representation and reality, or the slippage or perceived slippage or confusion between them is not
limited to women. In a comic moment, which serves to emphasise George's inability to distinguish art from reality, he looks
for reassurance that the spaghetti which Thomas (Robbie Coltrane) has cooked for him is real, and not one of the plastic
ornamental kitsch sculptures which Thomas, in an earlier scene,
had shown him. The identical job lot of spaghettis, which is like
an Andy Warhol reworking of Claes Oldenburg's plaster "Two
Cheeseburgers, with Everything" (1962), is a multiple image of
mockery and frustration of desire which sums up the cheapness
and banality of their world, and highlights George's difficulty in
reading art and reality.

Interestingly, the other consignment that Thomas has in his
garage is a "choir" of illuminated plastic Virgin Marys. This fits
neatly into Jordan's critical engagement with religion, spirituality

or belief and miracles, which is brought to the fore in a number of his films, not least in *We're No Angels*, which is "an extended joke on the irony of religious belief" (Glicksman, 1990: 11). More importantly, the figure of the Madonna at that film's centre, is a *statue*. In short, it makes literal what is only suggested in *Mona Lisa*, that religion itself is a commodity.

The film represents a dark fairytale that traces George's adventures in a strange contemporary environment which he never fully understands or becomes comfortable with. In a sense, it follows him down a version of the magical rabbit hole of *Alice in Wonderland* — and out again at Brighton, when he no longer clutches the white rabbit that he (unwittingly) uses as a ticket into the seedy urban world. At the end of the film, he walks away from the rabbit and its dead owner, Mortwell (Michael Caine). If the image seems surreal, it nonetheless betrays Jordan's interest in the fairytale, which found more explicit expression in, notably, *Company of Wolves* and *In Dreams*.

On his release after seven years in prison (for a crime he may not have committed), George, a petty criminal, walks across a Thames bridge at dawn to experience the city anew. The bridge as metaphor of transition is used repeatedly in the film and looks to another bridge, that of *We're No Angels*, where it serves the same purpose. In this case, the bridge brings him literally and metaphorically to a new world, something made clear once he is rejected by his ex-wife (Pauline Melville). Refusing to let him speak with their teenage daughter Jeannie (Zoe Nathenson), she slams the door in his face. He responds to her insult and display of power by hurling abuse and throwing a rubbish bin at the door. This domestic scene, to the annoyance of the racist George, takes place in front of the racially mixed neighbours. During his absence, the area has been transformed with many "darkies" living there. Their presence as well as their disgust at his violence, and his wife's independence and rejection of the nuclear family, function as the first signs of threat to this representative of traditional working-class masculinity, which is under siege throughout the film (Hill, 1999: 168).

After he causes another disturbance on the street by deliberately knocking over a bin, he is rescued from the ensuing fight by his friend Thomas who, in effect, becomes his "wife" and who has a house — a caravan within his warehouse. George shares with Thomas an interest in the cult thriller writer John Franklin Bardin (*The Deadly Percheron* is commented on during the course of the film) whose complex plots serve as a form of *mise-en-abyme* to the events in George's life, just as Rose's writing does in *The Miracle*. Indeed, both he and George seek to incorporate George's adventures into that story and one written in the same style. As Jordan has commented, the film is not so much a *noir* story as about someone (George) who is obsessed with narrative and "who sees himself as a hero in a *film noir* story" (Barra, 1990: 41) and Thomas, like Rose does for Jimmy (*The Miracle*), helps him to do this.

George, complete with the aforementioned white rabbit, goes in search of his former crime boss, Denny Mortwell, who owes him a favour, George having apparently taken the rap for one of Mortwell's crimes and not implicated him. However, as Thomas warns, the rules of the game, and the game itself, have changed. George, like Jimmy, refuses to heed the advice, and enters this new criminal world that disgusts him. The old bar is now a sleazy stripjoint with prostitutes upstairs and computers in the office. It is part of a much bigger operation that, as Mortwell later smugly (if not fully true) points out, is legal. George is re-employed and when issued with a "bleeper", his initial reaction to it sums up his alienation and separation from his new abusive capitalist "family".

Though one of his jobs is to deliver pornographic videos to Soho sex shops, it is his role as driver, and later, unconsummated lover, of young black prostitute Simone which dominates the film. His task is to act as a respectable cover or "date" and take her to appointments with her rich clients, mainly in expensive hotels. One of her nightly visits includes to the home of a wealthy Arab, Raschid (Hossein Karimbeik), which causes Mortwell to be suspicious. At her request, he also drives her to the crude "meat market" of King's Cross.

The pair are poles apart culturally, racially, and financially. Simone has risen above her working-class origins, and is unimpressed with George's vulgarity and cheapness, which is epitomised in the new loud clothes he buys with money that he reluctantly accepts from her. She later dresses him to her taste so that he can appear like the "civilised" men who nevertheless, despite appearances, invariably enjoy more perverted sadistic violence than the physically aggressive George, who is simultaneously an old-fashioned and "moral" romantic.

They gradually settle down to a normal working relationship, and as he begins to mistake her kindness for love, he becomes interested in her and her clients. Simone, taking advantage of this, asks George to help her in her search for Cathy (Kate Hardie), another prostitute who is a heroin addict, and whom she had looked after when they were both working for the same abusive pimp, Anderson. They lost touch when Simone spent a summer in Brighton after being brought there by a client, and through which she transformed herself from a street-walker to a classy call girl.

In Jordan's classic reliance on the image and the photograph, she shows Cathy's picture to George. He subsequently agrees to help her out of love, but also because the young prostitute reminds him of his own daughter, who is the same age. He searches for her in Soho clubs, where a member of Mortwell's "family" arranges a meeting with her. It turns out, in an aside to the Irish migration narrative and the fraught economic and cultural relationship between Ireland and Britain, later touched upon in *The Butcher Boy*, that she is a fifteen-year-old Irish girl, May (Sami Davis), who is regularly abused by her pimp "Mr Smith". However, Lester Smith turns out to be Simone's (and Cathy's) previous pimp, the extremely violent black Anderson — an "animal born in a butcher shop" according to Simone — who likewise controlled them by beatings and seduction. This private history George discovers when he finds a porn video, *Kitchen Kactus*, featuring Simone and Anderson, and in which George shows perhaps too great an interest.

In the meantime, Mortwell asks George about the nature of the relationship between Simone and Raschid, but she only reveals that they "have tea", a cheeky subversion of that most English of rituals. A photograph is presented to him by Simone of them literally drinking tea as a form of verification. Photographs, like all representations, Jordan seems to be saying, are fictions, even and especially while they are offered as documentary proof of reality, further evidence of Jordan's distaste for "facts", or his deconstruction of established and seemingly "natural" truths which are moreover ideological fictions.

George trails Anderson to Cathy. Later, Anderson goes to Simone's home, where he attacks both George and Simone, who are like trapped animals in a caged lift. Jordan returns to this image again when George reinterprets for himself and Thomas his relationship with Simone. He tells him she was not to blame, but like the actress in *Vertigo*, herself only a pawn, or a bird (albeit an exotic one) trapped in a cage. After she bandages him, he takes her to stay with Thomas. George then rescues the stoned Cathy from an elderly "gentleman" client who is being hosted by Mortwell in his big English mansion. Hiding in the adjoining room, behind the one-way glass, which houses video cameras to capture the sessions, George pulls her through the revolving door.

Waiting for Simone to join them, he takes Cathy to a roadside café where she tells him that he knows nothing and hints at the nature of Simone's attraction for her, telling him that "She likes me. She *really* likes me." Thomas brings Simone, who goes to meet Cathy alone. He remains outside, holding Simone's bag and cosmetic case. Satisfied, with his lover and "daughter", or his new nuclear family, he looks to the child's tree house and playground, where a magical white horse stands, suggesting that everything may have turned out fine. This is not the film's only reference to the world of the fairytale and the mystical, though the horse is also a reference to the Bardin novel. However, this fairytale is not destined to have a happy ending.

They go to Brighton to recover, but this particular seaside is not a place of redemption, but of violence and betrayal, if at the same time understanding or acceptance. At their hotel, George comes across the two women holding hands in adjoining beds and realises the full meaning of Simone's "confession" in the lift, that she is "*different*". He later angrily tells Simone that he "sold out for a couple of dykes". As a consequence, his

own infatuation with Simone is misplaced. George drags
Simone to Brighton Pier and in a violent mock seduction echoed in Jimmy's rape of his mother (*The Miracle*) or Vivian's embrace of Claire (*In Dreams*), forces himself on her and shouts a
tirade of abuse on the nature of heterosexual relationships.
Looking into the sea, Simone touches his hand.

Anderson and his henchmen arrive, and George and
Simone escape back to the hotel where Mortwell with the rabbit is waiting for them. Simone draws the gun that George had
given to her for protection and kills Mortwell after he hits her,
saying it really hurt. Likewise, she kills Anderson when he appears. She also seems to be on the point of shooting George,
who is upset at her violence and destruction of male power,
particularly as embodied in his white working-class boss. He
disarms her and leaves to renew his friendship with Thomas,
with whom he finds work as a mechanic. The pair incorporate
George's adventures into a fictionalised "past tense" narrative.
They are joined by Jeannie, whose relationship with her father
has gradually improved, and the film ends as the trio, arms
linked, take a walk in a park in a jaunt recalling Dorothy and
her companions setting off on the yellow brick road to the Emerald City (*The Wizard of Oz*). It is a nuclear "family" emptied of
the threat of adult female sexuality or, as in Mortwell's version,
abuse, power and sexuality.

The original idea for the film came from a newspaper article
about a pimp charged with "Gross Bodily Harm" who claimed
he was trying to save a young girl from "a life of perdition". Jordan wanted to make a love story where an obsessive man falls
for a woman for "the utterly wrong reasons", and where there
was "a total gap in understanding". Self-deprecatingly, Jordan
remarks that such a scenario was "something I was familiar with
at the time". Television dramatist David Leland, who shares the
film's writer credit with Jordan, wrote the first draft of the
script, which, according to the director, "came out really violent" without any "romantic saving graces to it". Bob Hoskins
rejected this version and only after Jordan went to see him to
find out what the actor objected to, was the script rewritten by
Jordan. Hoskins liked the new draft which, according to Jordan,

focused on the theme of "yearning" and was "about [a] man who wanted to love somebody". As would happen three years later with the very different *High Spirits*, where Peter O'Toole's role was written with Sean Connery in mind, so, too, Jordan originally wrote *Mona Lisa* with Connery in the Hoskins role, though, as he later put it, "now you can't think of [*Mona Lisa*] without Bob Hoskins" (Dwyer, 1997: 3).

In terms of the film's design, for Jordan one of the main tasks was to make London "look other than everyday drab" and where the visual would blend with the emotional. Indeed, the whole film is predicated on looking and watching, especially by George as he cruises the streets and clubs. Thus, a lot of work went into turning the city into "some kind of Dante-esque place", a London unfamiliar to those who know it as a cosmopolitan city, and like *Angel* and *The Crying Game*, even *The Miracle*, it resonates with "the world of *film noir*" (Dwyer, 1997: 4), though as Barra suggests, it goes beyond the usual sensuous *noir* so that it becomes "perhaps the first phantasmagorical *noir*" (Barra, 1990: 41). In what is a Jordan trademark already evident in his two previous features, the realist dimension is quickly subsumed in its fictional world, which creates a new psychological and sexual topography or streetscape (Dwyer, 1997: 4).

Critics commented most positively on the film's segments where it suggested a new contemporary British *film noir*. These included scenes with the young prostitutes at King's Cross, which, as Julian Petley put it, "have a genuinely infernal, *Taxi Driver*-ish feel about them[;][1] the plush-hotel foyers which conceal less salubrious goings-on behind their luxurious facades[;] Michael Caine's . . . nasty gangster Mortwell"; "the final bloodbath in Brighton"; and "George's endless traipse through the strip joints, peep shows, and hostess clubs of Soho".[2] As a result, it was championed as containing "the perfect recipe for a British thriller" not least because "it pulls off the difficult trick of seeming to work to an American dynamic while having obviously imported nothing"[3] — except its Irish writer and director! The further irony is Jordan's comment that "Britain is bourgeois — I don't want to insult that country, but it's a very sedate and prosaic place in many ways" (Glicksman, 1990: 71).

The view of human relationships, though, as Petley comments, "which emerges from this urban nightmare is as black as anything produced by Hollywood in the 1940s". The bleakness or the impossibility of the relationships, of course, is directly linked to the hopeless attraction George has for the woman who is not just a prostitute, but is black and lesbian. For Jordan, this made it "an anti-erotic film" which deals with "misplaced passions and emotional devastation".[4]

When Jordan met Cathy Tyson, she commented that unlike in the USA, black British actresses were primarily asked to play nurses or "hookers" — arguably she plays both in this film — nevertheless, her certain "knowability", as Jordan put it, helped to displace her role as such from its clichéd antecedents. Another feature of Tyson's screen presence is how closely she resembles, in terms of physique, dress and hair style, the transvestite Jaye Davidson in The Crying Game.[5] Indeed, Jordan did a screen test of her for that film as a fall-back situation, should the inexperienced Davidson not work out. Thus, Mona Lisa's most fruitful area of exploration from the viewpoint of Jordan's career is the nature of Simone's characterisation and its combination of prostitution and lesbianism, and, ultimately, thwarting of male desire. Unsurprisingly, it is this aspect of the film which has received most serious critical attention.

In an analysis of Jordan's Mona Lisa and The Crying Game from the perspective of African-American representations in the cinema, Joy James regarded Jordan's cinema as exuding "a sensitivity and abhorrence of violence against black females and feminized blacks". However, she went on to say that by linking black women to sexual violence, Jordan's films "project the notion that intermingling with 'blacks' increases not only the possibilities of violence and excitement for whites but also provides opportunities for the expression of white humanity and self-restraint vis-à-vis an unfettered black sexual and physical aggression". Acknowledging that, unusually in the cinema, Jordan gave leading roles to black people, nevertheless, he also "sets the stage for the seduction of the audience via the body of the 'desirable' hybrid black female" in which "white males exude ethical agency as feminized blacks personify pathological sensuality, loyalty, and deception, bordering on violence and chaos" (James, 1995: 33).

While *Mona Lisa* (and later *The Crying Game*) appear to break racial and sexual taboos, nevertheless, "racism and sexism remain fixtures" (James, 1995: 34) throughout because of the cultural clichés used which undermine Jordan's rejection of racism and homophobia. James reads Simone and Dil as mulattas, or hybrids of African and European origin, a status which makes them the most desirable of black women because they are the most (visually) white.

Thus, the tragedy of the mulattas represented in such films as *Imitation of Life* (Douglas Sirk, 1959) where the "hybrid" tries to pass herself off as white as she seeks to love a white man, inevitably ends in sadness and rejection. Miscegenation was one of the most forbidden taboos of commercial cinema until the 1960s, and when barriers to inter-racial relationships were challenged in the cinema, it was usually within the bourgeois constraints of middle-class discourse, as in Sidney Poitier's black middle-class role in the breakthrough film, *Guess Who's Coming to Dinner?* (Stanley Kramer, 1967). By the 1970s, blaxploitation films focusing on black criminality were an important genre, but even in such films as *Shaft* (Gordon Parks, 1971), the relationships (and often explicit sex scenes) were between black people. Even in contemporary soap operas, if Asian and black characters have relationships with people not of their own ethnic group, criticism, usually from a family member, becomes a major obstacle to their union and happiness.

Thus, the context for reading the relationship between George and Simone is conveniently made impossible not because he does not, as he says himself in Brighton, have a "tan", but because she is a lesbian. Indeed, even within the terms of the lesbian affair between Simone and Cathy, it appears that Simone is in the subsidiary position, in that it is she who clearly wants Cathy more than Cathy desires her. The tone of her comment to George that Simone "really likes" her suggests she will take advantage of Simone's love for her. Shortly afterwards, when Simone gives her a chaste kiss on the forehead, it is not reciprocated, nor a hug given. Indeed, in the later scene where

George comes across them and realises that he has no hope of a relationship with Simone, the two women are in separate beds, and though holding hands, there is an absence of an erotic charge between them, or even the hint of a "post-coital" rest. (Jordan, in his commentary on the DVD edition of the film, has described their poses as two statues in "death-like tranquillity".)

As a result, the double tragedy of Simone (and Dil in *The Crying Game*) is that while white, male characters fall in love with these "queer" black, "female" characters, and in the process breach castes and taboos, "these falls into unrequited, unconsummated love signal a plummet into chaos and danger greater than 'normal' sexual obsession". In these films, black female sexuality "is portrayed as pathological and violence is coterminous with sex" (James, 1995: 35). Consequently, the bloody killings by both Simone and Dil reinforce this sense of pathology. As bell hooks notes, the acceptance of difference and the crossing of boundaries "does not disrupt conventional representations of subordination and domination" (quoted in James, 1995: 36). Indeed, as noted, Simone's preferred relationship with Cathy seems also to remain unconsummated, or at least chaste, and potentially exploitative. In fact, after Simone kills the two criminals, her final look, a frozen, almost enigmatic one to Cathy, contains the realisation that she is now the complete outsider and is most likely to end up in jail, losing everything, including Cathy (whom, it must be remembered, never asked to be rescued) and her own freedom.

This ending is significantly different from early drafts of the script retained by Jordan until shortly before the film went into production. In one such version, George, the eternal loser, once more in prison, is bailed out by Thomas and is greeted by Simone, for whom he is taking the rap, as he had earlier for Mortwell, an idea which would find its place at the end of *The Crying Game*, when another loser, Fergus, takes the rap for Dil. In these draft scripts of *Mona Lisa*, after his release from prison, George is taken away, variously to meet either Jeannie or Cathy. One short-lived script idea was to explain Simone's love for Cathy by saying that she was her daughter and her colour was because her father was white. Within a few weeks, this improbable idea was dropped, although it does make explicit George's fantasy of a new nuclear family.[6]

The film's closure as regards Simone reinforces the belief that it is not just the violent pimp and the crime boss on whom she wishes to take revenge, but *all* men, as is suggested when she turns the gun on George, who has risked so much to help her. Though he clearly loves her, he nevertheless has been verbally abusive, remains controlling and over-protective, and also hits her. (He has already reacted with violence to his wife, and his explanation to his daughter that he was a "bad lot" ambiguously suggests that he was "bad" both in the domestic and non-domestic spheres.) He disarms her by hitting her and before leaving, says to her, "You would have done it" and calls her "a fucking cow", the same term he applied to his ex-wife at the beginning of the film. Thus, while the film concerns how (black) women betray men, in the process it is the women who are brutalised since the men retain their (white) humanity. It may appear that women get their wings, but it is men, the film argues, who are the angels.

Indeed, George and Thomas re-construct George's adventures with Simone as something that is over and unimportant: "He was just the driver, just for a little while and that's the story." And his final comment to Jeannie indicates that he will not change. There will be no reconciliation with Simone and, unlike in *The Crying Game*, there will be no transformation: "No. I'll never grow up." It is the trio of whites, Thomas, George and Jeannie, who close the film. As a result, George achieves redemption and a relationship with Jeannie (the "good" side of the other two blond teenagers, Cathy and May) without the dehumanising use of violence, as happens to Simone, even if the gun was supplied by George, what James describes as "the desire to retain innocence by containing violence within the spectacle of the 'sub-human'" (James, 1995: 39).

However, Jeannie has inevitably been "contaminated". This can be seen at a number of levels, firstly in the connection George makes between his daughter and the (innocent) street girls; George cruising by the school looking at her, and later "picking-up" Jeannie; but, most of all, by her bizarre inquiry:

"Do you know any *tricks?*" — the slang term of prostitutes for their clients. He pauses, confused, and kisses her on the cheek. That's a good trick, she tells her father, and leaves him.

The Nat King Cole song "Mona Lisa", which provides the film with its theme tune, suggests that Simone is potentially many things, most of all, an enigma, "the lady with the mystic smile". Certainly, the well-known face painted by Leonardo da Vinci appears as a poster in Thomas's garage, but, as the song asks: "Do you smile to tempt a lover" or "Is this your way to hide a broken heart?" For George, Simone is a virgin and a whore: "A tall thin black tart. But she's a lady", he tells Thomas, as if Simone is a character in one of their stories. But, when he voyeuristically enquires about her clients' relationship with her, she replies: "Sometimes they fall for what they think I am." He asks what, to which she replies, what you think I am, "a black whore". He corrects her, "Let's say you are a lady", to which she replies, in mock formality, "I thank you".

This playing of a role is, of course, at one level what all prostitutes do, as is most pointedly shown in the opening scene of *Klute* (Alan J. Pakula, 1971), where Jane Fonda cries in apparent pleasure for a client as she looks at her watch to determine the end of the session. In the one scene where Simone is seen with a client, she is performing a sadomasochistic role and is clearly annoyed that concerned George has burst in to "save" her, because she already told George that no one hits her.

Hitting then becomes like kissing in *Pretty Woman* (Garry Marshall, 1990): it is a familiarity reserved for male intimates (heterosexual father figures) including her pimps, Anderson (and by extension Mortwell) and George. She is also seen to be "performing" in the video with Anderson, who, of course, she tells George, had beaten her up and threatened to cut her with a knife, but the audience is spared such gruesomeness. While the enigma remains, the song concludes, "Are you warm, are you real, Mona Lisa / Or just a cold and lonely, lovely work of art?" pointing again to an abstract, or representational, notion of women, rather than "real" human beings.

While Joy James comments that "it is unclear how seriously Jordan takes his own morality plays" (James, 1995: 43), perhaps the question really should be: In the end, how sympathetic is Jordan to his female characters, of whatever hue? As with many of Jordan's films, there is a degree of irony, sometimes allowing for (unexpected) distance, even at the most painful moments in the narrative, though in *Mona Lisa*, it is placed in the context of a scene which "is the apex of sadistic viewing" (James, 1995: 42). When drug-addicted Cathy is being sodomised by an elderly man wearing surgeon's gloves, the soundtrack plays a duet from *Madame Butterfly*. In the adjoining room, George looks through a two-way mirror door in shocked disbelief at the brutality of the rape, yet the camera moves from his perspective to a camera placement behind the man in which the audience alternatively watch George watching Cathy being abused and seeing the reflection of her contorted and pain-filled face in the mirror. The assault ends when the man turns his back to Cathy and George rescues her by pulling her through the revolving door.

In cinema, the mirror usually serves to signify (women's) narcissism, but the use of the convention in this scene (as well as the music) suggests something less than sympathy for the young girl's plight. Indeed, any sympathy for Cathy is undermined in the scene prior to her incarceration, when she is picked up in a church by Anderson, suggesting that even this spiritual sanctuary cannot protect such a degenerate person, the "one place no one ever goes", Simone tells the shocked George.

Irony is central to the post-modern condition, and as a filmmaker who is far from immune from this uncritical virus, Jordan often layers his films with irony. Thus, in *Angel*, the killer with the orthopaedic shoe works in a shop selling such shoes. More lightly, perhaps, other ironic moments in Jordan's cinema include the playing of popular songs which sum up the mood of the film or a key scene such as "When a Man Loves a Woman" and "Stand By Your Man" at the beginning and end, respectively, of *The Crying Game*; "When I Fall in Love" as George becomes tender towards Simone; the Rolling Stones' song (sung by Stone Roses) "Sympathy for the Devil" at the end of *Interview with the Vampire*; "In Dreams" in *In Dreams*; and "Haunted Heart" in *The End of the Affair*.

The same applies to a degree to his periodic Irish jokes in *Mona Lisa* and other films. In early drafts of the script, Mortwell's Christian name is Tony, but in the film it is transformed to the Irish abbreviation of Daniel, Denny, while the young prostitute May tells George that she is Irish, even though her accent is totally English. For no apparent narrative reason (except perhaps that she has just been rescued from an old man), Cathy starts singing in her drug-induced reverie: "There was an old man called Michael Finnegan / He grew whiskers on his chin again", while the dwarfs on Brighton Pier (a comic reference back to the novel George is reading) dance to "It's a Long Way to Tipperary". (Similarly, in *The Good Thief*, Irish accents were dubbed on to the "American" twins.) Additionally, in George's and Thomas's "fiction within the fiction" musings, George comments to Thomas that the "Simone character" was a Sister of Mercy in disguise, a reference, perhaps, to the Irish order of nuns.

As in *Angel*, where *L'avventura* and other films are alluded to, Jordan, in common with developing cinematic practice in the 1980s, adds obligatory cinematic references to *Mona Lisa*, especially in the bedroom scene where *They Live by Night* (Nicholas Ray, 1949) is on the television. Here, the young lovers-on-the-run (Farley Granger, Cathy O'Donnell) are seen walking up the garden path to the marriage office door. This is designed to draw a painful parallel to George, just before he confronts Simone with his own desire for marriage and family, but the scene is used ironically just after George discovers that she is a lesbian.

Reading the film as part of a corpus of films allegorically reflecting Thatcherite England, which also includes *Company of Wolves*, and the end as a "reconstruction" of the white family with the independent and threatening adult woman now excluded, John Hill argues that "in turning the working-class male gangster into an emblem of 'old England', and pitting him against a new — ethnically charged and increasingly sexualized — 'England', the film locks into a strand of (Thatcherite) traditionalism preoccupied with the decline of family and nation" (Hill, 1999: 168). This concern with the family (if not always the "nation") has remained a central preoccupation of Jordan's work.

Notes

¹ Jordan has dismissed comparisons to Martin Scorsese's 1976 film, pointing out that "That's a film about a man going mad; *Mona Lisa* is about a man finding himself" (Barra, 1990: 41).

² Julian Petley (1990), *International Dictionary of Films and Filmmakers 1*, 2nd edition, Nicholas Thomas, ed., Chicago/London: St James Press, 591.

³ Richard Combs (1986), *Monthly Film Bulletin*, 279.

⁴ Quoted Petley (1990), op. cit., p. 591.

⁵ Likewise, it could also be argued that Niall Byrne's (Jimmy in *The Miracle*) facial structure and colouring is not dissimilar to Honor Heffernan's (Deirdre in *Angel*). Jordan comments on the DVD edition of the film that he viewed Cathy Tyson as "asexual". Indeed, this film is an early example of an "androgynous" film text; such films (including *The Crying Game*) became increasingly popular in the 1990s, where gender is deliberately blurred through the actor's physiognomy.

⁶ The version of the script dated March 1985 includes this explanation, but by the version of 3 April 1985, the notion was removed (National Library of Ireland, Manuscripts Accession No. 4761, Box No. 1).

Chapter Five

High Spirits (1988)

Summarily dismissed by critics and the cinema-going public as a limited and even offensive effort which delights in the clichés of American and Irish identities,[1] and rejected by writer-director Jordan as a compromise made for the "scumbag producers from hell" (Dwyer, 1997: 5) (see Chapter Fifteen), *High Spirits* neither was, nor is, a successful film. In part, this owes to the constantly evolving definition of a genre, the need for that which is being parodied to be recognised, and the fact that, notwithstanding the commercial success of the special effects fest *Ghostbusters*, the supernatural or demonic horror, as defined by Derry, had, by the 1980s, lost "the relevant cultural energy or the sincerity of [its] forebears".[2]

However, *High Spirits* is certainly an interesting and rich film whose paternity, despite Jordan's protestations, and indeed nationality, remain, if not always clearly visible, at least detectable. As such, it demands critical reappraisal. It must also be remembered that texts exist beyond the author's intentions, and as Todorov points out, "intentionally or not, all discourse is in dialogue with prior discourses on the same [or related] subject[s], as well as with discourses yet to come".[3]

Generically at odds with itself, *High Spirits* begins as a comic supernatural gothic horror but retreats into domestic melodrama and romantic love. Nonetheless, this hybrid form is shared with other horror films in which the house comes to life and seeks to (re)establish its own identity.[4] *High Spirits* tells of

Peter Plunkett (Peter O'Toole) who, unable to make the payments on his ancestral home, is on the brink of suicide. Just as he is about to hang himself, he decides to market his dilapidated castle-home to American tourists as a haunted hotel. However, his ghostly entertainments, inspired by (American) contemporary horror as much as by native folklore, prove disastrous, and when one of the guests turns out to be Sharon (Beverly D'Angelo), daughter of his American creditor Jem Brogan, who was himself born there, his fate is apparently sealed.

Later that night, Sharon's husband, a drunken Jack (Steve Guttenberg), encounters some real ghosts caught for two hundred years in a traumatic loop of murder and death. His interaction with the past, by saving Mary Plunkett (Daryl Hannah) from murder on her wedding night at the hands of her husband Martin Brogan (Liam Neeson), results not only in a bond between Jack and Mary, but also between Martin and Sharon. In short, and as already inscribed in the figure of the Big House/Castle and the familial lines, present and past fuse.

The following night, All-Hallows' Eve, Jack and Mary consummate their love, but their relationship is disapproved of by the spirit world, which as a consequence enjoys a night of terrorising the other guests: the parapsychologist Dr Malcolm (Martin Ferrero), his wife Marge (Connie Booth) and their three children; the handsome religious Brother Tony (Peter Gallagher); and the attractive Miranda (Jennifer Tilly). The result for Mary of her unholy union is rapid ageing, so that, like the mythic Oisín who breaks the other-world rule by physically touching the earth and therefore cannot return to Tír na nÓg, her body assumes its actual age; but in this case, the transformation may be undone by love.

Meanwhile, Sharon, in incestuous ecstasy, jumps to her death and to union with Martin Brogan. She and Mary swap places so that there is a live happy couple (Jack and Mary) and a dead happy couple (the Brogans, who are consigned to history, though not erased), normality is restored, the guests, most especially Brother Tony and Miranda who have become amorously intertwined, leave "satisfied", and Plunkett, whose castle will be recommended as the most haunted in Ireland, saves his home.

It had been Jordan's initial intention to make a small movie — a "character study of a community" — which drew on "Irish literature of the absurd and the fantastic", such as the metaphysical ironies of James Stephens, or the surreal Flann O'Brien (Jordan, 1989b: x). Unsurprisingly then, the film, like so much of New Hollywood cinema, was envisaged as a generic hybrid, one which married the Gothic tradition to theatrical farce — the worlds of Stoker, Boucicault, Feydeau, Molière, but, most of all, Oscar Wilde — and which was to be infused with the "magical and worldly" sensibility of Irish mythology and legend.

However, the film was hijacked by the producers and became something else, at once bigger (the effects) and, according to Jordan, smaller (the meaning) (see Dwyer, 1997: 4). There is, unfortunately, no "director's cut", even though Jordan, encouraged by the *New Yorker* film critic Pauline Kael, had wanted to re-edit the film with Pat Duffner. Shepperton Studios would not release the film to Jordan because the producers had allegedly defaulted on payment (Dwyer, 1997: 5).[5]

While this, together with the similarity of the published script to the film, appears to make it impossible to "distinguish" Jordan's input from that of the producers, the draft scripts and an early outline of the project entitled "Hotel D'Esprit"[6] in the Neil Jordan Papers at the National Library of Ireland, clearly give access to Jordan's vision, which could have been a most interesting film. A number of elements are immediately obvious, such as a concern with image, performance and representation, and how they relate to "reality". For example, the ghosts appear because they are outraged at the poor imitations of themselves. When they do appear, they are mistaken for fakes, and finally when the humans accept them, the humans choose not to believe in them, which causes them to vanish. When the spirit and human world meet through the unholy love of the seventeen-year old wraith who had died in childbirth during the famine and the American youth already out of love on his honeymoon, a monster from the prehistoric past is conjured up. This terrible force, feared by humans and ghosts alike, is eventually destroyed by the hotel owner's ingenious idea to destroy it with its own image. When the prehistoric monster gazes into the mirror, it devours itself and its reflection, leaving the beautiful wraith returned in her place. (This draws on the Greek mythological creature, the basilisk, whose gaze or breath could kill and who ultimately was killed by its own reflection.) The narrative ends two years later, with a finely restored hotel and the grateful ghosts as the supernatural but efficient staff.

If that gives some indication of Jordan's original conception, the point remains that interpreting the film according to the author's intentions, or by reading it through his clearly bitter (though understandably so) commentary is less rewarding than approaching the film on its own terms. In short, this chapter will regard the film as both a complete and incomplete text, and as part of a broader metanarrative on cultural production and the construction and fixity of identity.

In this regard, Jordan's introduction to the published screenplay is illuminating. Firstly, he situates the film's idea — the fake haunted castle — as a perfect instance of the Irish national character, in that it displays "enterprise, ingenuity and an inexplicable attachment to an utterly useless idea" (Jordan, 1989: *vii*). The result of this negating of the rational or the functional allows, broadly speaking, for the verbal and cerebral labyrinths of the Irish psyche to manifest themselves in "a thirty-two-county republic whose writ runs in only twenty-six. Or, a national language spoken by nobody. Or, a state legislature wherein divorce is only available through ecclesiastical authorities [annulment or dissolution of a marriage] who are themselves opposed to it. Or, . . ."[7] (Jordan, 1989: *vii*). Nothing is what it seems, yet despite or as an extension to this, the apparently opposite, the phenomenological "we are what we are", informs his films. Such a characterisation of the contradictions and love of the riddle is not unique to Jordan. Indeed, this refusal of the linear/rational is often defined, as Jordan does in *Sunrise with Sea Monster*, as a peculiarly Irish trait. Jordan continues in his introduction by concluding in a self-deprecating ironic mode that, of course, the end product — the film — is similarly "another great monument to uselessness" (Jordan, 1989: *viii*).

It is such double coding, which characterises much recent artistic production, that typifies Jordan and his work, and when undetected has allowed for an unfavourable comparison between his work and that of the more overtly political and socially engaged texts of the indigenous filmmakers of the 1970s and 1980s, who included Bob Quinn, Joe Comerford, Cathal Black, Pat Murphy and Kieran Hickey. It is interesting to note that a similar questioning of the value of theatre/cinema takes place in Quinn's breakthrough and formally complex *Caoineadh Airt Ui Laoire* (1975), but here it is not presented as ironic, but as part of a dialogue. The staging of the eponymous poem and the representation of reality by art is challenged throughout that film.

Secondly, in the introduction, Jordan questions the nature of comedy, arguing what should be obvious: that the tragic and the comic are/can be "two sides of the one coin, that awfulness becomes most awful when it is almost comic" (Jordan, 1989: *ix*). Perhaps better termed black irony, it is such "humour" which is evident in *Angel*: a deaf girl goes to a dance hall to listen to the saxophonist, while the club-footed murderer works in an orthopedic shoe shop. While arguably Jordan's marriage of horror, the tragic and comedy in *High Spirits* is an uneasy one and provides a less successful balance to that achieved elsewhere such as in *Interview with the Vampire* or *The Butcher Boy*, such a discourse is relevant in its wider application: the appreciation of mutability and transformation, which is a key trope in Jordan.

Finally, the reference to the film *The Quiet Man* (John Ford, 1952) in his prefacing poem "Lines Written in Dejection" is an important one, not because *High Spirits* makes use of the same quaint Irish landscape, the local "colour", the customs — though here marriage takes on an even more violent aspect — which it does, but because it never presents anything naïvely. Both films delight in actively undercutting, or, in theoretical terms, deconstructing that which is assumed natural. *High Spirits*, like *The Quiet Man*, belongs to the world of masquerade, whereby playing with masks, or deliberately revealing the constructed nature of something, such as the theatrical apparitions (in *High Spirits*) or the "Protestant community" led by the Catholic priest (in *The Quiet Man*), makes impossible the verification or fixing of identity.

While frequently contemporary cinema operates within the reflexive mode — the celebration of spectacle, the articulation of

film as artistic enunciation, the questioning of (the film's) reality
— it is most apparent in the musical, and, increasingly, in the
send-up comedy, comic-horror and horror genres. At its most
basic, it is presented as a problem of vision, wherein perception
and reality are questioned. Or, put another way, the ocularcen-
tric discourse of Western society, in which the eye is privileged
amongst the senses, and sight becomes equated with cognition, is
undermined.[8] Bruce Kawin has argued that in the horror film
there are two possibilities: resolution of the problem by confirming the existence of the monster/horrific vision, or, in the second
case, aperture, or openness, where the question is left unresolved.[9] Kawin concludes that the first type is conservative, the
other is radical. However, moreover, much recent horror uses
the second model as a cynical device to allow for a sequel.

High Spirits unproblematically fits into the first category.
That said, not only is the film's "vision" not coincident with the
characters' vision, and the non-rational infects everything from
the television transmission to the mounted fish-head, but despite the "happy" ending, the supernatural refuses to be contained. Given this, a third category is needed, one that
foregrounds the film's form and deconstructionist aesthetic
over its basic (conservative) thematic content; one that regards
as radical the surreal logic whereby the inanimate becomes
animate, two dimensions become three. With a nod to Baudrillard, the spoof spookies create the blueprint of a history that
entraps the real ghosts: Jack saves his wife from a sword-
thrusting fake ghost only to repeat a version of this the following night, this time saving his wife-to-be.

This double scenario, the fake and the real, itself is cinematically double-coded in so far as it recalls, albeit in an anodyne
way, the ultimate film of necrophilic romance, the blackly comic
mystery film, *Vertigo* (Alfred Hitchcock, 1958), which similarly is
constructed as a puzzle between reality and constructed reality.
However, in Hitchcock's film, the good girl and bad woman are
condensed into one figure, and when Judy dressed as Madeleine
(Kim Novak) jumps to her death at the film's end, Johnny (James
Stewart) ends up with nothing. By contrast, naïveté and gullibil-
ity, it would seem, are rewarded in *High Spirits*.

It is also possible of course to suggest that *High Spirits*, like *Candyman* (Bernard Rose, 1992), is a double film. In both, the first part explores the (supernatural) fantasy, while the second makes it real. In *High Spirits*, the real ghosts only appear after Jack and Peter Plunkett become inebriated, interestingly on brew that belongs to the past — the drink is Plunkett's father's concoction, described in the screenplay as a dusty "opaque, cracked, mysterious bottle" (Jordan, 1989b: 29). As such, one could see the events that follow as a wish-fulfilment alternative to the reality (and theatricality) of the narratives of Brogan foreclosing on the mortgage, and Jack realising he has married a cold, uncaring woman. (A similar repositioning of the real, or the morphing of real into the fantastic, occurred in *Company of Wolves*.)

Just as *The Quiet Man*, as argued by Gibbons (in Rockett et. al, 1987; see also Gibbons, 2002), plays with the dominant representations of landscape, so, too, does *High Spirits*. According to Panofsky, representation of landscape falls into two categories, which he terms "soft pastoralism" and "hard primitivism". The former is understood as a "dream incarnate of ineffable happiness" — "civilised life purged of its vices" — and the latter, as a raw primeval condition "devoid of all comforts" — "civilised life purged of its virtues".[10] Ford's film, considered by McLoone (2000) as "postmodern" without recourse to supernatural intervention and governed by an internal logic, juxtaposes both versions of the landscape so that they are seen as projected mythologies — the first benign, the second sublime. In this way, they are bound to the narrative and the notion of the Irish character and temperament rather than bearing any close relationship to reality.

High Spirits, more acceptably termed "postmodern", achieves the same result — the undermining of cultural perceptions of Ireland as a quaint non-modern world, yet recognising the use of these perceived values for marketing or other purposes — but through a technique less integral to the film: that of quotation. As the American tourists are driven to Castle Plunkett, they are stopped by a flock of sheep who slowly cross the road. This is a direct reference not just to the *The Quiet Man*, but to the countless representations and jokes of Irish roads being trafficked by animals rather than vehicles. (A similar scene occurs in *Michael Collins*.)

The implicit suggestion is that, in order to encounter the true (mystical) spirit of Ireland, one must reject modernity and rationality. This discarding of technology becomes literal in *High Spirits* when Jordan, in an aside to *The Luck of the Irish* (Henry Koster, 1948), has the bridge give way under the coach of tourists. In *The Luck of the Irish*, American visitors on their way to Shannon airport get lost and end up on a little bridge which gives way under the weight of their motorcar, which slowly sinks, thereby trapping them in a mystical landscape, where they encounter a leprechaun. More recently, in *Hear My Song* (Peter Chelsom, 1991), a flat car battery coincides with Mickey (Adrian Dunbar) actually seeing and being at one with the landscape. Earlier in *Hear My Song*, Fintan (James Nesbitt) explains to Mickey that the fairies have got them lost and that Irish roads are somehow like its people — not to be trusted — a comment not dissimilar to that in *The Luck of the Irish* where one of the travellers responds to the other's comment that the road "must lead somewhere", by telling him not to be "too sure" as "Irish paths are whimsical, like the Irish character". This stereotype, used ideologically by and against the Irish, which positions Ireland as non-modern, or anti-modern, arguably had (historically) a cultural truth. However, given that the majority of Irish people have been urban dwellers since the 1960s and that today over a quarter of the population live in the greater Dublin area, the recourse to such a stereotype is necessarily problematic.

If *Hear My Song* attempts to play it straight, the same cannot be said of *High Spirits*, in which we are given insight into the staging and construction of an "Oirish World" by Plunkett, to be sold to gullible Americans. One of these Americans, Jack, has already shown his lack of understanding of Ireland when he sums it up as his wife's homeland and location of the Loch Ness Monster. Though the nationality — Scottish — of the monster is a moot point, it is important only in so much as Ireland is represented not as an emerging modern country which in the 1990s underwent profound economic growth, but as a site of the irrational, or primeval.

Plunkett then is using the common perception of Ireland to his own capitalist ends. It becomes a postcolonial strategy whereby he sells foreigners back their own ideas of Ireland. In this way, Castle Plunkett becomes a fun house of mirrors, where each finds what they seek. In such a world, there can even be happiness for those such as Martin and Sharon Brogan who — in another genre — would, or should, be punished. In other words, the film presents us with a trite and clichéd world, but one in whose scenography we have been implicated. The wild storm, occasioned when the guests try to leave, must also be understood in these terms and is necessary only in so far as it is demanded by the narrative and the Gothic tradition.

The Gothic novel, of which Horace Walpole's *The Castle of Otranto* (1764) is seen as the first, celebrates fantasies of physical and psychological transformation. Generally, these take place against the aesthetic backdrop of the sublime, whereby terror "productive of the strongest emotion which the human mind is capable of feeling",[11] is used to provoke the required frisson, and the socio-economic backdrop of the declining power of the aristocracy. (It is no accident that in Jordan's next foray into the Gothic, *Interview with the Vampire*, the vampires feel at home in a Paris just prior to the uprising of the Paris Commune (1870), while Lestat, the ultimate vampire, is an unconstituted aristocrat who has no time for the emerging (American) democracy.) Terry Eagleton, noting the similarity of Irish Gothic to its British counterpart, where the "deadweight of property and inheritance moulds an upper-class world", remarks that "the encumbered nature of their estates was the true nightmare of many an Anglo-Irish landowner" (cited in Cullen, 1997: 113). Whatever about Plunkett being of the Protestant ascendancy — to which we will return — Jordan, in a time-trick, makes that Plunkett's contemporary nightmare. The last in his familial line, Plunkett clearly views his ancestral home as (literally) a noose around his neck. As he says during a confrontation with his ghost father, "you made me miserably useless, leaving me this place, staff to run, bills to be paid, and then dying on me just like that", concluding "I missed you, Daddy".[12]

The resolution of Plunkett's predicament depends on the uncovering and closure of the historical nightmare — the murdering in the 1780s of Mary Plunkett on her wedding night by her cheated and jealous husband following her refusal to give herself to him. Such a terrible deed committed in the past is frequently at the core of the gothic text, and is similar to so many novels of the genre where "a portrait play(s) a crucial role in exposing a hidden truth" (Cullen, 1997: 111).[13] In *High Spirits*, the idealised — pure, yet erotic — image of her which hangs in the main dining room gives us our first glimpse of a world that was. The picture does not come to life in the manner of the "restless" portrait found frequently in the gothic or ghost story. Neither does it do so within the context of early cinema's fascination with the screen image and how the image might preserve an animated and independent self;[14] or, become the repository of life as in Oscar Wilde's *The Picture of Dorian Gray*. Nevertheless, the picture's subjects — the diaphanously clad Mary and her white horse — become real, at least in proportion to the viewer's, especially Jack's, imagination.

Elsewhere, Jordan has fun with the more conventional (cinematic) trope of the rotten corpse coming to life when, on All Hallows' Night,[15] the ancestors emerge out of their open vaults, in a look that resembles a tightly hung gallery, as in Gilbert and Sullivan's *Ruggidore*. This image is used again in *Interview with the Vampire* during the Paris sequence, only in this instance, the honeycombed vaults are multiplied and more medieval.

In short, *High Spirits* not only fits into the Gothic paradigm but, in the power given to the dead, it shares much with specifically Irish Gothic. As Siobhán Kilfeather writes: "The moment of confrontation with the ghost enacts the terror of history and of the power of the dead which inflects so much gothic discourse about Ireland" (cited in Cullen, 1997: 111). Irish Gothic, it has been suggested already, is an Anglo-Irish Protestant phenomenon. This, Eagleton says, is because "nothing lent itself more to the genre than the decaying gentry in their crumbling houses, isolated and sinisterly eccentric, haunted by the sins of the past. . . . For Gothic is the nightmare of the besieged and reviled . . . of a minority marooned within a largely hostile people to whom they are socially, religiously and ethnically alien" (cited in Cullen, 1997: 106).

This definition lies uneasily with *High Spirits*. No matter how appealing, Plunkett cannot be simply read as the beleaguered Protestant and the Brogans as the Catholics who are in the ascendant, if also in exile from their native home and homeland. It is this refusal of traditional categories of wealth and religion that makes *High Spirits* at once interesting yet problematic, and perhaps can be taken as Jordan's refusal of the sociopolitical in favour of the human or metaphysical story, of individuals who act not out of ideology but out of something ultimately more powerful: their own natures. As Jody in *The Crying Game* explains to Fergus, the scorpion has no choice but to sting. It is this humanist, almost mechanistic, vision, that is also articulated in Jean Renoir's *La Règle du Jeu* (1939), and that is central to the understanding of Jordan (see Chapter Two).

Jordan refuses to give us sufficient history from which to understand the characters. The story of Mary and Martin remains resolutely a personal one; there is no broader canvas. Given that the traumatic event occurred when anti-Catholic Penal Laws were in place which disallowed (Irish) Catholics from owning landed property, it is difficult to see Plunkett as anything but Protestant. This is given further weight through the acting of Peter O'Toole and his eccentric mother, though the Scot, Sean Connery, whom Jordan had wanted to play Plunkett, might have undermined this. Nevertheless, Mary Plunkett prays to "Sweet Mother Mary" and St Bridget, clearly marking her as Catholic, even if this results from the "Oirish" broad strokes of the American producers.

The Plunkett name itself is ambiguous, and recalls equally the eighteenth Baron of Dunsany (County Meath), Edward John Plunkett, born in London, whose writings, coincidental with Jordan's, "created a dream-world, suffused with the quality of fairytales";[16] the poet and nationalist revolutionary Joseph *Mary* Plunkett (emphasis added) who was one of the signatories of the 1916 Proclamation of the Irish Republic; and, of course, the seventeenth-century Saint Oliver Plunkett, the Catholic Archbishop of Armagh and martyr, killed by Cromwellian republicans. So, if the film refuses to make clear the characters' religious and social backgrounds, it might be more interesting to try to understand Mary and Martin as representative of Irish types.

Mary is refined and willful only to the extent of protecting herself against the wild and barbarous Martin. His lack of refinement is marked not just by violence, but by Mary's description of her sensory experience of him as offensive: his warts, his smelly feet, his "squishing". For her, his grotesque body houses his animal soul. He is a beast whose lust is made clear in his chase of Sharon. If, as Miller suggests, to feel disgust is human and humanising,[17] that Jack and Mary feel it in relation to Martin sets them apart not just from him, but also from Sharon. Therefore, it appears that Martin and Mary represent two contrasting figures, that of the (physically bound) ape and the (idealist and spiritual) angel.

Within an Irish cultural context, these are necessarily loaded images and refocus the couple as only opposites of the same coin. They are the extremes of the Irish character, as has been portrayed in (especially British) literature and art over the last two hundred years. Fintan Cullen, in his discussion of Hamilton's painting "Lieutenant Richard Mansergh St George" (1796–98) cites Charles Maturin's reason for setting his romantic novel *The Milesian Chief* (1812) in Ireland as "the only country on earth, where . . . the extremes of refinement and barbarism are united" (Cullen, 1997: 104).[18]

Characterising Ireland thus becomes a way of distinguishing Ireland from modern Britain (and Europe). While this may owe to Ireland's lost nationhood and the Act of Union with Britain (1801), or to the Romantic sensibility and the desire to find in the exotic wild landscape — and in its natives — a counter to the rational and industrial, it must also be the effect of having a non-Irish (usually British) reader as the intended "consumer" of the various visual and literary texts.

Arguably, *High Spirits*, despite its late-eighteenth-century gothic narrative, has more in common with (Romantic) post-Act of Union work. Only in this case, "the sophisticated, reluctant and bored stranger [who is brought] into [the] romantic Irish setting and then [permitted] a love affair with a native"[19] is not British but obviously American. That the native is dead may say more about American nostalgia than Ireland's culture, while the fact that Jack, our idealist filter, chooses to remain in the realm of magical mysticism, rather than return to capitalist America, emphasises America's outdated perception of Ireland as pre-modern.

Nevertheless, this is a notion that arises from white American Anglo-Saxon prejudice against Irish culture, but is also a product of Irish migrant memory. This outside mediation is one with which the Irish are only too familiar. With the brief exception of indigenous filmmaking in the 1970s and 1980s, seen from a cultural perspective, it has been one of the most negative features of films based on Irish stories and characters. In *High Spirits*, not only are the "real live" Irish characters marginalised in relation to the narrative — Jordan has admitted that he was more interested in them than the stars — but made quaint and ignorant: when Plunkett introduces Malcolm as a parapsychologist, a baffled Katie (Mary Coughlan) responds "a para-what?" In short, at a surface level, *High Spirits* mutes the Irish voice as Ireland becomes the passive object of representation. However, as argued above, Jordan, in his playfulness, allows at least its echo to be heard above the smothering blanket placed on the project by the (outside) American producers.

The relationship between America and Ireland is one that is bittersweet. America, as represented in the first fiction films made in Ireland and produced by the American Kalem Company during 1910–12, may have been regarded as the Land of the Free, and Ireland's hope, but it must be remembered that the migrant, at least until the late twentieth century, rarely returned and in that way was forced into a type of self-imposed exile. The desire always remains for the home, the motherland, as explored in the most famous Irish-American film, and part inspiration to *High Spirits*, *The Quiet Man*. Sean Thornton leaves America's lousy money, the work, the hell that is the steel mills, and the boxing ring, to return to his mother's home(land). Jordan's Jack may not be Ford's Sean, but he puts into focus Sean's motivations, a dream to return to a land of the imagination that represents or offers everything that (American) capitalism is not. Yet, it remains the case that Plunkett's "business" idea not only reveals the nature of the fantasy world, but also highlights that which underpins capitalism and modern advertising. As noted, haunted Castle Plunkett is really not so different from Brogan's "Irish World". On the other hand, for those left behind, the feelings are inevitably also ones of loss, but are countered by the hope of remittance money. The "empty" letter (from America) was one without money. Of course, the returned "Yank" was also to be treated with suspicion, as in *The Quiet Man* or *The Field* (Jim Sheridan, 1990), as the outsider who may outbid the local in purchasing land. If *High Spirits* manages to hint at this Irish-American tension, Cathal Black's *Korea* (1995) is the most potent illustration of the complexities of the Irish-American relationship, summed up in the image of the American flag draped over the coffin of an Irish-born US Army soldier who died during the Korean War, and his "modernising" parents being compensated financially for his death.

A recurrent criticism of Jordan's films has been his treatment of women, and, unfortunately, *High Spirits* seems to do little to alleviate such a view. The two main female characters — Mary and Sharon — are drawn according to the stereotypical and extreme images of femininity: Mary is the passive, subservient and refined woman who addresses Jack as "Sir Jack", while Sharon is the cold, hard, yet neurotic and hysterical woman. Despite their differences, both yearn to be happy, and it is only a man that can make them so. *High Spirits* creates a conservative world where (female) transgression is punished and females (and ghosts) are (temporarily) contained. Mary, who appears to be passive, is murdered because she is not — she refuses the moral and legal obligation of sleeping with her new husband. She is given Sharon's life (and husband) only when she shows that she is capable of true love, but most of all, respect. Sharon, for her part, is punished (or rewarded) by death, but, ironically, finds more happiness and "life" in death than in life. Through her sacrifice-suicide, and by seeing Martin as a sexual man rather than as a disgusting, squishing, squelching wart-ridden "frog" who rises up from the mire-infested pond, she humanises both him and herself. Thus the love stories are complete.

That Mary is a ghost, and one that is crudely rendered — her pasty complexion jarring with her rich golden hair — and prior to which she was a painting, only confirms her as a projection of the (male) imagination, and by implication is an (unwitting) acknowledgment of her (and others') two-dimensionality. Even Plunkett's mother, who guides Jack and unwittingly helps Plunkett to conceive of the haunted hotel business, has no power in herself. Like all the female characters, including Miranda who in her aerobic exercises suggestively recalls Miss Torso of *Rear Window* (Alfred Hitchcock, 1954) (see Jordan, 1989b: 50), she is important only in what she provokes in or represents to the male.

Jordan's males, if less tied to the stereotype, are for the most part ineffectual, and caught in a pre-Oedipal moment of coming to terms with that which belongs to the symbolic (the world of the father). This is the story of *The Miracle*, but here nothing is ever allowed to be that serious. *High Spirits* simply posits a world where (heterosexual) romantic love produces the only real happiness. The children it might produce are another story.

High Spirits, in line with the trend of the 1960s and 1970s, and epitomised by horror films such as *Village of the Damned* (Wolf Rilla, 1960), *The Innocents* (Jack Clayton, 1961), *The Exorcist* (William Friedkin, 1973), or *The Omen* (Richard Donner, 1976), views children as little demons.[20] Or, at least, that is how they are described by characters within the film, which seems at odds with the actions of the children. Despite their knowing references to the Freddy Krueger series of films, and their feigned *ennui*, the children seem genuinely excited by the "awesome" coach ride, accept as real (and terrifying) the amateur antics of Plunkett and his staff, such as the walking suit of armour, and are stunned when the woman dressed in a leotard doing aerobics on television actually interacts with them. In short, the kids are not demonic, but nor do they fit into the (Victorian) cult of idealised childhood. They are spoiled, demanding, materialistic, and in search of the sensory thrill that is created and only briefly fed by the media monster of television.

As well as the television woman attacking them, another monster, a tentacled one, from a version of television — the theatre — also battles with one of the children. This creature, derived more from the popular fantastic imagination (of the Lough Ness variety) and Greek mythology, rather than being specifically Irish, is first introduced as a flatly rendered part of the fantastical water set that forms the background to the hotel's entertainments. However, it comes to (three-dimensional) life and attempts, in a revised allusion to *Poltergeist* (Tobe Hooper, 1982) to eat one of the children. But as with any genre, or self-enclosed world, an understanding of the internal logic and rules of that world enable a solution: in this case, the boy is thrown a cut-out life-buoy which is inflated magically and the boy is saved.

Elsewhere in the film, Brother Tony fails to embrace this world and instead and mistakenly chooses to pray. Finally, he gives up on the notion of auto-eroticism, the spiritual "treats"[21] and the masochism of Catholicism, choosing the body: the voluptuous, sexually aware, yet knowingly innocent and coy Miranda.[22] Again, Jordan's reference is Hitchcock. The Day of Judgement that Tony faces is that of Melanie (and Mitch) in *The Birds* (1963) only here the attacking birds are replaced by disembodied nuns' wimples. His spiritually induced but hypersensuous experience ends with an orgasmic escape through the window and down into the slime covered pool below, all the time steam rising from his groin. Miranda, in an attempt to save him, ends up, with the help of the nuns, likewise relocated by falling out of the window and into his arms. The Lord, after all, works in mysterious ways.

That the body should, with divine blessing, be chosen over the spirit in Catholic Ireland should not come as any great revelation. If scandals of sexually active and paedophilic clergy only came to be highlighted in the media during the 1990s, prior to that there was a type of hypocrisy that celebrated the "errant" ways of the sensuous body and the pagan or superstitious mind so long as the veneer of institutional Catholicism remained undisturbed. One only has to look to the traditional practices of the wake and the various unruly amusements and excessive drinking associated with it to see that Gibbons's suggestion that the Irish are pagan and only appear to act as Catholics is not unfounded (Gibbons, 1996a). If this is clear from J.M. Synge's early-twentieth-century writings about the Aran Islands and its people, in terms of recent culture, it is no less so.

Together with religion more broadly, this is explored in several low budget indigenous films, including *The Kinkisha* (Tommy McArdle, 1977) and Bob Quinn's *Budawanny* (1987) (later developed in *The Bishop's Story*, 1994) in which the institutional church is seen as a fragile construction which never fully eradicates the Irish sensuous relationship to the body and sexuality. In the first film, a Catholic woman follows a pagan belief that a child born on Whit will kill or be killed, and it will be spared only by having a robin crushed to death in the infant's hand. The latter films have a priest live openly with his housekeeper whom he makes pregnant. Here the church has a hollow victory when the bishop intervenes and brings the priest into line. Such a scenario is evoked in the granny's comment to Rosaleen in *Company of Wolves* when she tells the child that priests are not called fathers for no reason.

Perhaps one of the most potent images of the irrelevance of the church in contemporary Ireland is contained in *Poitín* (Bob Quinn, 1978), a film not about religion, but one which, amongst other things, set out to deromanticise the West. During a drunken brawl, the ubiquitous potato is thrown against and smashes a picture of Our Lady. In yet another instance of the juxtaposition of Catholicism and paganism, the priest in Brian Friel's play *Dancing at Lughnasa* (made as a feature film by Pat O'Connor, 1998), comes to embrace pagan practices during his missionary work in Africa. He returns to his home village as a "convert", much to the embarrassment of his sisters, one of whom is a teacher in the local Catholic school. Nevertheless, he can relish in the native Irish fertility festival, Samhain, an event which also recalls the sexually explicit sheela-na-gig stone carvings that decorated early Irish Christian sites.

With such a wealth of broader cultural references to draw on, *High Spirits* was tapping into, not just the rich Irish Gothic tradition, but the difficulties of Irish migration (economic and missionary), institutional versus popular religious practice, and, most of all, the complexities of trying to negotiate a subtle, multi-layered reading of Irish culture in the context of a powerful American film industry with its narrow focus on trying to emulate recent generic successes. That the film was not successful in steering a course through these shark-infested waters does not make the film any less interesting for attempting to do so.

Notes

[1] See, for example, Richard Combs's review in *Sight and Sound*, Vol. 55, No. 656, pp. 362–3.

[2] Charles Derry (1987), "More Dark Dreams: Some Notes on the Recent Horror Film", in *American Horrors*, Gregory A. Waller, ed., Urbana, Chicago: University of Illinois Press, 169.

[3] Tzvetan Todorov (1984), *Mikhail Bakhtin: The Dialogical Principle*, trans. Wlad Godzich, Manchester: Manchester University Press: x (orig. Paris, Editions du Seuil, 1981).

[4] "Haunted house" films are many and include the fast-paced comic *Beetlejuice* (Tim Burton, 1988); *The Haunting* (Jan de Bont, 1999), a remake of Robert Wise's 1963 *The Haunting of Hill House*; *The House on Haunted Hill* (William Malone, 1999), a remake of William Castle's 1958 film; and *The Others* (Alejandro Amenábar, 2001). Also included are "non-horror or supernatural" films such as *Pacific Heights* (John Schlesinger, 1990).

[5] See also "Neil Jordan" in *Donal McCann Remembered*, Pat Laffan and Faith O'Grady, eds., Dublin: New Island, 2000: 44–7.

[6] Accession No 4761. In Boxes 3, 5 and 6 (of 7) there is an extensive range of scripts and storyboards from *High Spirits* (see Neil Jordan Bibliography).

   Though Jordan places *High Spirits* (at least that which he initially conceived) within a fantastic Irish tradition, the (French) name given to the treatment, as well as the narrative of the hotel coming to life, also suggests the numerous popular transformation films at the beginning of the twentieth century which were, like Jordan's film, equally indebted to the new mechanical toys and special effects. In these, as in *High Spirits*, there is a juxtaposition between reality, effect or illusion, the rational (technology) and the irrational (supernatural). It is of note that in this draft, the technology lets them down, it behaves irrationally: the slide projectors do not work. In the film, the effects work, but they are not good enough; they cannot pass them off as real, and as such they are like the art forgeries in *The Good Thief*, which never transcend imitation. (Likewise, in *The Good Thief* technology is critiqued.) Therefore, a key element, the confusion of seeing or knowing reality, is diluted in the film.

7 In 1995, seven years after the release of *High Spirits*, a referendum of the Irish people narrowly approved the deletion of the prohibition on divorce inscribed in the 1937 Irish Constitution.

8 See Martin Jay, *Downcast Eyes: The Denigration of Vision in Twentieth-Century French Thought*, Berkeley, Los Angeles, London: University of California Press, 1993.

9 See Bruce Kawin "*The Funhouse* and *The Howling*" in Waller, ed., op cit., note 2 above.

10 Erwin Panofsky (1970), "Et in Arcadia Ego", in *Meaning in the Visual Arts*, London: Penguin, 340–67.

11 David Punter (1980), *The Literature of Terror: A History of Gothic Fictions from 1765 to the Present Day*, London: Longmans, 44.

12 Commenting on this scene, Jordan observed "how strangely personal and obsessively private things creep into something without one even knowing it"; in this case, he said that this speech was an unconscious response to his own father's sudden death three years earlier. "Things just creep in in spite of you . . . they just find their way into the structure of the thing" (Neil Jordan, *South Bank Show*, 1988).

13 A portrait is also central to the aforementioned *Vertigo*, and also Hitchcock's *Rebecca*, another relevant film. The cinema is rich with other such examples and belies the cinema's own obsession with the (fixed or fixable) image, and the gap between image or projected illusion and reality.

14 An example is Percy Stow's 1903 *Animated Picture Studio* where the cinematic image of Isadora Duncan becomes three-dimensional to the distress of the real Isadora (who is herself only another "copy" of the star).

15 In the treatment discussed in the first paragraph, the night is the more magical, and less gothic, midsummer's night.

[16] Henry Boylan (1978), *A Dictionary of Irish Biography*, Dublin: Gill and Macmillan, 299.

[17] William Ian Miller (1998; orig. 1997), *Anatomy of Disgust*, Cambridge, Mass.: Harvard University Press, 11.

[18] See also Joep Leerssen (1996), "The Burden of the Past: Romantic Ireland and Prose Fiction" in *Remembrance and Imagination*, Cork: Cork University Press; and for the representations of the Irish in Victorian cartoons, L.P. Curtis, Jr. (1971), *Apes and Angels: The Irishman in Victorian Caricature*, Newton Abbot: David and Charles. See also L.P. Curtis, Jr. (1968), *Anglo-Saxons and Celts: A Study of Anti-Irish Prejudice in Victorian England*, Bridgeport, Connecticut: Conference on British Studies; and R.N. Lebow (1976), *White Britain and Black Ireland: The Influence of Stereotypes on Colonial Policy*, Philadelphia: Institute for the Study of Human Issues.

[19] Barry Sloane cited in Leerssen (1996), op cit., 36.

[20] For a discussion of changing representation of children in horror, see Vivian Sobchack "Bringing it all Back Home", in Waller, ed., op cit., note 2 above. The irony, of course, which is made explicit in a draft, "Ghost Tours", by Neil Jordan and Michael McDowell, dated 13 August 1986, is that the misbehaving children are victimised by a poltergeist even more destructive than they are. The draft summarises the hauntings thus: "Each American receives a haunting appropriate to his personality and failings — the parapsychologist undergoes an intense and humiliating examination with his own paraphernalia . . . Jack's wife is proposed to by a ghost as hot-blooded as she is cold, and so on" (p. 3).

[21] In a Freudian slip to Miranda, he tells her he came to the Castle as a spiritual "treat . . . retreat".

[22] In *Miracles and Miss Langan* (1979), a television film adapted from a script by Jordan, Ben D'Arcy, who is due to take his vows for the priesthood, is seduced by an older woman who describes them as a "modern" priest and a "modern" spinster. She gives him a chance to play husband and wife but he cannot deal with it. She asks him to leave, but subsequently he returns to her. She rejects him.

Three men united in their defeat: Alan Rickman (left) as Eamon de Valera, Liam Neeson (centre) as Michael Collins and Aidan Quinn (right) as Harry Boland after the defeat of the 1916 Rising at the beginning of *Michael Collins*.

Julia Roberts as Kitty Kiernan, for whom both Michael Collins and Harry Boland compete, but they are, perhaps, too much in love with the world of men and politics and turn away from her.

"Is this what they taught you in convent school?", Stephen Rea's Danny asks Veronica Quilligan's Annie after they have made love outside the Dreamland ballroom in *Angel*.

In *Interview with the Vampire*, Lestat (Tom Cruise, left) introduces his partner Louis (Brad Pitt, right), his vampire creation, to society and "hunting".

In *The End of the Affair*, Bendrix (Ralph Fiennes) tries to make real his love and fix his future with Sarah (Julianne Moore), but she is already promised to the ultimate Father through disease rather than faith.

Steve Guttenberg's Jack finds that his ghostly, two-hundred-year-old lover, Darryl Hannah's Mary Plunkett, comes of age in *High Spirits* following the transgressive consummation of their love.

By the time they finally succeed in crossing the border/bridge, Molly (Demi Moore) has developed an unconventional relationship with a secular priest (Robert de Niro), while Sean Penn (right) decides to return to the religious life, in *We're No Angels*.

Vampire-child (Kirsten Dunst), complete with alter-ego doll, shares a coffin-bed with one of her "parents" (Brad Pitt) in a parody of normal family behaviour in *Interview with the Vampire*.

Apparent family harmony in *In Dreams* sees Annette Bening's Claire and husband Paul (Aidan Quinn) celebrate their daughter's (Katie Sagona) fairytale performance in *Snow White* before she is kidnapped and brutally killed by psychotic serial killer Vivian.

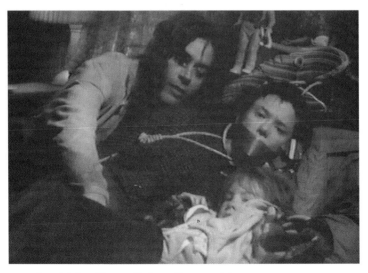

Serial killer Vivian (Robert Downey Jr) creates a perverse "normal" family with kidnapped Annette Bening and young Krystal Benn against a background of his childhood toys.

The Butcher Boy's Francie Brady (Eamonn Owens) clutches his kitsch Irish cottage, a present bought for his mother, who in his absence had committed suicide.

The rotting corpse of the beautiful and sensuous woman is exposed beneath a mountain of dolls, painful reminders of young vampire Claudia's trapped condition.

Julianne Moore and Ralph Fiennes go to the cinema in *The End of the Affair*, where they "enjoy" his novel as adapted for the screen.

During his trip to Dublin, Francie partakes in the cinema event as he watches the science fiction film *The Brain from Planet Arous* and consumes cinema food in *The Butcher Boy*.

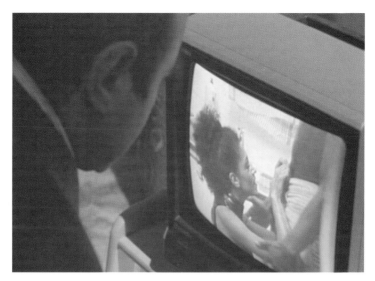

Too interested, Bob Hoskins's George is voyeuristically trans-
fixed by the porn video featuring Cathy Tyson's Simone and
her pimp in *Mona Lisa*.

Standing beside a video camera at a one-way window-mirror,
Bob Hoskins watches the rape of teenager Kate Hardie in
Mona Lisa, before he rescues her.

Chapter Six

We're No Angels (1989)

Neil Jordan's *We're No Angels* has an extensive pre-history on stage and screen. While Jordan's film is a screen version of a David Mamet script,[1] the origins of both can be traced to the French play *La Cuisine des Anges* by Albert Husson, which had been adapted for the English stage and been presented in London and on Broadway. A feature film version of the play, *We're No Angels* (1955), was directed by Michael Curtiz, in which little attempt was made to maintain the play's original French flavour. That film is set in 1895 on the French penal colony of Devil's Island, and concerns three convicts: a forger, Joseph (Humphrey Bogart), and two murderers, Albert (Aldo Ray) and Jules (Peter Ustinov), who escape to a store owned by the Ducotels, where they intend to steal clothes before continuing their escape by boat. However, the three escapees become involved in the Ducotels' family intrigue and help the family by altering the store's account books to make them more appealing, fairly divide their inheritance, save the daughter from a mean suitor and find her a nice boy. Before the convicts return to prison, they prepare an elaborate Christmas dinner for the family. Beyond the title of the film, Mamet retained little from Curtiz's film except an attempt to maintain its somewhat dissipated humour and basic premise of escaped convicts integrating themselves into the broader community.

Jordan's film is set in 1935 and opens in an American state penitentiary near the Canadian border where petty crooks Ned

(Robert De Niro) and Jim (Sean Penn) are cajoled by murderer Bobby (James Russo) to partake in a break-out in which he kills two guards after he has escaped from the executioner's chair. The scenes located in the prison set the tone for the film, with Ned and Jim being polar opposites, the former street-wise and mainly interested in himself, the latter "a sweet beatific kid", as Jordan describes him,[2] who develops his spiritual side. The comic interaction of the two becomes the mainstay of the film, but from the opening Jordan also establishes another of his intentions: the challenging of appearance and reality. The gritty social realism and interest in prison life is revealed to be an exploration of an aesthetic style. With extended crane shots of the prison's hell-like conditions and interior, set in a half-light of fog and molten steel, the film moves from "realism" to theatricality and stylisation.

This "non-realism" is particularly evident when Ned and Jim become spectators at the preparations for Bobby's execution after the brutal Warden (Ray McAnally) punishes them for speaking out of turn as he is berating Bobby, telling him that his soul will be in "that new place". He leaves it to their imagination as to which of the "new places" Bobby will go. Later in their prison cell, Jim initiates a conversation with the disbelieving Ned about the after-life in which Ned shows more interest in a nude female pin-up than Jim's tortured concern with what will happen after death. Fittingly, their journey together brings Ned to the woman and Jim to the church. The film's fairytale-like happy ending allows both characters to find their particular form of "new place", both figured within broadly religious terms — the holy family and vocational life. Jordan's vision is ultimately less optimistic in his later fairytale *In Dreams* where release is understood as death, and even death might not be the final answer.

Realism is further eschewed by the speed with which the film's many cinematic references are introduced. Jordan, as ever, enjoys what has become synonymous with postmodern practice — intertextuality. Not only are the opening scenes reminiscent of 1930s Warner Bros.' films with their commitment to "realism" in stories looking at the underbelly of the American Depression, but through its extensive quotations, other films are evoked, such as *I Am a Fugitive from a Chain*

Gang (Mervyn Leroy, 1932) in the rock-breaking scenes, the Expressionist *Metropolis* (Fritz Lang, 1926), in the long lines of prisoner-workers, while most particularly, the gangster characters played by James Cagney find an echo in Bobby. As he is being prepared for execution, Bobby looks directly ahead with an insolent smile recalling that of Cagney, and while Cagney shakes off the prison guards as he is being led to execution in *Angels with Dirty Faces* (Michael Curtiz, 1938), unlike in that film, where he feigns cowardice (off-camera) as he is being executed to dissuade his teenager acolytes from emulating him, Bobby escapes from the execution chamber following a gun-battle initiated by an accomplice.

A further parallel to *Angels with Dirty Faces*, but one which registers a shift in culture towards an increasing secularisation and disrespect for authority, can be seen in how the reverent representation of the Irish-American priest, played by Pat O'Brien, who convinces Cagney to scream from apparent fear, is substituted with Bobby kicking the priest in the stomach after being freed. In the prison's final scene after Ned and Jim have already escaped, and as Bobby is about to jump from the prison walls to the snow below, he shouts, "Ever hear the phrase, 'Top of the world'?". Such a phrase necessarily refers to Cagney, as it was one of his most famous lines, which he delivered just before the conflagration at the end of *White Heat* (Raoul Walsh, 1949). (Other cinematic references in the film include The Three Stooges, and John Goodman and William Forsythe in *Raising Arizona*.[3])

Though the landscape in which most such 1930s films were set was the Deep South, after their escape from prison, Ned and Jim find themselves in a no-man's-land, a frozen wasteland with "scenic" mountains and an "innocent" Sirkian deer. As they struggle through this inhospitable area, Jim finds his inspiration (in a scene prescient of Francie's engagement with the Blessed Virgin in *The Butcher Boy*; Bernadette in *The Song of Bernadette* (Henry King, 1943); or any of the number of cases where the "visionary" is coded as mildly dim and/or as an innocent child) when he sees a poster concerning the "Weeping Virgin", a Blessed Virgin Mary statue in the nearby town of

Brandon (hardly an accidental reference to the Irish mountain). The poster carries an inscription from Hebrews 13:1: "Do not neglect to show hospitality to strangers, for thereby some entertained angels, unawares." If this quotation, which in a potent way sums up Jordan's own concern with appearances, is appropriated by Jim (and Ned) later to the duo's advantage and helps in the farce of mistaken identities, it is fitting that Hebrews 13:3 continues, "keep in mind those who are in prison as if you are in prison with them, and the ill-treated as though you are suffering physically yourselves".

An eccentric old woman arrives in a pick-up truck, but she makes a lie of perception and removes all innocence from the landscape by killing the deer, and then by drawing a gun on the two escapees. Mistaking them for priests after Jim recites the biblical quote from the poster, she gives them her shotgun to finish the deer off, and while she looks away, they take the opportunity to shoot through the prison leg-irons that bind them. In a further shift from the realist mode, she says that "they" will be looking for them.

The irony is, of course, that the "they" refers to the clergy of the local monastery who have been awaiting the arrival of two eminent writer-priests. Jordan, it would seem, is drawing a parallel between the morally bankrupt and physically coercive institution serving public morality and its morally or ideologically coercive brother, also serving public and private morality. While elsewhere Jordan more fully explores the church and faith, here criticism is reserved for the clergy, namely the power-obsessed, snooty, rotund bishop who is outside/above the small religious community of the monastery. Nevertheless, the simple naïveté of this community and their willingness to believe and to forgive is nonetheless a benign and comic critique. Arguably, the monk (John C. Reilly) who becomes Jim's most ardent and holy follower is an early incarnation of the simple and childlike Dougal from the satirical British television series *Father Ted*.

Arriving in the border town of Brandon, Ned and Jim adopt the masquerade of priests and are believed by the monastery to be the missing theologians, Fathers Brown and Reilly, thus initiating the film's major themes: the nature of belief, identity, the (im)possibility of crossing borders, and the complexity of relationships. The pairing of Ned and Jim readily fits within the tradition of (asexual) male companions of the buddy movie, such as those made by Howard Hawks in classical cinema; Robert Redford and Paul Newman in George Roy Hill's *Butch Cassidy and the Sundance Kid* (1969) and *The Sting* (1973); or, its later reversal/subversion through the focus on female characters in *Thelma & Louise* (Ridley Scott, 1991); or the inter-racial pair of Mel Gibson and Danny Glover in the *Lethal Weapon* films (1987–98).

However, Ned and Jim are searching for some form of "nuclear" family relationships. This is evident from the idealised image of the family seen by Jim shortly after his arrival in Brandon when he looks through the window of a home to see a mother and two children eating, in a soft focus shot of traditional family life. Shortly afterwards, Ned sees an altogether more sensual image, that of Molly (Demi Moore), when he voyeuristically spies on her as she is semi-nude in her bathroom. His desire to escape the prison authorities or create a family is made difficult when he becomes interested in Molly, a single mother whose young daughter, Rosie (Jessica Jickels), is, like Annie in *Angel*, deaf and dumb. Molly is interested in men only to the extent that they will pay for sex so that she can support her daughter, or, ideally, that they are strong enough to be true to her and her child. Her policeman lover is clearly unequal to this ideal, with his moral deficiency, yet hypocritical relationship to, and need of, religious, moral or legal strictures. As a result, her interest in Ned, whom she believes to be a priest, is defined in those terms. So while it would appear there is no possibility of a sexual or loving relationship between them, equally, there can be no platonic or caring one as she is disinterested in religious "mumbo-jumbo", as it will not help Rosie. Ned, who shares her disregard for religious belief, is unable, because of his masquerade, to express his attraction for her.

In the meantime, Ned and Jim make repeated but futile attempts to cross the bridge which will take them to Canada and to freedom. Each time, the police, and later the prison warden and his officers, cause them to retreat to the town or the monastery. At the monastery, Jim becomes interested in the life of the monks, who, though normally remain silent, are allowed to speak as it is the Feast of Our Lady of Sorrows. Under his new identity, Jim, forced to deliver a sermon, draws inspiration not from the Latin bible from which he is expected to read, but from its seeming opposite, a capitalist promotional leaflet on an instrument of violence and death. From this advertisement for a Colt 32 Hammerless Automatic pistol, which posits the dangerous fantasy of "An Encounter with a Bear", he reads, "Have you ever felt completely alone . . . ? Alone in a world of danger and no-one to rely on . . . ?" His "existential" homily is greeted with sage-like nodding by the monks and confirms the young monk's admiration for the maverick and wise, though down-to-earth, simple impostor. Indeed, this pair become close, especially when Jim listens to the young monk's religious lessons, thus setting up an alternative "couple" to that of Ned and Molly. However, these relationships only become explicit at the end of the film.

In a further desperate attempt — their fourth — to escape across the border, Ned discovers that the procession of the Weeping Virgin will enter Canada before returning to the monastery. Needing an ill or disabled child to be allowed to participate in the procession, Ned cajoles Molly into giving him Rosie, but only after he agrees to pay $100 to "borrow" her. In the meantime, Jim is obliged, having won the right through a raffle — which he unwittingly entered, not knowing the prize — to give a public sermon to the community (religious and secular) before the procession leaves.

In a further narrative twist to enable the missing third escapee to re-enter the film as a kind of *deus ex machina*, Bobby is captured in female disguise[4] in the town after a shoot-out and Ned as priest is brought to administer the last rites. Threatening to expose him to the authorities, and falsely charging him with his own killing of the police officer, Ned is forced to help the injured and irredeemable Bobby escape from the police cell and hide him under the ornate canopy which surrounds the statue of the Weeping Virgin. As the procession crosses the bridge,

Bobby is discovered as his blood drips from the Virgin's hand and a shoot-out occurs during which he is killed.

In the mêlée, Rosie, who is aware of Ned's true identity having seen a picture warrant for his arrest but is unable to communicate this, falls into the raging waters below when she is hit by the statue. Ned jumps to her rescue while the statue also tumbles into the river. Underwater, as Ned with Rosie in his arms sinks beneath the torrent, the statue appears beside them and Ned holds out his hand to the extended hand of the statue, which floats to the top and saves them. It is the ideal (and silent) mother with whom Ned and Rosie are united who saves and cleanses them — Ned of his lies, while the trauma and/or Our Lady restores Rosie's speech and hearing. The child uses her new gift from her "father" (and the Virgin) to utter the word "convict" as she points at Ned. The monks, perhaps realising what she has said, choose to elevate the "miracle" of their saving over the "truth" of the word and believe Ned's "confession" to them that sadly, he is, indeed, a sinner. He is a "convert" from Lutheranism to Catholicism (itself, of course, a form of "Reformation" joke). Nevertheless, Rosie's "betrayal" does not stop him becoming her surrogate father.

After this episode, Ned harries Jim to leave the monastery, now that they have a clear opportunity to cross the bridge. Hesitant, Jim does not want to leave the young monk and reluctantly goes with Ned, looking back at the monastery all the time as the monk waves from the door. As they approach the bridge, Molly and Rosie appear, and both men slowly separate as Jim drops behind to return to his "partner" still waiting at the monastery door, while the new "family" — Molly, Rosie and the still clerically dressed Ned — cross the bridge. While the male (religious) couple go back into the monastery and close the door, the nuclear family are the only ones to successfully cross the bridge to freedom. To get there, though, it is not just religious belief, but miracles which have come under scrutiny. Despite the film's interrogation of faith and the church, ultimately a kind of secular functional or Pascalian belief or optimism is celebrated. It is this comforting support system that allows the various characters the freedom to explore their own desires and identities.

Jordan has commented that his vision for *We're No Angels* was like *Il Miracolo* (The Miracle, Roberto Rossellini, 1948, released as part of *L'Amore/Love*), a controversial film in which a deranged Italian peasant (Anna Magnani) meets a mysterious stranger (played by Federico Fellini, the film's scriptwriter) whom she imagines is Saint Joseph. After his departure, she discovers that she is pregnant, calls the child a miracle, and upon being rejected by the community, retreats to a deserted sanctuary to deliver the baby. Perhaps what Jordan found in this film was the clash between sincere religious belief and the lack of belief in the modern, secular, everyday world. While *We're No Angels* may be "a parable on people's need to believe",[5] it is not the success or otherwise of the priests' masquerade which needs to be highlighted, but the transformative nature of belief for the sceptical Molly, the inspiring Jim, and even by Ned.

While Jordan's next film, *The Miracle*, is not overtly concerned with religious belief, as is discussed in the following chapter, the notion of divine intervention in human affairs, essentially a definition of a miracle, is central to *We're No Angels*, despite its comic pretensions, and, as is discussed later, is key to interpreting *The End of the Affair*. The "miracle" of the Weeping Madonna, which is under the control of the monks in the monastery, the institutional church, is shown to be a sham when one of the monks points out to Ned and Jim, after the former appears, momentarily, to believe in something beyond himself, that the Virgin's tears come from a hole in the roof which lets in rainwater. But, just because it is not real in a supernatural sense does not detract from its meaning or value. As Jordan writes in *Sunrise with Sea Monster* about another set of tears, "the tears were real, even though they arrived on cue" (Jordan, 1994:7). Likewise, in *End of the Affair* Bendrix's embrace of Sarah in front of the hotel window in Brighton is clearly a performance for Parkis, but it is, nonetheless, sincere and real. Put another way, if you believe, and are open to the non-rational, miracles happen, and it ultimately becomes a question of interpretation, and of how one chooses to see the world. This has most recently been explored cinematically in M. Night Shyamalan's *Signs* (2002).

By contrast, during Jim's lengthy, populist, and emotional "sermon" to the townspeople prior to the procession, in which he once again chooses as his point of departure the text from the Colt 32 leaflet, and goes on to say: "There's nothing there, it's all in your head", and while you never have enough money or power, "everyone has sadness" in their hearts, a cut-away shows that Molly has been moved by his words. Jim ends with a meditation on "comfort": "People have guilty secrets. If you want to believe in something, that's not so bad. If it comforts you to believe in God, do it." By this time Molly is crying with new-found belief (in herself? in God? — it is not explained, but then, that would be to miss the point). Indeed, the often contradictory gobbledegook spoken by Jim which proves inspiring to the community — they applaud wildly at the end of his speech — shows that it is the sincerity of his tone as much as its content which is most valued. In that sense, this simple philosopher echoes the fool in *La Strada*.

Later, when Rosie has been saved by Ned, Molly calls it a miracle and is told by him, "Believe what you want to believe", a coda, perhaps, by Jordan against the materialist world where belief of any kind is deemed "old fashioned", certainly not fitting into the world of floating signifiers of postmodernity, such as Bobby's final clichéd words, "So long", with the final word "sucker", blotted out in a hail of police bullets.

Nevertheless, the clergy's belief in the Madonna as manifest in the statue proves yet again to be misplaced, when the head monk believes she now bears the stigmata as blood streams from her hand, only to be disabused shortly afterwards when the wounded Bobby appears from underneath the canopy and begins shooting. To balance the earlier scepticism towards the Madonna, Ned's bible stops a bullet fired by Bobby, thus, perhaps, reinforcing the notion that a secular (or at least materialist) miracle has occurred, just as it did when she delivered a mountain of shoes to Ned and Jim in answer to Jim's childish prayer (which prefigures that of Jimmy in *The Miracle*). These mysterious happenings are coded as being as valid and as important as the "mundane" (Jordan, *Sunrise*, 1994: 40) miracle of transubstantiation. As they successfully cross the bridge, Molly, with Rosie asleep on her shoulder, says to Ned that she is thinking of taking "Holy Orders", a term mostly applied to men who wish to become priests, but when scoffed at by him she asks him to think of a better idea. He replies, "Maybe I can", but it will all be in "good time", a reference perhaps to his imminent "revelation" that he is merely an impostor priest and is thus available to become the husband for whom she has been looking.

High Spirits and *We're No Angels* unambiguously proved that Jordan's forte was not in light comedy, and particularly not in directing De Niro (who played Ned) in a comic role. Indeed, Jordan has commented that a comedy should hardly have been expected given the principals associated with the film: himself, Mamet, De Niro and Penn (Dwyer, 1997: 5). Happily, Jordan learnt his lesson, with his work during the following decade and beyond favouring more serious drama, whether tragic, optimistic, or even darkly comic, or a combination of these.

Notes

[1] In the Neil Jordan Papers, Manuscripts Accessions 4761, Box 4, National Library of Ireland, there are draft copies of David Mamet's script for *We're No Angels*, and the storyboard of the Ned and Rosie scene when they fall into the river.

[2] *Sunday Tribune*, 25 February 1990.

[3] Pam Cook, *Monthly Film Bulletin*, Vol. 57, No. 677, June 1990: 179.

[4] Interestingly, Jordan's other prison escapee who dresses in women's clothes is Eamon de Valera (*Michael Collins*).

[5] Neil Jordan, *Sunday Tribune*, 25 February 1990.

Chapter Seven

The Miracle (1991)

I Say Hello

Too late for words
Too late, too late to try
There's nothing left for me to say
But hello and goodbye.

I say hello, I don't mean hello
I mean, Oh how I could have loved you
I try to smile, and yet all the while
My arms are aching to take you, hold you

I say goodbye, I don't mean good bye
I mean, darling, why must I go?
Oh how I could have loved you
Now you'll never know

Oh how I could have loved you so
Once, too long ago.

— From *Destry Rides Again* (1959)

The Miracle was written after *We're No Angels* as a "tiny little movie", but one with "integrity", as a way of somehow returning "home" and erasing the terrible experience of losing artistic control which had happened with both that film and *High Spirits*

(Jordan in Dwyer 1997: 7).[1] Indeed, the return is literal, in that the film was partly shot in his own house in the seaside town of Bray (just south of Dublin), but, in terms of the film's narrative, also symbolic in that the film, as an oedipal fantasy, is concerned with origins.

Such a fantasy, though not unique to Ireland, seems most favoured in Irish culture. Even the most cursory glance at Irish film (and literature, particularly of the post-independence period) would indicate a certain predilection for this type of narrative. Arguably, in a colonised state, where the land (or even the process of production) is not the father's to give to the son, resolution of the oedipal crisis is frustrated. If there has been a return to this theme (and its ineffectual and castrated male) since the 1980s so that it is, as McLoone notes, a dominant strain of "Celtic Tiger" cinema (McLoone, 2000: 174–83), it may be related to the emergence of the woman's voice within culture, as suggested by Gibbons (1992: 13).

Though based on his short story, "Night in Tunisia" (1976),[2] from his first published collection of stories, *The Miracle* is also richly textured with themes from all of the stories, most notably "A Love". It also clearly looks back to *The Past* (1980) and forward to *Sunrise with Sea Monster* (1994) which is similarly concerned with a son falling in love with the woman who marries his father.[3] (Indeed, the familial home is the same one as that in *The Miracle*.)

If "Stardust" is Renée's song and the symbolic thread that connects and situates the central players of *The Miracle's* oedipal triangle, for those who are familiar with the stage musical *Destry Rides Again* (1959), in which Renée stars as the brassy Frenchy, perhaps the more potent musical expression of (her) loss, regret and ambiguous desire becomes "I Say Hello". But then, like Renée, whether as a woman or a mother, the musical is simultaneously present and absent. When the film's narrative intercuts with and counterpoints *Destry Rides Again*, it is not Harold Rome's 1959 musical, but the more tragic 1939 film Western directed by George Marshall and starring Marlene Dietrich and James Stewart.[4] In Rome's version, Frenchy is allowed to find love and happiness, but in the film, though she removes her "paint", she is ultimately punished by death for her transgression. That she is an active agent in her death — she takes a bullet intended for Destry — only gives it a further poignancy. Restoration of law and order to Bottleneck is dependent on her removal as much as on the removal of the corrupt Kent. Her "disappearance" ensures that Destry remains free to marry the pure Janice Tyndall.

Though Jordan re-enacts the film on stage, his selective use of it nuances it differently. What Jordan disregards is as important as what he uses. Left out are Frenchy's "heart of gold" and her sacrifice, so all that remains of her is her sexy, though masculine, aspect. She is represented as a woman who chooses to be one of the boys rather than to be a "lady" (something made explicit in her rendition of what became Dietrich's signature song, "See What the Boys in the Back Room Will Have"); one who is given to excessive desire and lack of restraint (expressed in "You've Got That Look"), and who eventually is shot.

Also absent is the source film's proto-feminist celebration of female solidarity which emerges when Frenchy motivates the townswomen to ignore their differences and to come together in order to march on the Last Chance Saloon and (literally) fight Kent and his henchmen. Other aspects of Destry the film are re-interpreted or are ironically juxtaposed within the context of The Miracle's reality, so that Frenchy's open relationship with her maid Clara is mirrored in Renée's relationship with her dresser — both women serving to bring into focus the nature of Frenchy's/Renée's connection with her "son" (Jimmy Stewart's Destry/Jimmy) — while the two callers to Frenchy's dressing room, Kent, the bad patriarch, and Destry, the good son, are invoked in the visits to Renée's dressing room by Sam (Donal McCann), the inadequate father, and Jimmy, the confused son.

Before further exploring the mise-en-abyme of The Miracle (and Destry), it is necessary to provide an outline of the film's narrative. The film follows the psychosexual development of seventeen-year-old Jimmy Coleman (Niall Byrne) during the summer months when he loses his innocence and unwittingly returns to the oedipal moment when the boy's love for the mother becomes sexualised and the father becomes a rival.

Normally, this is resolved through the threat of punishment (symbolic castration) by the father, which leads the child to reject his mother and identify with the father. The child then accepts and becomes part of the male world of the symbolic and is free to love other women. In psychoanalytical terms, the dissolution of the Oedipus complex is that the boy is permitted to possess a penis which comes to stand in for the phallus or power for his adult life.

In *The Miracle*, however, Jimmy, because of his mother's absence, his father having told him that she died, is locked out of this developmental stage and, not having experienced the first object of desire — he has even been refused a photographic image of her — is incapable of loving other girls. As he cannot reject that which he never had, he is unable to identify with his musician father with whom he lives and so simultaneously desires and hates him, while he cannot embrace Rose (Lorraine Pilkington), a girl of the same age with whom he shares his days and creative energy. Despite her desire for a romantic involvement with him, she sums up their relationship thus: "Too friendly to be lovers, too close to be friends, together they lived in that twilight zone." Together they fight the "empty, musing, poignant smell" (Jordan, 1993a: 10) of the seaside town by weaving narratives about the various people they come across. While Rose acts as author, with Jimmy as her helper, it is Jimmy's personal narrative which ultimately takes over. Only after he has unravelled his familial emotional knot does power return to Rose, and once again, she speaks the new narrative, which we believe, will become hers and his.

Disruption to their lives happens when a beautiful woman in her late thirties arrives by train. She is clearly out of place and the storytellers, most especially Jimmy, decide that she is a "specimen", and begin to create her backstory. Although Rose, already jealous of his interest in the stranger, dismisses as gauche his fantasy of her as a French woman who, having killed her husband, is "on the run from her past" and awaiting her inheritance, it turns out, in typical Jordan fashion, to be an ironic inversion of a past and present that involves Jimmy. It transpires that Renée (Beverly D'Angelo) *is* "Frenchy", is returning to her past, has been "killed" by her husband, Jimmy's father, and is awaiting her inheritance — Jimmy.

However, the inheritance becomes excessive; her boy, as she tells him, very clearly plays "Stardust" "much too good", and so doing returns to her in an incestuous embrace[5] of plenitude (or more crudely, Destry, the son, "rides" again). This is played out several times, first, compositionally following their performance of "Stardust" when the camera frames them so that their faces touch like lovers bound in a complete circle; second, in his dream, when he holds the rope/umbilical cord on which she as an acrobat swings around, before they kiss; and finally, when he actually rapes her on the seafront as he talks about his desire and his own conception.

He becomes his own father; an actor in the primal scene, comparing his "performance" to his father's. Like the Irish-Americans in Back to the Future (Robert Zemeckis, 1985), the son Marty McFly is better than the father, but in that film, the son's fantasy is also his nightmare which if realised would result in his undoing — should his mother choose him over his nerdish father, he could never be born, and so would cease to be. This is visually summed up in a photograph he carries of his family, which fades in relation to his mother's growing infatuation with him.

Though time travel in The Miracle is not literal, a similar scenario is played out, only now the positions of knowledge are reversed. It is the mother who is aware of the mother–son relationship, while the photograph, this time of the mother and father, only propels the son in the opposite way — to make love to the forbidden object.

The photograph, or rather its content — for as Roland Barthes points out, the photograph as an artifact is "always invisible"[6] — is central to both narratives (and is instrumental in other work by Jordan such as The Past, Angel, Mona Lisa, The Crying Game, The Butcher Boy and The End of the Affair). This fits the contemporary paradigm whereby (analogue) photography replaces history and memory, and comes to serve capitalism's reification of people into packaged icons of desire. In a culture fixated on the image, the photograph necessarily becomes a way into the past and the place where truth resides. "I went to the photographer's show as to a police investigation."[7] The photograph, in effect, is stripped of ideology and meaning and becomes an unproblematic, but violent[8] referent of the real, which destroys memory as it does the future, even if it is deliberately staged or fake, as in the cases of *Mona Lisa*'s tea-drinkers and the self-consciously amorous Bendrix and Sarah in Brighton (*The End of the Affair*). Simultaneously, it can bring us to another place, for the photograph's power is not its referent, but the image itself.

In *The Miracle*, Jimmy's encounter with the photograph is of a different register than that of *Back to the Future*'s Marty or the replicants of *Blade Runner* (Ridley Scott, 1982 and 1991) who collect photographs to (re)insert themselves into history. For Jimmy, the photograph stirs in him a madness, whereby he moves beyond that which was, a place that defiantly excludes him yet produces him, in order to enter the spectacle and "tak[e] into [his] arms what is dead."[9] After he replaces his father and "loves" his mother, he assigns both her and the image to history, and having learnt what he no longer consciously knew about himself,[10] that she *was* his mother, produces what could be termed a counter-memory of himself as an infant gazing up at his mother from his pram. (This is the image over which the opening credits play.) This idealisation is only the flipside of Jimmy's material expulsion of her whereby she is forced into a kind of death — she returns (emigrates) to America — and becomes again, as Rose suggests, a ghost. If Jimmy compliments her on her stage death — "you died well" — the irony is that it is Jimmy who actually kills her.[11]

Even though the early meetings of Renée and Jimmy seem more driven by his general curiosity rather than a specifically sexual one — though this is always present — his tender comment following their first conversation, that "she wouldn't hurt a fly", together with their age difference and the fact that his father does not fulfil his symbolic function in the home, hints at the traumatic and sexualised events to follow. The "fly" comment can be read as an allusion to *Psycho*'s (Alfred Hitchcock, 1960) ending when Norman Bates, locked into his mother's identity, refuses to hurt a fly. In short, Jimmy transforms Renée from the mysterious murderess to his romantic ideal, no less mysterious or more related to reality, whom he wishes to seduce by summer's end.

Meanwhile, his relationship with Rose becomes strained, or, at least, more asexual, while his interest in their fictional subjects, such as the nuns, begins to wane. She, on the other hand, hoping to provoke Jimmy, makes advances on Jonner (Mikkel Gaup), a brutish elephant trainer. Jimmy, already captivated by Renée and, like so many of Jordan's male protagonists, on the brink of relishing the fulfilment and emptiness of adult desire, facilitates their introduction, believing that Rose simply wants "to humanise" the beast and enjoy his physicality. From the start, Jonner is marked as different, and largely through his poor command of English, and the way in which he is so easily manipulated by Rose, is represented as a point of comic relief, not unlike O'Callaghan in *Destry Rides Again*. However, the most obvious reference is that to the gypsy boy in Jordan's short story "Sand". In it, a young half–naked bronzed gypsy trades with a young adolescent male a ride of his donkey for a "go" on his sister. In *The Miracle* Jimmy repeats that trade, though it is one which Rose acquiesces to, and seems to enjoy, at least in so far as it helps her to win Jimmy, with whom, as she confesses, she so longs to swim out (to sea).

The importance of the sea should be understood in the context of Jordan's other work. In *The Miracle*, the sea becomes more than a backdrop to the events; it becomes the site of fantasy. It is where Rose desires to be; where Renée continually gazes to, as articulated by Jimmy; while various sensuous, violent or romantic encounters happen by the seafront, including the nuns' swimming, the meetings of Olivia Strange (Cathleen Delany) and Mr Beausang (J.G. Devlin), the rape of Renée, and the parade of liberated circus animals. The seaside also appears as a dominant trope in the *Night in Tunisia* collection of short stories, where it is invoked in seven of the ten stories, as well as in *Mona Lisa*, *The Crying Game*, *The Butcher Boy*, *The End of the Affair* and *The Good Thief* (while water is also central to *In Dreams*). To varying degrees, water and seaside are treated as the *mise-en-scene* of desire and sexual liberation, so that it becomes a metaphor for the ultimate desire, which is to return to the maternal waters and total plenitude, a place where one is "seal[ed] . . . magically from the world outside" (Jordan, 1993a: 9).[12]

Sadly, the dream is rarely realised. The seaside holiday town is unrepentantly tawdry; a place of mechanical desire and pleasure, impersonal and empty, where "bodies are [not] free" (Jordan, 1993: 47), and suffer hurt and shame; "skirt and pants sagging with their burden of water" (Jordan, 1993: 56). Even if these seaside encounters and experiences prove to be unsatisfactory (painfully so for the young Francie Brady in *The Butcher Boy*, who longs to retrace the steps to the seaside town where his parents honeymooned and when happiness was possible), these images, understood from an Irish visual cultural context, are refreshing, as they provide relief from the dominance of the landscape. As noted by Ruane, "landscape is the single most important element that distinguishes Irish art from international mainstream",[13] while according to Gibbons, "landscape has tended to play a leading role in Irish Cinema" (Rockett et al., 1987: 203). This is especially evident in the very first fiction films made in Ireland by the American Kalem company, and their practice of identifying, through intertitling, key tourist spots such as "The Gap of Dunloe" and "The Lakes of Killarney".

From the film's beginning, Sam and Jimmy's relationship is dysfunctional. If their mutual loss serves to bind them as father and son, the structuring absence — the wife/mother — tarnishes the bond with resentment and hate. This is not helped by Sam's excessive drinking (frequently represented as an Irish way of sublimating sexual desire), and his effective abdication from his responsibilities as a father. That he has failed is expressed in a dream. In this, the first of five graphic image bursts which punctuate the film, Sam imagines himself by the shore at twilight. Three men dressed in black are selling coffins. The method of payment is decided according to the buyer's palm. After the men look at Sam's hand, they demand cash upfront.

While Jimmy dismisses his father's fears, the dark austere images succinctly sum up Sam's real crisis: the crisis brought about by his failing to respect the patriarchal world of the symbolic. He has refused to name things and put them in their proper places, and for that he must pay — in cash and in his death. Standing by the sea, he comes to understand that he can have no place there — he is about to be erased. Therefore, like

Renée, he, too, is out of place, but the difference is that it is not only within the man's role to define place, but it is his responsibility to do so. In "A Love" a lesser abdication occurs: the boy is unable to drive because his father never taught him.

Ironically, in the second dream of the film, Jimmy's, Sam suffers his projected destiny: death. Jimmy fishes him out of this same water, viciously hooking his mouth (an image returned to in *Sunrise with Sea Monster* in Donal's fantasy of catching something other than fish on his (and his father's) night-lines). In Jimmy's second dream, the film's third, an image of Sam, then Sam himself, is consumed by flames. Later, as already noted, Jimmy's encounter with his mother is a symbolic replacement by Jimmy of his father within the lovers' photograph. In short, Sam's sin has been his failure to explain to Jimmy his origin story, thereby condemning him, like the replicants of *Blade Runner,* to an existence outside of history, or more generally, outside the symbolic and into a problematic relationship with his mother and women.

Like in "Night in Tunisia", the troubled relationship of the father and son is filtered through music, with their sexual identities made manifest through their ability to play music. Unsurprisingly, the music of choice is jazz, which more than any other musical genre is figured in terms of the body and natural rhythms. This is especially true in relation to free-floating improvisational or bebop jazz, where obvious harmonies and rhythms are eschewed in favour of melodic fragments which though often drawn from standard (including musical) songs ooze a kind of nervous and racing energy.

The title of the source story, "Night in Tunisia", is taken from Dizzy Gillespie's bebop composition and it, as played by Charlie Parker, facilitates the son's entry into his own musical expression and, simultaneously, into the adult world of focused and heterosexual desire. The coupling of sex (or the sensuous) and music is implicit in the boy's description of the piece, building as it does on his earlier experience of hearing Parker perform "a rapid-fire succession of notes that seemed to spring from . . . falling water, . . . so much faster than his father ever played, but slow behind it all, melancholy, like a river" (Jordan, 1993a: 42). But now,

> [t]he notes soared and fell, dispelling the world
> around him, tracing a series of arcs that seemed to
> point to a place, or if not a place, a state of mind . . .
> stretching to infinity, . . . lap[ping] like water. He de-
> cided it was a place you were always in, yet always
> trying to reach, you walked towards all the time and
> yet never got there, as it was always beside you.
> (Jordan, 1993a: 46)

If this is undercut by the boy actually reaching, if only momentarily, that "place" with the open-mouthed Rita, figured as a
type of forbidden older sister, in *The Miracle*, these words are
given an uncompromising strength when Jimmy chooses heterosexuality (though homosexuality is never explored — or
rejected — as it is in the story) which, ultimately, is driven by
the impossible desire of self-annihilation through total union
with the woman (mother). And so, even if Jordan in *The Miracle*
moves towards conventional music by giving a "straight" performance of "Stardust", the transgressive power and excitement of Otherness, of Eastern things, of Africa and of Tunisia
(as rendered by Gillespie) remains palpable.

This association of music and the body and sex is made even
more explicit in the image of the phallic, shining saxophone
which Jimmy fetishistically works on, and is figured as an extension of a visceral expressive organic body: "the gold sheen of
the instrument became quickly tarnished with sweat, the sweat
that came off his fingers in the hot metal room. He fashioned his
mouth round the reed till the sounds he made became like a
power of speech, a speech . . . that sprang from the knot of his
stomach, the crook of his legs" (Jordan, 1993a: 47). "Night in
Tunisia" also sets up a parallel between blowing (the instrument) and the thin (homosexual) boy blowing a "French Letter"
(Jordan, 1993a: 38), and later, as the boy finds solace with Rita
and enters the void, he recalls the memory of how the lifeguard
"put his lips to [Rita's] lips and blew" (Jordan, 1993a: 49).

In *The Miracle*, Jimmy's musical performances are inextricably bound to sexual desire; for example, during his musical accompaniment to the one-fingered contortionist's act, he is

standing in the background and framed by her open legs. As already noted, his intimacy with Renée often takes the form of a musical conversation: "Stardust", when both see in each other their lost object of desire; and at the ballroom when Jimmy tries to serenade her through his father's band. If she helps him to discover love, the body and the saxophone, ironically, Sam's decline as a musician and retreat into alcoholism can be seen as a consequence of having lost her.

Similarly, Danny in *Angel*, having lost the mute girl and becoming increasingly involved in political violence, loses his saxophone, thereby swapping his ability to play many tunes for a gun, which plays only one. In *Destry Rides Again*, learning to use the gun is analogous to learning to play the saxophone in *The Miracle*. Indeed, the point at which Destry takes up arms when he realises Kent's men have killed Wash, who had been his father's deputy, the same way as they killed Destry senior, is re-enacted in Jordan's film, but staged such that the climaxes of both texts are literally bound together and criss-cross with one another. The theatrical scene is extended beyond the stage to include and mirror the real-life entanglements of the Colemans and Renée. Rose and Jimmy, left of stage, look across the action to the facing wing where Renée, removing her stockings, is talking to Sam.

Though it would seem that, while the sax might stand for, or be a prelude to sexual performance, in keeping with the boy's intuition of Parker's jazz describing an unattainable place, this experience ends up as something both more and less than (improvisational) jazz. For Sam, the result is pain and loss, and a masochistic relationship to sensuous jazz, while for Jimmy, it is incestuous transgression. Indeed, as Jimmy commits this, in a repeat of the father's sin, other attempts at heterosexual love are intercut, including Rose's empty encounter with Jonner, a couple dancing, and Sam playing, melancholically, "You'd Be So Nice To Come Home To".

It would appear that jazz and love are incompatible.[14] Yet, in order for love to be possible, one must enter the world of art, though not remain fixed in its alternative reality. (In this case love can be understood as approximate with empathy, companionship, mutual respect and acceptance of *difference*, rather than the all-consuming type of romantic love, for in Jordan's world, people seem condemned to live in their individuated bubble wrap of emotional and psychic isolation.) It is, Jordan suggests, through the "Players and the painted stage"[15] that we see and come to understand the labyrinths that we walk, but it is in being that we live. The sadness of Narcissus was that he loved the image too much. The miracle of the film's title that Jimmy undergoes is that he disengages from his night in Tunisia and grows up with his origin story "intact" and sees in the phenomenology of the elephant, what the fool and Gelsomina see in the pebble (*La Strada*). The reason is just to be, and such a justification is perhaps more divine, albeit secular, than the Church and the ultimate father — God. But, as the nuns' pellucid skin indicates, God never is really there. As Rose comments, only women who never see their husbands could look so young. With everything resolved, the film can end with A loving B and B loving A — no story at all. Or, put another way, Rose and Jimmy walk the promenade as she narrates her story, and Olivia Strange and Mr Beausang, on whom the two projected their own desire for each other, are finally introduced.

The reference to bebop, no matter how it is then perverted by and filtered through Sam and his commercial seaside band that plays to old timers and holiday folk who, according to Jimmy, do not appreciate it, serves another purpose. If the short story both laments and registers the passing of the big band and its replacement by three-chord showbands from the mid-1960s and later, in the 1970s, by disco and nightclub culture, *The Miracle* refuses to do so and allows it, or its ghost, to linger in a temporal limbo. In short, the film offers what has become a hallmark of much of contemporary cinema: a nostalgic world floating somewhere between the past and present, and suffering from what Frederic Jameson might term, a temporal schizophrenia. The music, Sam's showband, the dancing, the circus and its animals, the show business culture, the stage direction of *Destry Rides Again* and the show's poster locate the film in a theatrical or postmodern space that recalls another time, mostly the 1950s. This is also achieved through the representation of Renée as the enigmatic and punishable *femme fatale* of *film noir* who wears "old-fashioned" stockings, the apparel of Rose in *Sunrise*, which is set mainly in the 1930s and 1940s, instead of tights (see Butler Cullingford, 2000: 189; Pramaggiore, 1998: 286). Renée is, as all classical women are, little more than a screen for projected male fantasies.

Despite this recourse to another time, this is most definitely not a coming-of-age 1950s film of the type which Ireland produced during the 1980s and 1990s, which included *My Left Foot* (Jim Sheridan, 1989), *All Things Bright and Beautiful* (Barry Devlin, 1994), *Circle of Friends* (Pat O'Connor, 1995) and *Dancing at Lughnasa* (Pat O'Connor, 1998), where a (perhaps) self-consciously plastic image of Ireland is presented which celebrates in an uncritically nostalgic mode a past figured in terms of tradition, family, the landscape, Catholicism and conservative moral values, but with nationalism and its attendant reality of political violence avoided. *The Miracle*, while it celebrates images and sounds drawn from the 1950s, and in so doing gives weight to Gerry Stembridge's observation that in small-town Ireland there lingers a "sentimental attachment to the showband era",[16] like Stembridge's *Guiltrip* (1995) it not only refuses to endorse the promise and exoticism of the past — the night in Tunisia — but points to its emptiness (most potent in the "You'd be so nice to come home to" sequence)[17] and pain. Perhaps the more powerful articulation of the rejection is that Jimmy "kills" the (1950s) mystery by raping his mother, and seems in the end to take Rose as a (modern) lover, who, unlike Renée, is finally allowed by Jimmy to control her own representation.

Moving away from the woman–mother–sea trope that Jimmy would impose, Rose describes how, during her encounter with Jonner, she had her hair spread out "like a fan", not Jimmy's "seashell". However, even though Jordan suggests the ultimate failure of such things to overcome reality, and shows art only as a way to circumvent, but never fully transcend the tragedy of human desire and loss, he reminds us through Rose of the importance of imagination — in her words, doing something, to have a plan.

It remains somewhat irrelevant that the animals she frees, with the keys stolen from Jonner as he was having sex with her, will all eventually be caught. The intervention is both magical and artistic and creates a time and space beyond, yet bound to, reality, and in that sense, is, like all art, a miracle, if not quite that of the film's title.

Arguably, the real miracle is that Jimmy, despite the trauma of losing his mother, having her miraculously reborn and then raping her — his summer nights in Tunisia — becomes an emotionally complete person. In that sense, the (super)natural event of grace that befalls Jimmy, symbolised by the elephant who enters the church as he sits and waits for God to do something about his family predicament, has more in common with the appearance of the mechanical robin at the end of *Blue Velvet* (David Lynch, 1986) which symbolises a return of love and normality to the world. In that film, it coincides with Jeffrey's successful entry into maleness (and heterosexuality) which has been dependent on his rejection of the older woman/mother Dorothy, who, by the final scenes, has been repositioned as a mother, and the sadomasochistic and homosexual world that he encounters through her. But if the two films share much in terms of their postmodern nostalgic aesthetic — the look and the sound — and in that their protagonists are young adolescent males who undergo oedipal journeys from which they emerge "normal" and ready to embark on love, *The Miracle* refuses the cynicism of *Blue Velvet* — the elephant is after all real — and, at least in part, *Blue Velvet*'s regressive gender politics.

While Renée suffers the fate of classical cinema's trangressive women, it must be understood in a context of generic conventions, and in that she never is a real woman, only Frenchy, or a glistening projection of Jimmy's (and Sam's) fantasy. Rose, on the other hand, is very much alive and is allowed to be a creative rather than an interpretive artist, and she, despite her own difficulties with her golf-playing father who has little interest in her,[18] is clearly in control of her life, is never represented as simply a spectacle as are Renée and the contortionist, and is rewarded by getting what she longed for all summer — Jimmy.

Though Rose functions in part as the good girl, her ability to read situations, make plans and manipulate, and her sexual performance as Masoch's dominatrix, mean that she cannot be seen

simply as the natural and pure Janice Tyndall as Butler Cullingford suggests. Given the fact that she throws the keys (back)
into the sea after freeing the animals, means her power or intervention is that of transgression or disruption, and so cannot
be seen as another incarnation of Mary Kate (*The Quiet Man*)
whose feistiness and independence wanes once she gets her
man. Rose, though giving up the whip, remains in control.

The oedipal scenario within which Jimmy is central, is, as
Rose tells him, the oldest story, and as such cannot be seen as
specifically an Irish one. Yet, for all the debts that Jordan owes
to American culture (as Jimmy does to his American mother),
and the fact that ultimately Jordan is interested in the (alienated)
self, the body and concepts of mutability and the inbetweenness
of dualities rather than some geographical place, the film not
only is set in Ireland, but speaks with a decidedly Irish voice and
intersects with Irish culture. It does this by confirming and challenging traditional notions of Irishness and by reflecting debates
which came to the fore during the 1980s that centred on
women's bodies and the family. Although it might be said that
these shared in a more generalised (postmodern) preoccupation
with the feminised body (male and female) which had been de-
centred by technology, particularly reproductive technology,
they went far beyond this. If, more broadly, the body, culturally
speaking, symbolically lost its "private halo" of resistance, in Ireland — where women's expression of sexuality, control of their
fertility and access to abortion were controlled or altogether
denied — there simply could be no resistance.

Conceivably, the one place that the *Night in Tunisia* collection of stories could go metaphorically — the teenagers' encounters with various Mother figures — could have been made
literal only in a culture that placed the maternal body under the
media spotlight, as a "specimen" for the patriarchal institutions
of church and state. This was especially evident during the 1983
abortion referendum[19] which constitutionally resulted in the
unborn foetus being given equal right to life as the mother, but
also, in 1985 with the death of a teenager, Anne Lovett, who,
having concealed her pregnancy, died giving birth in front of a
statue of the Virgin Mary at Granard, County Longford, and

"the Kerry Babies" tribunal, the same year. The tribunal was set up in December 1984 when Joanne Hayes took a case against the Gardaí for falsely arresting her for the murder of an infant washed up on a Kerry beach in April 1984. However, the tribunal focused in a most voyeuristic, moralistic and offensive way on her sexual activities. Similarly, inter-family and church and state relations were aired in what was a divisive campaign prior to the defeat of the 1986 divorce referendum (Pramaggiore, 1998: 287–8).

The Miracle, in its defilement of the mother's body, is unambiguously an attack on the family, the basic unit of the State as defined in the 1937 Constitution. In this, it continues the work of the first wave of contemporary Irish filmmakers, who as part of a corrective or alternative vision of Ireland, proffered a version of the family, which, in a manner not dissimilar to much post-*Psycho* (Alfred Hitchcock, 1960) horror, became the site of repression and instability. For the first time, it could be seen as a fragile construct subject to abuse, oppression, hypocrisy or divorce. Such films included *Wheels, The Kinkisha, Exposure, Criminal Conversation, Maeve, Traveller* and *Pigs*.

Part of the achievement of these films was the deliberate complication of Ireland's emotional and psycho-sexual landscape, and *The Miracle* also exists in this framework. Renée is not simply the bad, promiscuous mother, who "knew" them all, but she is also the heroine, who returns to save her boy and help him discover the truth. She is at once the hard callous mother who left him and the woman of his (and Sam's) dreams, whose screen image is signalled by the sultry and sensuous saxophone. Sam, on the other hand, while he remains Jimmy's only parent, is, when it counts, unequal to the job. By refusing to position Jimmy within the oedipal triangulation, he becomes an all-too-Irish father: an ineffectual drunk.

Such a problematising of the father, and the desire of Jimmy to commit (if only in his dreams) patricide, can be seen as yet another instance within Irish cinema of a crisis of paternity. Examples range from the irrelevant and largely silent father of *Hush-a-Bye Baby* (Margo Harkin, 1989) which, though set in Northern Ireland, Derry especially, uses the Southern Irish de-

bates on abortion and other related events as its backdrop, to
the more commercial *In the Name of the Father* (Jim Sheridan,
1993) in which the son rejects his father's political passivism.

This may have its roots in the post-famine period when, in
order to stabilise the social fabric, the principle of primogenitor
became the primary means of passing land from one generation
to the next. This led to adult males, who, though sexually ma-
ture, were forced to live in the parental home as children until
both obstacles in the way of fulfilment (through marriage) were
ideally dead. The alternative was emigration. The eruption of
the tyrannical, or its mirror, the ineffectual, father, within
1980s' culture has been seen by Gibbons and others as a hysterical response to the growing power and independence of
women, as epitomised by the election of Mary Robinson as
President of Ireland in 1990, and the overwhelming presence
within public discourse of the visuality of women's bodies and
women's issues (McLoone, 2000: 177, Pramaggiore, 1998: 287–
8; Gibbons, 1992: 13).

Though the intergenerational conflict of father and son is
present in "Night in Tunisia", because they do not love the
same woman, it is not as central or as vicious as in another
story of the collection, "A Love". There, as in *The Miracle*, the
son becomes jealous of his father, and wants to destroy him. In
both, the confused and developing son mistakes his own
mother as a first — the ultimate — lover, but desires her, not
least because she "belongs" to the father. Indeed, for Neil, the
son (and writer) of "A Love", his affair with the woman who
"could have been anyone's mother", might have begun with her
smile, "[b]ut what perpetuated it was something outside, my
mathematical *father* lying sleepless . . . your civil war gun, rosa-
ries, that rain-soaked politician with his fist clenched" (Jordan,
1993a: 74; emphasis added).

Likewise, Jimmy knows that Renée is his mother, but refuses
to deny his desire, as he believes it is the father's role to do so:
"I knew, but I couldn't tell myself — I needed you to tell me, I
knew, but I didn't know I knew . . . even though you're a piss
artist, you're my father, and all I needed to hear you say was that
she was my mother." Like previous young Irish men who were

trapped by their mothers and the church, or more broadly, the process of modernisation following the Great Famine, to have the woman is not enough, fulfilment can only be known by triumphing over and literally replacing the hated father.

Accordingly, partial resolution for Neil comes when he has destroyed his father's possibility of romance, and this is also the case for Jimmy. Notwithstanding how the son of "A Love" hates the father as one would hate a rival of the same age (Jordan, 1993a: 82) and Jimmy's public taunting of his father's sexual prowess — "You want to fuck her, but you're too old, so you won't let me" — in a way that recalls Renée's words to Jimmy — "From a woman who is too old" — once they have taken what the father desires, the woman loses her function, for neither woman is allowed to have meaning in herself. Neil's muse is nothing more than a "blown-up photograph . . . a still from a film", who plays Ava Gardner to his James Dean (Jordan, 1993a: 76), while Renée is the exotic poster image that Jimmy hangs on his wall, and who fades into a memory of a beautiful woman pushing a pram. Neither knows what "woman" means, a predicament that Jordan views as a problem specific to Irish men (Jordan, cited in Pramaggiore, 1998: 288).

If, as noted, the church and spirituality seem to be self-consciously grafted onto *Blue Velvet*, the same could not be said of *The Miracle*. Even when Jordan (over)uses the image of the nuns, it is done with a sense of sincerity to the work as a whole in order to set up an easily read symbol of the church which has become somewhat invisible because it is such an integral part, if an increasingly declining one, of Irish society and an alternative form of desire. Interestingly, while he points to their difference — the double difference of the tall nun — by heightening their visibility, the nuns enjoy the sensuous feel of the water in perhaps the same way as the housewife in "Skin", the boys in "Night in Tunisia", or the man in the shower in "Last Rites". This is contrary to the contemporary representation of the Catholic Church in Ireland as being wholly repressive of pleasure. Jordan partly critiques the nuns, just as he critiques religion and the Blessed Virgin in *The Butcher Boy* (as noted by Butler Cullingford) — for example, they are seen to travel as a gaggle of schoolgirls (which suggests an immature sexuality) — but he refuses to crudely dismiss the pleasures and comforts of religion and belief. It is the nuns' sense of serenity or oneness, their "pellucid" skin, that draws the two teenage friends into the church, where Jimmy asks God to help him seduce Renée, and Rose, more aware of "Catholic barter", lights a candle and prays for this to happen.

Despite such entreaties to the Divine, as is the case in *The Butcher Boy*, the miracle is ultimately a secular one: the church, it would seem, provides only the *mise-en-scene*. As suggested elsewhere, the church deals in illusions (some of which give ambiguous comfort): we would do well to follow the advice of Fathers Brown and Riley in *We're No Angels*, who remind us of the nature of a miracle, and that divine intervention, or in that particular case, the weeping statue, is nothing more or less than a hole in the roof.

Finally, the sense of inferiority, of Ireland, or Bray, being a "God-forsaken place", while typical of a youth's rejection of the home, is given more meaning in a post-colonial country which both resents, yet secretly respects, its coloniser. Such ambivalence is central to the understanding of Francie Brady's relationship to the "English"-tainted Nugents, the too-proper family that he longs for, yet destroys. Jimmy's destruction of the outsider, figured as American and fittingly bound to popular culture (both cinema and theatrical review), though less graphic, is no less violent. But his is more explicitly the destruction of the bad mother. Bad not just because she is sexually promiscuous or because she left Jimmy, but because, notwithstanding her desire to give him his history and free him, she threatens, in her mouth-on-mouth kissing, to engulf him, to literally swallow him. "Los Angelesation" it would seem might indeed be a greater threat to Ireland and Irish identity than Anglicisation, as James Montgomery, the first Irish film censor, feared.[20]

This transgression, while brought in line by Jimmy's "punishment" of her, could have been resolved much earlier through Sam's intervention. It is Sam's presence outside the "hall of mirrors" — the place where the imaginary or the world of maternal plenitude gives way to the symbolic and the father — that causes Renée to stop Jimmy's seduction of her. As a result, Jimmy is unable to unite with his mother, and is left with shattered images of her as she flees from him. The father's subsequent ineffectual action allows for the infatuation to grow and results in the traumatic ending, making impossible the restoration of the family.

If *The Miracle* can be summarised as a simple story of a young man falling in love with his mother, and his return to grace, it can equally be seen, like the *nouvelle roman*, as a metanarrative on the construction of stories and reality and one informed by film history, which partially allows Jordan to defend himself against feminist criticism of his characterisation of Renée. Despite the tight literary composition and his extensive use of dialogue, particularly through Rose who acts to (re)articulate reality, and who becomes a kind of interpreter both for Jimmy and the audience, even though she herself is unable to communicate with her family, the film never loses sight of the more sensual (and erotic) elements of cinema, which are most pronounced in the moments of theatrical, musical and circus performances and their respective *mises-en-scene*. However, his use of images never simply provides a break in or disruption to the narrative, but as in a well-integrated musical, serves to expand it and offer other levels of texture, seeing and immersion.

Notes

---

[1] Jordan said he was almost going to retire after *High Spirits* (Glicksman, 1990: 10).

[2] This was produced as a television drama which was directed by Pat O'Connor (1983), with script by Jordan. It is a slimmed-down version of the story, with some additions. It does not capture the twilight magic of either the story or Jordan's film, even if Luke and his friend Nick dance at dusk, as the two boys do in *Sunrise*. Instead, it is a somewhat pedestrian coming-of-age tale in which there is a certain complicity of father and son. The father pays him to learn and plays with him, and facilitates his becoming a man. After "performing" in a suit, Rene dances with him and invites him outside where they make love. Their love scene is intercut with the father and Luke's sister Rita. He makes use of music throughout.

3 *Sunrise with Sea Monster* is set against a backdrop of political violence (the Republican movement in Ireland and the Spanish Civil War). The interweaving of past and present, reality and imagination, and the personal psycho-sexual familial ties between father, son and stepmother, are explored through the son-narrator, Donal, who attempts to recount the inevitability of his betrayals. The son's relationship with his stepmother, which predates his father's with her, finally ends when the invalid father (her husband), visits the spa in Lisdoonvarna, a location (if not exactly the same oedipal configuration) already familiar from *The Past* (whose central character is also called Rene and in which the narrative, like in *The Miracle*, is partly played out in Bray). There the father is touched by the seventh son of a seventh son, disappears and is presumed drowned. The possibility of a miracle — of the father walking to his suicide — is finally rationalised as a secular miracle by the son who encounters his father's ghost when he partakes in their shared ritual of nightline "fishing". Following their reconciliation, the removal of Rose back to her home, the father joins his first wife on the beach. Desire is fulfilled. As with *The Miracle*, music is central to the narrative, but here the piano replaces the saxophone as Donal says, "the piano became my way to her" (*Sunrise*, p. 25). Although jazz is also replaced by classical music, it is of the Romantic period, or the arbitrary "melodies" of Erik Satie, which are preludes to and accompany their lovemaking. The novel is best summed up in Donal's words: "Rose, myself and father as a triangular cocoon, an equation known only to ourselves that related to no known numerical system" (p. 116).

4 Ben Stoloff's 1932 film of the same name starring Tom Mix is very different to Marshall's, although both were based on the novel *Destry Rides Again* by Max Brand, New York, 1930.

5 In the Neil Jordan papers at the National Library of Ireland (Accession no. 4761) there are draft scripts of *The Miracle* in Boxes 3, 4 & 7 (of 7). Included in these are scenes which make explicit the mother–son relationship and register the "companionable incest" of the maternal embrace, "where everything is suspended: time, law prohibition: nothing is exhausted, nothing is wanted: all desires are abolished, for they seem definitively fulfilled" (Roland Barthes (1977, trans. 1978), *A Lover's Discourse*, London: Penguin, 104).

In one script (undated), Renée is in her hotel room wearing a kimono and is watched from outside by Jimmy (prefiguring Claire in *In*

Dreams, when she dressed in her red kimono and is being watched by Vivian). She allows him in. He wants to seduce her, but settles for the calm of her loving arms (Duparc in Barthes, 1978: 104). She then sings softly "Stardust" — "Sometimes I wonder how I spend the lonely nights / Dreaming of a song, / The melody haunts my reverie / And I am once again with you". She stops, he is asleep, and she says that she is his mother.

In another draft ("Stardust, Lost Sex Story", Box 7), this "innocent" infantile embrace is again invoked, but it follows rather than leads to genital desire which Barthes suggests (Barthes, 1978: 105) might be understood as "the lover . . . as a child getting an erection: such was the young Eros." Jimmy walks home by the beach, Jean [Renée] is there waiting, and she tells him that she wants to talk to him. He asks what about, and allows her to come in. Once inside he kisses her and she tells him that he can't, though refuses to give a reason, and he continues to seduce her. When the seduction is over, he tells her that he knows she is his mother. "She holds him, then in her arms like her own child, Jimmy sleeps. When he wakes up she is gone."

6 Roland Barthes (1993), *Camera Lucida*, London: Vintage, 6. Indeed, the photograph of the dead father is central to understanding Sarah Langan's sense of oppression which she finally manages to overcome (*Miracles and Miss Langan*).

7 Ibid., p. 85.

8 "The photograph is violent: not because it shows violent things, but because on each occasion *it fills the sight by force*, and because in it nothing can be refused or transformed" (Ibid., p. 91).

9 Ibid., p. 117.

10 Ibid., p. 85.

11 Another ending (Box 7, in the Neil Jordan Papers at the National Library) suggests a reformation of the family. It is dawn and Jimmy is with Rose on the promenade. Jean [Renée] walks by and he introduces her to Rose as his mother. His dad arrives after Jimmy releases the "divine" sign. He allows his dad to put his arms on his shoulder.

While Jordan is often criticised for how he treats women, or in this case ultimately excluding or punishing the woman, an interesting reversal happens in his *Miracles and Miss Langan*, made for television by Pat O'Connor in 1979. Though aesthetically the piece is dull, a number of interesting Jordanesque tropes are present, not least a preoccupation with appearance, representation and reality; seeing; religion, "miracles" and ritual; faith and ideology; the overbearing oppression of society and institutions; and most of all the (sexual) inter-relationships of men and women. In this short piece, it is the man who is expelled and dejected, while the woman has broken out of her "virginal" status. The problem is not Sarah, but, as the other teacher, obsessed with her appearance reassuringly tells her, "men". Like George (*Mona Lisa*), or Rose (*The Miracle*) she too narrativises her life and like George, characterises her "romantic" involvement as unimportant. But then, it is from books — French novels — that she "learnt about men and suspenders" — and when she makes love for the first time, she feels like she is "copying" someone like those frail girls in *Vogue*. Like in *Miracle* (and all of Jordan's miracles), the miracles of the title are not of divine making, nor is it totally clear as to what the "miracles" are. Clearly one of the miracles is the breaking out of the prison "cage" of Irish conformity, repressed sexuality and religious morality (whether Protestant or Catholic — her comments are echoed in Danny's inquiry in *Angel* as to whether Bloom is a Catholic or a Protestant Jew), and, indeed, the miracle of seduction by the older atheist — whore and virgin — of the young priest.

[12] In "Night in Tunisia", Rene (the girl known as Rita in the story) tries to commit suicide by drowning in the sea, in order to understand how the brown-bodied boy priest must have felt when he did this (following an encounter with her). In *Miracles and Miss Langan* the priest as a thirteen-year-old boy enjoys all the more the "sin" of looking at a woman undress because it is on the beach. As well as the name change of the object of desire to Rene, it also includes nuns, who are not mentioned in the story but are prominent in *Miracle*. They are the only type of Irish unmarried women who are "satisfied" in their virginity. Theirs is not enforced, as Miss Langan's is. The image of the sea or immersion in water which perhaps finds its most explicit and visually beautiful rendering in *In Dreams*, also draws on the "sexual" apples of "Night" (Jordan, 1993a: 45) is, of course, not unique to Jordan.

[13] Frances Ruane, *The Delighted Eye: Irish Painting and Sculpture of the Seventies* (Exhibition Catalogue), unpaginated.

[14] In Pat O'Connor's adaptation, Luke's (Jimmy's) friend, who is clearly figured in terms other than straight heterosexuality (he uses the same "chat up" lines to Luke as he does to a young girl when Luke is busy performing with his dad and subsequently dancing with Rene) makes the comment that music and love songs are a con. They promise illusions that can only lead to disappointment or heartbreak. While this may not be a revelation, it is something to which Jordan frequently returns: the non-identity of representation and art and the reality.

[15] W.B. Yeats, "The Circus Animals' Desertion" in *W.B. Yeats Selected Poetry*, A. Norman Jeffares, ed., London: Macmillan, 1962. The image of the circus animals and Yeats in relation to *The Miracle* is discussed in Gallagher Winarski, 1999. However, Yeats and Jordan use it to different ends. The similarity is in the image, not in its meaning.

[16] "Family Affair: Stembridge interviewed by Shane Barry", *Film Ireland*, No. 50, Dec 1995 / Jan 1996: 25.

[17] In *Guiltrip* the music ("I Love You In My Own Peculiar Way" and "Chapel on the Hill") ironically inform the abusive relationship that Liam has with his wife Tina.

[18] In both Jordan's story and O'Connor's screen version the golf course is a place where the young Rita/Rene, "Queen of the fairway" goes to meet her "clients". Given the association of golf (and tennis) to sex, it is interesting that the only time we see Rose's father is when he is on the course.

[19] Further referendums were held in 1992 and 2002. The current situation is that it is illegal to procure an abortion in the Republic of Ireland, but that one has a right to abortion information and to travel abroad to get one. However, clearly the right to travel is problematic if the female is institutionalised, in state care, or simply cannot afford it.

[20] See Kevin Rockett, *The Los Angelesation of Ireland* (forthcoming).

Chapter Eight

The Crying Game (1992)

The point of departure of *The Crying Game* is the kidnapping in Northern Ireland of a black British army soldier, Jody (Forrest Whitaker), by the IRA (Irish Republican Army). The paramilitary organisation hopes to trade him for one of their senior members being held in Castlereagh interrogation centre. This scene, and the subsequent imprisonment and killing — ironically by his own side — of Jody, carries a clear echo of a key literary text dealing with Anglo-Irish military activities, Frank O'Connor's War of Independence short story "Guests of the Nation" (1931), which explores the detention and eventual execution by the IRA of two British soldiers, Belcher and Hawkins. Like Jody, they too are being held as hostages in the hope of exchanging them for two IRA men due to be executed in Mountjoy Jail, Dublin. During the course of the captivity, the IRA men and British soldiers come to empathise with one another, not so much as soldiers of opposing armies, but as people whose common humanity transcend their national or political allegiances. In *The Crying Game*, the IRA leader Peter Maguire (Adrian Dunbar) makes explicit the reference to O'Connor's story by calling Jody one of their "guests", while his confinement in a farmhouse is similar to the location used in O'Connor's story. A few years after the story was published, playwright Denis Johnston made a silent film adaptation of the story (see Rockett, 1987: 60–2).

Belcher and Hawkins, a Communist, are both working class and without any particular allegiance to the British army. Their precursors, as Elizabeth Butler Cullingford outlines, can be traced back to Dion Boucicault's "Irish-loving Englishmen", or "decent chaps" who visit Ireland (Butler Cullingford, 2001: 37ff). They become, as the cliché has it, "more Irish than the Irish themselves". This includes them learning Irish dancing, which leads narrator Bonaparte to observe that they could take root "like a native weed" in Ireland.

While the relationships between the men becomes increasingly friendly, the homosocial world of male bonding remains totally chaste. This is not the case in Brendan Behan's *The Hostage* (1959), a translation of his own Irish language play *An Giall*, which was inspired by O'Connor's story. As befits a bisexual author, Behan discards the limited concerns of O'Connor's story with national allegiances in favour of an exploration of male sexuality. Yet, as Butler Cullingford notes (2001: 58), while the "prudishness of the IRA and the Gaelic League was a prime target in *An Giall*", Behan knew that "overtly gay characters" would not be acceptable in a 1950s' Dublin theatre, whether the play was in Irish or English. Consequently, it was at Joan Littlewood's Stratford East Theatre, London that the English-language version of the play was first performed.

In this production, set not in O'Connor's and Jordan's farmhouse, but in a brothel, a male prostitute, Rio Rita, and his "coloured boyfriend", Princess Grace, are introduced. This "queer" duo set out to seduce the soldier-prisoner Leslie, who is quite aware that he is dispensable to the upper-class British authorities. Rio Rita, Princess Grace, and Mulleady, a homosexual undercover policeman/informer and civil servant, try to free Leslie and in doing so are seen to challenge the political allegiance and sexual puritan morality of the IRA officer, but, in the process, the prisoner is accidentally killed in crossfire, a fate somewhat similar to what happens to Jody.

In *The Crying Game*, the gay discourse is quite explicit when Jody sets out to seduce Fergus (Stephen Rea), a reversal of what is known variously as "The Patty Hearst Syndrome" or "The Stockholm Syndrome", whereby a prisoner begins to identify with a jailer. Jody engages with Fergus through a series of mildly flirtatious comments, such as telling him that he is the handsome one with "killer eyes and baby face", before inviting him to look at a photograph (a typical Jordan device) of his special friend Dil. This leads, in an echo of IRA woman Jude (Miranda Richardson) holding Jody's hand while he goes to the toilet at the fairground just prior to his capture, which excites him, to Fergus accompanying and helping a handcuffed Jody to urinate outside the farmhouse. Though Fergus is reluctant to take out Jody's penis, which Jody reminds him is only a "piece of meat" when they return indoors, they both find the whole affair humorous, insisting to each other that "the pleasure was mine". Following this physical bonding, Jody warns Fergus that "women are trouble" and that he may "think" of Dil too. This permission to "know" or take pleasure in his "woman" clearly marks the homoerotic nature of their relationship. Fergus's subsequent involvement with Dil, particularly when he, as Dil notes, dresses her like Jody, is a confirmation of that.

Like in "Guests of the Nation", when the British refuse an exchange of prisoners, Jody is taken outside to be executed. Unlike in the story, it is left to one of Jody's captors, Fergus, to execute him. By then, though, and like in O'Connor's story, Fergus has befriended Jody. Indeed, Jody running away from Fergus is a dramatisation of what Bonaparte imagines might happen with his prisoners. In O'Connor's story, Bonaparte is shocked when the IRA officer arrives and orders the execution. Hawkins asserts their friendship — "Weren't we chums?" — and Bonaparte wonders what would happen if they "put up a fight or run for it, and wishing in my heart they would. I knew if only they ran I would never fire on them."

However, The Crying Game combines this imaginary event from O'Connor with the scene's denouement, which is more akin to that of The Hostage. Unable to kill the unmasked Jody, Fergus, in effect, allows him to escape, only, ironically, for an arriving British Army Saracen personnel carrier to knock him down as he is fleeing, while the vehicle behind runs over him and kills him. With help from an old man, Fergus escapes to Britain and the very different world of London, which, as in Jordan's earlier films, is marked by a noirish glow and where the characters lack the "realism" associated with their Irish counterparts.

Jordan's script for *The Crying Game*, originally known as *The Soldier's Wife*, goes back to a 1982 outline in which the soldier Lewis is killed by one of the IRA men after Louis (later called Fergus, perhaps after the similarly named character, Feargus, in *The Hostage*) fails to carry out the execution. Like in Jordan's finished film, Louis also goes to London; thereafter, important differences emerge. In the earlier, more convoluted set-up, Louis exchanges correspondence with the soldier's wife and confesses to a priest his role in the soldier's death. After partially revealing his role in Lewis's death to his widow, Louis leaves her, sleeps rough on the streets, and meets a transvestite, Caroline, in a bar. Comforting each other, they spend the weekend together at the Notting Hill carnival — Jordan's magical nostalgic playground that invariably leads to pain — with Caroline "being both the soldier's wife by day and the soldier himself by night" (Giles, 1997: 21).[1]

Jordan chose not to finish the script following the publication of Bernard MacLaverty's novel *Cal* (1983) because of the parallel between his script and MacLaverty's with regard to the narrative's central relationship. In *Cal*, the eponymous IRA driver participates in the murder of an RUC policeman and subsequently has a love affair with the policeman's widow. Jordan's project was put on hold because he felt that "his idea had been usurped" (Giles, 1997: 21). When Pat O'Connor released a feature film adaptation of the novel in 1984, *The Soldier's Wife* was shelved. However, Jordan felt liberated by the fact that O'Connor's film "had prioritised politics and realism rather than the personal odyssey of its protagonist" (Giles, 1997: 25).

Unsurprisingly, the film has been approached by many critics as a tale of two parts: the first set in Ireland, largely within the enclosure of the glasshouse, which focuses on the relationship between Jody and Fergus, and the second, set in London, where Fergus falls in love with Dil and tries to disentangle himself from the IRA. However, this division, which is ultimately debilitating, perhaps has been accepted too readily, as the film is constructed with a very tight set of binaries which cross both sections of the film, just as the various triangular relationships interweave and bind both sections.

Though Fergus goes through a psychic transformation unlike anything seen before in a film about Ireland, he is far from being a new character. Within the first section of the film, the IRA unit includes Fergus, Maguire, Jude and two lesser characters who are killed in the British army attack on the hideout. Fergus and Maguire can be seen to fit within the established characterisations of the binaries of good and bad IRA man offered by British commercial films since the 1940s. Fergus is cast within the tradition of the reluctant and sensitive IRA man who, after participating in or witnessing an act of violence that repulses him, consciously rejects military action as the means by which to achieve a free Ireland and advocates a parliamentary route. While this may be seen in Johnny (James Mason) in *Odd Man Out* (Carol Reed, 1947) who realises his mistake too late, the first complete expression of this is through Terence (John Mills) in *The Gentle Gunman* (Basil Dearden, 1952) and continues through to Cal (John Lynch) in *Cal* (Pat O'Connor, 1984). The representation can also be found in *A Prayer for the Dying* (Mike Hodges), released in 1988, four years before *The Crying Game*, where Martin Fallon (Mickey Rourke) leaves the IRA for London after taking part in a bombing designed to kill British soldiers but which causes the deaths of school children.

By contrast, Maguire is the cold-blooded, emotionless IRA fanatic for whom the cause is everything, irrespective of who gets hurt, including himself. This is made explicit in his "suicidal" attack on the almost infirm judge leaving the London brothel. Though this carries an echo of *Mona Lisa*, where the elderly British "gentlemen" are seen to sadistically exploit young girls, here it is given a more political and moral edge. The judge becomes a "legitimate target" not just politically in his representation of the autocratic British Empire (also crippled and near death and with a veneer of respectability), but, from a puritanical IRA point of view, morally through his sexually colonising or oppressive and degenerate behaviour. If this "repressive" attitude to sex and the body is registered in other films, notably in the pathological James Cagney character of *Shake Hands with the Devil* (Michael Anderson, 1959), or even in Shinto's disinterest in the seductive Maureen in *The Gentle Gunman*, it is also alluded to in *The Crying*

Game, ironically by Jude who says that there are certain things that she wouldn't do for her country — i.e. have sex (with Jody).

Similarly, in Jordan's *Michael Collins* (see Chapter Ten), de Valera is less than pleased with Michael Collins dressing him up as an "old whore" in Collins's aunt's fur coat on his escape from Lincoln Prison. As he says, "there are certain things that one should not do for one's country". Here, as elsewhere, it is not just the body, but "pleasure" to which the nationalist fanatic objects. More generally, of course, the male world of violence operates to deny heterosexual intimacy. This is suggested several times in *Michael Collins*, not least when Collins and Boland witness a wedding party and can only imagine a wedding to each other along with the G-man, Ned Broy, who is tailing them on behalf of the British Government.

Returning to Maguire, in summary, he can be placed within the tradition stretching from Dennis (Robert Beatty) in *Odd Man Out* to Shinto (also Robert Beatty) in *The Gentle Gunman*, Lenihan (James Cagney) in *Shake Hands with the Devil*, and to the coldly distant Skeffington (John Kavanagh) in *Cal*, who has photographs of other "fanatics" such as Patrick Pearse on his living room wall.

Fergus and Maguire, like those before them, are so locked into an external and repetitive history that their narrative necessarily leads them "across the water". For all of those characters who have sought to leave "the Organisation" after committing an initial and irreversible error (Hill, 1987: 153), and go to England (or in more recent versions, America, and even Australia), the IRA seeks them out. As Jude tells Fergus when he is tracked down, "You're never out, Fergus". But then that is also the condition of family which elsewhere Jordan explores, even in non-nuclear families of crime and prostitution.

While these sets of binaries are well-established tropes within (primarily) British representations of Ireland, discussion of *The Crying Game* has not fully appreciated that Jude, also, fits within this tradition, as well, of course, as within *film noir*. The IRA woman taking up the gun and participating in military activity is a relatively rare cinematic representation, though the popular imagination was fuelled by the killing in Gibraltar in March 1988 by the British army's SAS of Mairéad Farrell as a member of an unarmed three-person IRA unit on a trial run for a bomb attack.

However, if we look back again to the early British films about Northern Ireland, we find Kathleen (Kathleen Ryan) in *Odd Man Out* drawing the gun and firing at the police, whose return fire kills her and her boyfriend Johnny — an act which is not, however, inscribed as "political". In *The Gentle Gunman*, Maureen (Elizabeth Sellars), though she does not handle a gun, carries perhaps the clearest echo of Jude with her promotion of IRA violence and her fascination with guns. According to Terence, her children would be born with a Tommy gun as a rattle. Maureen shifts her emotional allegiance from Terence to his younger brother Matt (Dirk Bogarde) when the former abandons the military struggle, and in the earliest representation of the IRA supporter as *femme fatale*, Maureen is seen emerging from the shadows into the light at the moment Matt comes of age with the (phallic) gun pointing (lovingly) at her. Jude's transformation to *femme fatale*, of course, occurs when she goes to London in search of Fergus, an issue to which we will return.

Nevertheless, in most of these films, IRA violence is characterised as destroying domestic harmony; thus the "good" woman occupies the private sphere, such as through Kathleen's grandmother (Kitty Kirwan) in *Odd Man Out*, who had abandoned a boyfriend involved in the struggle, and Maureen's mother Molly (Barbara Mullen) in *The Gentle Gunman*, who laments the loss of her dead IRA husband; during the course of the film, her young son Johnny is shot. (The issue of how the domestic sphere is adversely affected by the male world of the violent public sphere is returned to in the discussion of *Michael Collins*.) Pat Murphy's *Anne Devlin* (*Anne Devlin*, 1984) is interesting in this respect. Even though she is inextricably linked to republican violence, acting as the confidante and "house keeper" of the 1803 leader Robert Emmet, in her subsequent torture and imprisonment, the British authorities are unable to break her, and she remains a "real" woman who chooses to act rather than be seen as a sexualised agent of provocation (see Gibbons, 1996a).

It was not this issue or the world of IRA military activities in *The Crying Game* which fuelled the imagination of cinemagoers and critics alike. That privilege was reserved for the moment when Jody's lover Dil (Jaye Davidson) is revealed to be, not as the film's working title had it, the soldier's wife, but a male transvestite. With a brilliant marketing campaign, the film's American distributor, Miramax, succeeded in gaining the collusion of those who had seen the film, critics included, into not revealing the film's "secret" that Dil was a man. This had the (intentional?) effect of dampening down critical assessments of the film, especially its key interface of race and sexuality, because without exposing the "secret", such discussion was worthless. While the publicity campaign had the desired effect — *The Crying Game* took more than $60 million at the American box office, making it the most commercially successful non-American film released in the USA up to that time — the response by reviewers was usually to laud its "daring" theme, or as *Variety* put it, the film offered "a fearlessly penetrating examination of politics, race, sexuality and human nature".[2]

Additionally, the view was canvassed that it challenged stereotypes, though some feminist critics in particular took exception to the fact that the one "good" woman in the film was a man, and condemned the portrayal of Jude as "misogynistic". In an interview, Jordan responded by suggesting that what women (critics) find threatening or offensive is not Jude, whom he wrote "quite consciously as a monster" (Burke, 1993: 18), but that the choices which the men make exclude women. The "film creates a more viable and more attractive image of a woman through a man than through a woman" (Burke, 1993: 19). For Jordan, that is the real challenge of the film. Jude, he argues, is simply a logical projection of his schema that, in order for men to survive, they must make female choices while women make male choices (Burke, 1993: 18). Unfortunately, while one can accept Jude as monstrous rather than as a "representative" or real woman, his argument draws the viewer back into understanding her in strictly gendered terms.

Nevertheless, if the male as a woman is explicit in Dil, who becomes a parody of the clinging masochistic female, this is equally clear in Fergus's expression when Dil gives him sexual pleasure in her flat. The camera focuses on his face, his head is tilted back and his lips are parted in what is now the clichéd cinematic representation of female orgasm.

The issue of "woman as dangerous" is explored by Sarah Edge, who questions the film's ability to challenge stereotypes, Irish, racial or sexual, and argues that the film ought to be viewed within the context of contemporaneous commercial films such as *Fatal Attraction* (Adrian Lyne, 1987) and *Basic Instinct* (Paul Verhoeven, 1992), with their punishing of transgressive women and the parallel search within Hollywood for a new form of masculine identity "based on compassion, respect and love between men", which can be found in films such as *Parenthood* (Ron Howard, 1989) and *Hook* (Steven Spielberg, 1991). (Edge, 1995: 183). A more refined exploration of sexual and national identity is offered by Amy Zilliax (1995), who disentangles the binaries which, as noted, operate across both sections of the film. As Jordan has said, he conceived of the second half of the film as "a mirror of the first half" (Burke, 1993: 18). ⸺

⸺ The film is in the first instance a tale of deception. From the opening scene, where Jude lures Jody to the trap which sees him become an IRA prisoner, it follows a trajectory which includes Fergus deceiving Maguire by not carrying out the execution, through to Dil's (unintentional) deceit of Fergus that she is a man. These deceits are articulated in the first instance by Jody when he tells Fergus the fable of "The Scorpion and Frog", first used cinematically in Orson Welles's film *Mr Arkadin* (aka *Confidential Report*, 1955).

> There are two kinds of people: those who give and those who take . . . Two types, Fergus, the scorpion and the frog. Ever heard of them? A scorpion wants to cross a river, but he can't swim. Goes to a frog, who can, and asks for a ride. The frog says: "If I give you a ride on my back, you'll go and sting me." The scorpion replies, "It would not be in my interest to sting you, since I'll be on your back, and we both will drown." The frog thinks about this for a while, and accepts the deal. Takes the scorpion on his back, braves the waters, halfway across, feels a burning spear in his side,

and realises the scorpion has stung him after all. And as they both sink beneath the waves, the frog cries out, "Why did you sting me Mr Scorpion? For now we both will drown!" The scorpion replies: "I can't help it, it's in my nature."

It is tempting to read this tale as carrying an Irish/British metaphor in the film, with both peoples dragging each other beneath the waves, and, indeed, the reference to "nature" readily fits within the British cultural tradition that constructed the relationship between Ireland and Britain in terms of the character "flaws" of the Irish. This, of course, was a British ideological strategy to displace attention from its imperialist project and made regular appearances, especially when Irish resistance to British rule took on a military aspect (see Hill, 1987; Curtis, 1984). Like the British in general, for Jody, it would seem, the Irish are also the scorpions. Thus, as he says, it is in the nature of "your people" (the "tough undeluded motherfuckers",[3] the IRA) to kill him.

However, when the story is told for the second time, by Fergus to Dil at the end of the film, he, too, is a prisoner, this time an Irishman in a British prison. By then, their identity has become interchangeable. As if to underpin the Jody/Fergus mirror, both stories are told to their lover/alter-ego in their respective "glass house" prisons, locations which mock the clarity of the relationships between the people.

While Fergus does not share Jody's love of cricket, as Monsewer, the elderly owner of the house, does with the soldier in *The Hostage*, Fergus, who favours the Irish game of hurling, comes to appreciate cricket. His journey to London brings him in close proximity to the game. There is a cricket pitch in front of the building site on which he works and later, overseen by the smug employer, he "performs" batting — in response to Jody's "shit hot" bowling. Despite their race or even competing ideologies (which are ultimately external to them) they, confirming Jody's belief in their similarity, have simple tastes. Fergus learns to be imaginative and trade his pint "on a rock" for Jody's pint in the Metro.

Jody also tells Fergus that it is not in his nature to kill him, a prediction which proves right. Indeed, for Jody there are two kinds of people, "those who give and those who take". Fergus/ Stephen Rea, as Jordan's alter ego (similar, as Jordan put it, to François Truffaut's use of Jean Pierre Léaud, in Burke, 1993: 20), fits into the former category, thus associating Fergus with the humanist values which can come to the fore once the public sphere of male military activities is abandoned. Indeed, for Jordan, Fergus "only survives by becoming a woman", by taking on "feminine virtues" of understanding and compassion (Burke, 1993: 18).

Thus, when he meets Dil, following Jody's insistence that he visit her after his death, the film shifts register towards an exploration of sexuality in the triangular male world of the dead black soldier, the white man whose national identity is irrelevant to the transvestite male, Dil, who thinks he could be American before settling on Scottish — his "treacle" voice being the tell-tale sign. (Jordan had enjoyed a similar joke in High Spirits.) All three of them carry feminine characteristics, making Fergus the mirror image of Jody between the two imprisonments. Indeed, he seeks to become Jody as he intensifies his relationship with Dil (who also becomes Jody and later occupies Fergus' space in the prison).

In this configuration, the issue of race is also foregrounded, from the first shot of Fergus in London. On a building site, his face is covered in the white powder of builders' dust from his jack-hammer demolition of a wall, an action which reveals a new (superior?) white vista to him and to the film's audience, on to the world of upper-class English cricket. "It's a toffs' game", the fast bowler Jody tells Fergus shortly before his death. It is also the game played in the colonies (Jody's family came from Antigua), but even though he was born in Tottenham, he felt excluded from the game, thus making the photographs of him in cricket attire and his recurrent appearances in Fergus' dreams take on a symbolic (resonant of race, class and imperialism) rather than "real" aspect. Jody might have gone on to say that the game being played is "crying", or as the song of the film's title explains, crying comes "when love disappears".[4]

As Dil puts it in her version of the song: "Don't want no more of the crying game."

Now that her true love Jody is dead, it is for Fergus to fill the void and provide her with true love once more. Even before she realises Fergus's relationship to Jody, and Fergus's desire to be with her because of him, in order to re-embrace him, Dil's sixth sense or superstitious belief in the hereafter, tells her that Fergus and Jody are the same, they are both "*gentle*men". Even now, through Fergus, he is looking after her, Fergus continues to accept this role as Dil's protector and life-companion, even after he discovers Dil's true gender. But then, Dil tells Fergus when she visits him in prison, in a corruption of the biblical quote, "Greater love hath no man than this, that He lay down His life for His friends", delivered in a slightly sarcastic, even cynical tone, "No greater love, as the man says". This leads into Fergus' telling her it is in his nature to do time for her, and the retelling of "The Scorpion and the Frog" story. It remains open as to whether the pair will eventually drown each other, too.

While Jody becomes aware of Jude's deception with the arrival of her IRA colleagues, this occurs immediately after the shot of Jody moving his hand up Jude's thigh and under her skirt. A similar version of this is replayed when Fergus slides his hand up Dil's leg and beyond her short skirt. Though she unwittingly delays the moment of his realisation of her (unconscious) deceit, by stopping its movement, the echo of the previous scene is such that we may read the dark "secret" of successful masquerade. A portent of something between the characters may be found in the scenes in which Jude strikes Jody during his captivity in the greenhouse and Fergus strikes Dil, also drawing blood. Similarly, when Dil draws a gun on Fergus after she discovers the extent of his deception and relationship with Jody, she says "I should blow you away", a phrase identical to that uttered by Maguire (the jilted IRA lover?). Indeed, as Zilliax observes, "so indistinguishable is the political affair from the romantic one . . . that Fergus initially mistakes the IRA car for one belonging to Dave (Ralph Brown), Dil's former boyfriend, who acts the deceived lover in turn" (Zilliax, 1995: 31–2). She goes on to note that

> Characters who would appear to be radically different
> from one another are doomed to repeat the same pat-
> terns. The film sets up, and returns to, innumerable
> structural parallels, large and small, seeming to insist,
> again and again, on the dominance of organization (and
> with it ideology) over the individual, of narrative over
> identity, and on the radical insignificance of human
> agency (1995: 32).

As a result, should the film even be considered in (the necessarily limiting) terms of issues of gender or race? Arguably, this
is a version of *Angel* where straightforward political readings
seem to limit the film. Might not a reading that focuses on the
mutability of identity and masquerade be more productive?

Dil, a hairdresser, is preoccupied with her *appearance* —
hair, lipstick, makeup — a series of foregroundings of feminine
"narcissism" which parallel Jude's transformation from blonde
bait for Jody at the fairground to her seemingly "real" nationalist IRA self as an Aran sweater-wearer at the hideout. In turn,
the status of the "real" Jude is challenged or subverted by her
adoption of (male-influenced) 1980s' "power dressing" when
she becomes a *femme fatale*. As she explains to Fergus, "sick of
being a blonde", she "needed a tougher look". Ironically, as a
blonde, she used her "vulnerability" and soft curvaceous sexuality to trap and thereby kill Jody.

With such superficiality of gender position and identity, or
the ease with which it can be discarded and a new persona
(even gender) adopted, it is unsurprising that Dil does not regard the fact that she is not a woman as important for her reality: "details, baby, details", she tells Fergus. Even barman Col
colludes in this, when he responds to Fergus's comment that
Dil is a man, "Whatever you say", just as he accepted Fergus
(as Jimmy) as a Scot. As Zilliax observes, race is represented as
a similar kind of masquerade (1995: 33). Jordan's message is
that appearances are precisely that — appearances — and yet
people (and very often his male characters when it comes to
women) insist that they somehow have an unproblematic rela-

tion to the real, or that, in other terms, there is no slippage between the signifier and the signified.

Jody spends most of the time at the hideout with a black hood over his head. It is occasionally removed to reveal the "real" (black) man beneath it. Fergus, as noted, is first seen in London with "whiteface" at the building site. In both instances, race can be seen as "radically external to the subject — literally a deposit on the skin, rather than the psyche" (Zilliax, 1995: 33). (Such an interpretation has, of course, significant implications for a reading of Jordan's use of African-American music. Is it also external to the subject?) Like gender, race, too, can become a "visible, external construction: [a] barrier, potentially, but one that can be removed, discarded". In this way, Zilliax argues that a flexible notion of identity could be liberating.

Depending on what "mask" is worn, all an oppressed subject has to do is "to stand in another place, put on a different mask". Thus, for Dil to become a woman, all he has to do is stand where a woman stands, "allow herself to be constructed as a woman", while Jody only has to take off the hood to escape from his signification. Since any one individual can be substituted for another, Fergus only has to turn up at the Metro, order Dil a margarita, and thus continue where Jody left off. Of course, such "political glibness", for which the film has been criticised, allows for "one character to collapse easily into another, each conflict to prove nothing more than a metaphor for the next". Thus, as Zilliax says, the film depoliticises the IRA, desexualises homosexuality and de-feminises gender studies (Zilliax, 1995: 34). In that way it achieves a kind of "purity" so that like the bat and the narrator in *The Dream of a Beast*, it takes flight. Similarly, national difference is eschewed, with Dil thinking Fergus is Scottish, another "Other", which could equally be Irish. She knows he is not English. Such a view, though, fails to take into account the overt racism, or invisibility, of Fergus's stereotypical English employer(s) who refer to him variously as Jimmy (the Scot), Pat (the Paddy) and Fergus.

What then is left? A humanist sense transcending all national, racial and gender differences, or a postmodern (cynical) mélange that allows everything to be mixed: there is no anchor, no position. Just as *Angel*, as read by Jordan and Kearney, suggests that all violence is bad, it would seem that there can only be a metaphysical or phenomenological approach. In the end, Fergus takes the rap for Dil, but is this just the ending that never was in *Mona Lisa*, where George might have been bailed out by Simone? With everyone imprisoned in one way or another, it doesn't really matter who is in jail at the end, especially when cross-dresser Boy George sings the final version of "The Crying Game" over the film's credits. Nevertheless, Fergus's incarceration allows him to become Jody, but also to acquire the masochistic or feminine role of Dil.

If race and gender are just interchangeable postmodern masks, unsurprisingly, Jordan intersects them with one of his recurring tropes, that of performance. While Dil *performs* (though she does not sing) "The Crying Game" at the Metro, it is an exaggerated and self-conscious performance, as her arms are seen from behind a screen. *The performer is not even performing.* Even sex is merely a performance, as Dil tells Fergus that her ex-boyfriend Dave wants her to perform for him. Indeed, when Fergus voyeuristically observes Dil and Dave in her flat, they are seen in the window, also "performing" for Fergus, who observes them from the street. Later, of course, Fergus and Dil similarly "perform" their romance for Dave, just as Bendrix performs with Sarah for Parkis's camera in *The End of the Affair*.

The film appears unconcerned with the issue of the church and its hostile attitude to homosexuality. However, one of the last shots of the hideout under attack from the British army features a statue of a Madonna and Child smashed in a hail of bullets. This destruction of the icon of the Christian family is, of course, a prerequisite for the new "family" to be formed by the men in London. Ironically, there is a church-like entrance to the building where Dil has her flat. To get there a pedestrian "bridge" has to be crossed from the street, perhaps echoing the bridge across which Jody is taken into captivity, or even the one which features in the credit sequence. The film opens in a familiar Jordan location, the carnival with the Percy Sledge song "When a Man Loves a Woman" playing over the film's credits as the camera pans very slowly (contemplatively) with the car-

nival framed in the distance beneath the arches of a railway
bridge. For Jordan, the choice of this particular bridge was very
personal, because it was the bridge beneath which his father
died while fishing.

The Crying Game marked a decisive shift from the political
arena to the intimacies of the personal which had not been approached in such a bold manner prior to this. As a result, it
was a landmark film not just for Irish cinema, but in the manner
in which the personal and the political were so intertwined.
Perhaps only such a previous film as *Kiss of the Spider Woman*
(Hector Babenco, 1985) inserted such a highly charged discourse on sexuality into the politics of nationhood.

Notes

[1] Draft scripts of *The Soldier's Wife*, some undated, most from June to
September 1991, are in Neil Jordan's papers, Manuscripts Accessions
4761, Box 2, National Library of Ireland.

[2] *Variety*, 14 September 1992: 47.

[3] Arguably, such a comment acknowledges the rationalist aspect or
social/cultural/political context of the IRA activities. This understanding of paramilitary violence or the necessity for violence in general is
explored in *Michael Collins*. (Of course, that film is nonetheless an attempt to present the futility of (continued) violence and its negative
effect on the personal.) In this way, both Jody's insult and *Michael
Collins* answer the criticism against *Angel*, which was seen by many,
most particularly John Hill (1987), as endorsing British or establishment violence (see Chapter 2).

[4] The choice of this song can be said to go back to the "Night in Tunisia" story, where reference is made to it: "It galled his father what he
played. 'What galls me', he would say, 'is that you could be so good.'
But he felt vengeful and played them incessantly and even sang the
tawdry lyrics. Some day soon, he sang, I'm going to tell the moon
about the crying game. And maybe he'll explain, he sang." (Jordan,
1993: 35; orig. 1976).

Chapter Nine

Interview with the Vampire (1994) [1]

An erotic bloodied mouth speaks of love and desire. The black face to which it belongs remains hidden by a balaclava. In this way, Jody sucks Fergus into a world that refuses to accept the certainties of identity figured in terms of culture, race, gender, and sexuality. Throughout, *The Crying Game* remains focused on this, both narratively and cinematically — not least through performance and masquerade, most especially those of Jude and Dil.

However, it is the complex and ambiguous image of the *vagina dentata* just described that captures the secret and fluid world of desire to which Jordan as an artist is drawn. This messy image displaying the identity of desire and terror, or attraction and repulsion, is at the source of *Interview with the Vampire*. Notwithstanding the vampire's metaphoric relationship to capitalism, the media and its technologies of replication and transmission, consumerism, and disease, particularly AIDS as it is culturally represented, or its use as a philosophical tool of enquiry into good and evil and the meaning of humanity, vampirism at its core is a conceit to revisit the mother's body.

As Moretti has argued, at the root of vampirism "lies an ambivalent impulse of the child towards its mother" (Moretti, 1995: 157). The child longs for the mother "whom he loves, and yet hates, because obdurate to his sex-love for her in infancy" (Bonaparte, 1949, cited by Moretti, 1995: 155). Of course, this displaces (or represses) the child's fear of retalia-

tion by the mother against his "cannibalism": the fantasy of biting the mother's breast.[2] While the dominant mass cultural
depiction of the vampire as male[3] goes someway to distance
itself from the unconscious fantasy of the alluring yet threatening mother, *Interview*'s interest in the family and the lost
mother, returns us to the feminine, always present, as Moretti
notes, in Dracula's name. Indeed, Williams, too, in her influential article, "When the Woman Looks",[4] also highlighted this
feminine "essence", arguing that the woman victim enjoys with
her seducer a proximity and desire that derives from and is
ultimately displaced by her identification with him as a (monstrous) deviation from male (hetero)sexuality. The monster's
power, it is feared, extends to giving and taking human life, and
is mirrored by the woman, as is his status as an object for
voyeuristic or scopophilic investigation.

The film opens and indeed closes in present-day San Francisco. A vampire, Louis (Brad Pitt), tells a young reporter, Malloy
(Christian Slater), the story of how, in 1791 at the age of twenty-
four, he came to be a vampire. Having lost his wife in childbirth,
he turns his back on life and (civilised) humanity and the large
Louisiana plantation of which he is master. Too cowardly to take
his life, he behaves recklessly. However, just as he is about to be
killed by a robber, the vampire Lestat (Tom Cruise) "irrationally"[5] appears and orgasmically saves him. Sinking his teeth into
his neck, the two float upward, before Lestat drops him into the
amniotic fluid of the sea. He then offers Louis the Faustian bar-
gain of his human life and soul in exchange for eternal life purged
of misery, but isolated from humanity. This Louis accepts.

Despite the initial wonder at his new being and enhanced
sensory awareness — whereby even inanimate statues seem to
be imbued with life, but which the film, with the exception of
the statue that looks around and lowers her eyelids, barely registers[6] — he fights his predatory vampire nature, preferring to
feed on rats' blood rather than humans'. He longs to return to a
sympathetic interaction with humanity, and comes to hate
Lestat, whom he regards as material and cruel. Meantime, his
(black) slaves, belonging as they do to the alternative (and more
primitive) world of sensory engagement, of voodoo and dance,

suspect their master and his companion, and en masse, with burning torches, confront Louis. Having already yielded to his instincts by attacking his house servant — his first kill, which is clearly coded as a metaphorical rape and from which, guilt-ridden, he runs away — Louis tells them that he is indeed the devil. He frees them from their bonds and burns down his house and with it a portrait of his wife.

The pair move to New Orleans, where, again, he feeds on animals (rats and poodles), but walking in the path of the plague, sees, by her mother's rotting corpse, a little girl, Claudia (Kirsten Dunst), whom he cannot resist. Lestat interrupts Louis's furtive kill; Louis, ashamed, flees the now laughing Lestat, who dances a tarantella with the corpse.[7] When Louis eventually returns home, he is relieved to discover that Lestat had not killed the little orphan, but Louis's refusal to allow her to die means that he allows Lestat to transform her into a vampire, even though he utters a soft "No" in response to Lestat's act.

The three live together for thirty years (some thirty-five years less than in the book) in a parody of the nuclear family, which Jordan exploits to its full black comic potential, until the demon child, resentful of her maker, who has given her a damned and dependent existence, trapped as she is in a child's body, tries to murder Lestat, the abusive father. She does this by presenting him with identical prepubescent boy twins who appear to be in a drunken stupor, but are in fact dead, having been poisoned with laudanum, which also has had the effect of keeping their blood warm. The promise (of multiple pleasure) that they embody — prefiguring that of modern advertising[8] as well as displaying Jordan's interest in the copies and imitations more fully explored in The Good Thief — turns out to be a visual (and vicious), ironic joke. This is not least because they are children, but also because their completeness in each other mocks the vampires' isolation and the impossibility of their desire. Claudia then slashes the throat of a weakened and apparently dying Lestat, and with Louis's help, dumps him in the swamp.

Free, the two plan to leave for Europe with the intention of seeking their origin story, but on the night of their departure, a ghoulish and decrepit "living dead" Lestat returns for vengeance.

Louis sets fire to him and their town house and escapes. In Europe, they find nothing, only the myths of a "demented Irish man" (Bram Stoker), but in Paris, the *mother* of New Orleans, or the original to the fake copy, at last they find their own, only to realise that the new family is no more comforting than that which they have destroyed, but threatening and predatory, more decadent than Lestat, and for all their art, without emotion and knowledge; in short, empty. The literal parallel of this may be found in Henry James's *Portrait of a Lady*, in which Europe delivers only *ennui*.

These vampires, the oldest of whom, Armand (Antonio Banderas), is 400 years — the oldest of all living vampires — live in the uncanny world of the theatre, and pass themselves off as actors pretending to be vampires, staging their real kills as illusion. Though Armand desires Louis (in order to spiritually rejuvenate himself), which causes Claudia both fear and jealousy, the other vampires, led by the trickster Santiago (Stephen Rea), who is perhaps the most theatrical of the vampires, are suspicious that Louis and Claudia may have committed the only crime amongst vampires, that of killing one of their kind. The troupe forcibly capture the two in their hotel rooms, as well as the new vampire Madeleine (Domiziana Giordano), whom Louis, on Claudia's insistence, made so that she could look after Claudia should he go to Armand. The vampires then expose Madeleine and Claudia to sunlight, which burns them to ash, and, in a nod to the tales of Edgar Allan Poe, put Louis into a coffin, seal it and bury it behind a wall. Armand frees Louis, who in revenge kills the vampires by direct decapitations, and by burning the theatre and the coffins of resting vampires, so that by the following morning they will perish like his daughter in the sunlight.

It is interesting that Jordan did not choose to include Lestat in these scenes; in the novel, Lestat has connived with Santiago and the others to punish Claudia. If this seems to be a strange decision, it serves at least two purposes. Firstly, it allows the ending to have greater impact, and secondly, gives to the vampires another dimension to their power — that of reading minds, something that Lestat displayed at the society party. Louis, now on the street outside the theatre, is rescued for a second time by Armand, whom he later, notably in the *fin-de-siècle* art gallery in front of an expressionist portrait, rejects as passionless and already (emotionally) dead. Clutching his mortal conscience, he returns to the New World. In America, the cinema allows him to vicariously experience life (and sunrises) again. It also brings him home to Lestat, who, unable to cope with modern life, is near death, and has been reduced to eating rats and fouling his own space.

Malloy's response to Louis's story is an unsuccessful request to become a vampire, after which Louis vanishes. Still high on the narrative and listening to the taped voice of Louis in his car, Lestat suddenly attacks the reporter, clearly with the intention of turning him into his new vampire companion. "Feeling better", Lestat drives down the highway listening to Louis "whining on", as, in typical Jordan fashion, "Sympathy for the Devil" blares on the soundtrack. Whatever the incongruity of this ending from a narrative point of view, it does at least create the rock-and-rolling leather-clad Lestat of Rice's sequel.

The film is based on Anne Rice's 1976 cult novel of the same name, and though she receives sole script credit, Jordan made extensive contributions to it. Jordan's decision to cast Tom Cruise as Lestat provoked a public outcry from Rice, who took out an advertisement advising her fans not to see the film. She, in keeping with the Hollywood tradition of casting Europeans as villains, had wanted Daniel Day Lewis to play Lestat. However, when she saw the film, she loved it, praised all the actors, and, delighted, took out another advertisement in *Variety*, this time suggesting the public should flock to the cinema.

The film is faithful to the novel and its (in)action in a number of key respects. These include the interrelationship of sex, desire and death, and of dependency or need and love; the refusal of much of the genre's mythology (even if the vampire as aristocrat and the need for the coffin remain); the melodramatic elements; and, most importantly, the central interest in Louis's pact with the "devil" Lestat and his subsequent fall from grace and exclusion — like all the other vampires — from humanity, which, given the lack of interest society has in their murders, seems mutual. (After all, there is no Van Helsing character or crimi-

nologist who follows their murderous trail.) Indeed, there is also
the sense that the usual aesthetic of fear and identification with
the victim of the traditional vampire film is necessarily absent.
This is because the narrative is unusually told from the perspective of the monster who, by its nature, cannot be harmed.

like The
Butcher
Boy.

However, the film is clearly more than a straight adaptation.
This is most obvious in relation to the foregrounding of the
mother and the family; the irony and black humour, a defining
feature of contemporary horror especially, as Brophy (1986)
notes, when used as "an undercutting agent"; the celebration of
the visual (and voyeurism) both in terms of the vampire and art,
most particularly, the cinema and the related trope of mirrors
— played out in the *mise-en-scene*, character interaction, and the
narrative — and the consequent downplay, relative to the novel,
of the (vampires') other senses; the vampire killings as exhibi-
tionist and exploitative performance rather than mundane and
efficient practice, and the grouping of (mimetic) art, sterility and
vampirism.

In the novel, Louis's self-indulgent grief that occasions his rejection of humanity is over the death of his young brother, who
takes his life following a row with Louis after he claims to have
seen (religious) visions and requests Louis to sell the plantation
in order to fund his missionary work in France. This, and the
subsequent discussions, provide a context to Louis's (and the
novel's) religious or metaphysical musings. It also points to, and
critiques, in a way the film does not, the powerlessness of
women (the mother and sister are totally dependent on Louis),
which Rice revisits and challenges through Louis's love for
Babette Freniere.

To have Louis mourn his wife (and child), without any mention of other family members, alters this considerably.[9] Firstly, it
suggests that he has successfully negotiated the oedipal journey
and has, in choosing a wife, become a man; secondly, it suggests
that with their deaths he is left in an emotional vacuum without
any responsibility to family or humanity; thirdly, it reinterprets
his subsequent drinking and desire for death as romantic; and
finally, like the mother's body that haunts Claudia, it makes sense
of his search for the lost family. Interestingly, Lestat, too, is

stripped of his family, for in the book he gives Louis the dark gift not out of random homosexual desire or because of Louis's "passion and anger", but for the mundane reason of wealth and land so that his *blind* father may live in comfort and ignorance of Lestat's vampire nature.

As soon as the novelty of vampirism wanes, Louis comes to understand the detachment with which he must view humanity. Both novel and film, in different ways, figure this as Lestat as sadistic predator and Louis as the cinematic equivalent of voyeur. It is only through the (re)creation of a family that Louis is not only persuaded but compelled to stay. Notwithstanding that in the final scene which Louis and Claudia share, she calls him "father" and from a twentieth-century perspective it is *Lestat* who functions as the mother, giving, as he does, his own blood (milk) to make her a vampire, Lestat is positioned as (hysterical) father and Louis, in a nod to Irish cinema, as the long-suffering silent mother.

If one regards Lestat's making of Claudia from earlier understandings of creation, it is the father's essence that provides life (while the mother provides the body and the incubation).[10] As such, it is not surprising that Claudia is more Lestat than Louis, who is reduced to the role of minder rather than teacher, and with whom she sleeps. This picture of Claudia, complete with doll, snuggling up to Louis in his coffin and later, when she has her own coffin, creeping back into his, is a comic touch which Jordan uses to highlight the normality of this perverse "happy family".

Yet at the same time, this coffin-hopping of child to parent's "bed" causes Jordan to become complicit in Claudia's entrapment. If *Interview* raises consciousness of the ultimately narrow and disabling perception of human emotion and intelligence as body-based, in that a link is formed between the physical body — its form, beauty, gender, growth, and the way it moves and ages — and how a person thinks and feels, the film, in keeping with mainstream cinema, which has largely failed to offer positive images of people with disability,[11] also succumbs to this problem. It refuses to see her beyond the limits of her (child's) body.

This is not the case in the equally amusing scenes of Claudia playing the demon daughter before she has learned the house rules, such as when she sucks the dressmaker's pricked finger before killing her and when she does away with her piano teacher. That Lestat finds the bodies and interacts with her on these occasions is important, because it is through these — fashion and music — that she breaks out of the domestic (and Louis) into the public world (of Lestat). It is, for example, Claudia who is pictured in the library researching Europe and vampires, rather than Louis, while their passage through Europe is chartered in her charcoal drawings which seem to emphasise night, darkness and emptiness.[12]

If in the novel there is a sense that Louis appreciates beauty and life in a way from which Lestat is excluded, in the film there is a parallel set up between Lestat and Claudia as aesthetes who consume and use art as a form of empowerment, and Louis who is moved by it. It is Louis's empathy and human emotion that mark him as an imperfect vampire with a mortal soul, yet, ironically, which make him desirable to Lestat (who loves his passion) and Armand (who needs to embrace his broken soul, which defines the modern age). While Claudia, with critical distance, can comment on the theatrical performance of the Parisian vampires (from the old world) as "avant-garde", Louis shares more with the man in the audience who partially screens out the frightening pleasure by turning away and shielding his eyes from the murder of the woman, but whose action simultaneously heightens for the cinema audience the anticipation of the monstrous image.[13] Louis is repulsed, yet fascinated, while Claudia is simply curious. Like Lestat, she is matter-of-fact about life and death and has accepted her vampire nature. While she uses her piano-playing to gain access, with Lestat, to the homes of rich families, whom they then finish off with a deathly performance, the old vampires use theatre.

This equation of art, intelligence, and detachment is made elsewhere, notably within popular representations of serial killers (when they are not simply cast as mindless psychopaths) such as Hannibal Lecter in *Silence of the Lambs* (Jonathan Demme, 1991), or the killers in *Se7en* (David Fincher, 1995), and *The Bone Collec-*

tor (Philip Noyce, 1999). But then, the vampires are little more than serial killers; Louis's "problem" is simply that, though he comes to know and understand his nature, he does not enjoy his "symptom".[14]

For a time, this abnormal (but nonetheless normal) family knows happiness,[15] and through their choice of kill, deaden their pain by projecting it outward and turning it to resentment and rage against that which is most desired. For though they need any human blood to maintain themselves, the killing, or the killings that are shown, are rarely random. Claudia, for example, chooses to polish off whole families (in a way that is repeated by Francie Brady in his tormenting of the Nugents and his killing of Mrs Nugent in *The Butcher Boy* (1997)), but also women who promise or embody the maternal, such as the overweight doting woman whom Claudia, acting as the lost little orphan, calls "Mama" before she snuggles up to her and bites her neck.

She also kills the young woman whom the trio glimpse undressing in the window because she has what Claudia most desires: an adult female body.[16] In the novel, a version of this scene is present, but interestingly, Claudia refuses to kill the woman because she reminds her of her own mother. However, in the film, Claudia partakes in her own objectification (of the woman's body), which is bound up with notions of the male gaze. This becomes explicit in her attempt to touch (or appropriate) the body through drawing, and finally by killing her. But if, unlike the killer in *Silence of the Lambs*, she does not try to wear her skin, what she does is no less neurotic. Claudia buries the body in her bedroom under a pile of dolls she has been given (by Lestat) and has obsessively collected, which mock her own status as an eternal doll, "the eighteenth-century equivalent of Barbie".[17]

While this is an instance of Jordan favouring the visual, to which we will return, this time over the narrative's logic — surely the vampires, who have more acute sensory powers, would smell the decaying corpse — it is undeniably a powerful image which points to the complexity and the multiple meanings that a doll embodies. At its most basic, the doll is a metaphor for how women are (within the dominant patriarchal order) perceived as passive subjects to be looked upon. Amongst other things, the doll functions to trigger nostalgia and childhood memory (for the adult); to display contemporary fashions; to encourage in the child a proto-maternal role of nurturing; it is central to role-playing through which the child can make sense of reality; and it fulfils the child's desire for companionship.

However, because of this intimacy, coupled with its vulnerability — despite its immortality, it is the ultimate dependent, which cannot even scream — ironically, the doll is also potentially subject to abuse. In this scenario, as when Claudia destroys her doll mountain, it becomes nothing more than an alter-ego (or a fetish) against which the child focuses its pain and suffering. Indeed, Claudia's rejection of her dolls is an expression of self-loathing, in which her own abuse at the hands of Lestat (in making her a doll who cannot ever be independent) is projected back onto the consolatory but mocking gifts which he gives her on her vampire birthday. As Rumer Godden writes in her novel *The Doll House* (1947), "It is an anxious, sometimes a dangerous thing to be a doll. Dolls cannot choose; they can only be chosen; they cannot 'do'; they can only be done by; children who do not understand this often do wrong things, and then the dolls are hurt and abused and lost; and when this happens the dolls cannot speak, nor do anything except be hurt and abused and lost" (cited in Kuznets, 1994: 111).

Through the doll, Claudia attempts to speak by cutting her hair; later, taking vengeance against Lestat, her status as a doll remains, such that she chooses as her new mother a doll-maker, Madeleine. (In the novel, this is developed with her making for Claudia — her immortal but animate doll substitute for her dead daughter whose image she wears around her neck and through whom, in an attempt to preserve her as multiple doll replicas, learnt the art of doll-making — miniature furniture and other accessories. In this way, Louis becomes Gulliver trapped by enchantment and fear in her spider's web that is a doll house.) In the end, wrapped in the Madonna and child pose, they turn to a type of dust sculpture that recalls images of charred victims of the atomic bomb in Nagasaki, before crumbling to nothing under Louis's touch. Their feminine threat is disavowed (for all, not just the vampires). A more solid version of these burnt forms is used in the post-nuclear scene in *The Butcher Boy.*

The image, then, of a horrified Lestat looking on as the out-of-control vampire doll violently wades through the mound of dolls to reveal a beautiful if decaying corpse, becomes a literalisation of his fear of the threat that the doll and femininity embodies, as one signifier refers to its more monstrous other, with which it is intimately linked. The engulfment that the doll promises is realised in the dead woman.

This doubling (in this case tripling) is common within Jordan's work, whether played out in relation to the character's psyche or actions in, for example, *Angel, The Crying Game* and *In Dreams*, or in terms of repetition of events or images, as in *Company of Wolves, Mona Lisa* and *The Butcher Boy*, or the double robbery of *The Good Thief*, and reappears elsewhere in *Interview* as a deliberate play with mirrors. This is most explicit in the scene when Santiago meets Louis and his theatrical actions copy Louis's, which problematises or mocks subjectivity, something also evident in the scenes which compositionally (ironically) recall earlier ones. These "mirror" scenes include Louis, centre frame, having given up on his search for family, walking down a Parisian street and meeting his Old World relations, Santiago and Armand, in a shot that mirrors an earlier one in New Orleans, when he longs to know (familial) peace. Another such example is of a "resurrected" Lestat who, baying for Claudia's blood, is seated at the piano, playing the same Haydn piece, only slower, which he had played on the eve of his "murder". On both occasions, he is framed by net curtains in the same way she was on the night of her creation, which also carries a trace of the bedroom scene just prior to Louis becoming a vampire. Yet it is the image of Louis as Narcissus captivated by his own reflection which is central to *Interview*.

The malady that afflicts Louis is not just vampirism, or his exclusion from the family (and the plentitude that union with the mother promises) but self-obsession (something that Louis is aware of, at least in the novel in his critique of his treatment of his brother). This interest in the self and his attempt to articulate his psychic pain, which has become a commodity in contemporary culture through the popularisation of Freud's ideas and the psychiatry service industry where "patients" have become "clients", and the popularity of television and radio talk/confessional/phone-in shows, is at the heart of *Interview*. After all, notwithstanding that the film is not technically told using Louis's point of view,[18] it is presented as a "confession".

In this, Malloy, who describes himself as a collector of lives — a media vampire — becomes an accomplice. In their different ways, their lives depend on the opening up of bodies. As such, they are intimately bound up with contemporary wound culture which Seltzer, in his discussion of serial killers, describes as "the public fascination with torn and opened private bodies and torn and opened psyches, a public gathering around the wound and the trauma" (Seltzer, 1998: 100). Consequently, it is hardly surprising that Malloy should desire to become a vampire; but he, one suspects, will be a far better vampire than Louis, who for all the gothic trappings, is little more than a "Pinocchio", who only learns what humanity and beauty is when he has become the wooden puppet. The pity is that, while Claudia can never grow up and can only remain as a doll who, even in death, is locked into a sentimental and non-threatening representation — the dyad of mother and daughter — Louis, who has spiritually grown, such that he hates what he is and will not make another vampire, still refuses to die. In short, it is the problem of the body–mind (body–soul) condition.

The image of Louis gazing into his own reflection also points to a philosophical choice which Jordan makes: that of placing emphases on "detached" (if sumptuous and *seemingly* engulfing) seeing, rather than celebrating or trying to visually render the power and visceral experience of the other vampire senses. Only rarely are we presented with moments that seem to go beyond visual description, such as in the scenes of carnival excess in New Orleans on the night Louis and Lestat share a waitress, but it is put to ironic and misogynistic service (a rape is simulated in the background); images of the black slaves enjoying frenzied revolt and turning to voodoo; when Louis turns on the light in the hotel room;[19] when the ecstatic experience of Louis been taken by Lestat is figured as levitation; or when Louis sees with his vampire eyes the statue move her eyes and, later, the vein popping in Yvette's neck.

Nevertheless, even amongst these images there is a refusal to disorient or overwhelm the viewer. The experience is mediated (or controlled) firstly by Louis, and secondly by Jordan. The film favours the baroque aesthetic, associated with the tactility and unreadability of the sublime, which is at the heart of gothic. But it falls somewhat short of rendering it, and returns us simply to the surface and the art of description and comment. In other terms, Jordan's film does not belong to a postmodern "acinema", which the French cultural theorist Jean-Francois Lyotard defines as a celebration of the irrational or free-floating image (figure) over rational and meaningful narrative (discourse). Jordan's images, though beautiful in themselves, always have significance and are embedded with meaning. Paradoxically, Louis himself, though possessing vampire eyes which should give detachment, remains too connected with humanity.

However, debates around vision seem to be overly concentrated on the scopic regime most associated with the seventeenth century and Descartes: the distant, sadist and reifying male gaze. Arguably, this is the gaze of Lestat. But Louis's is ultimately one that overwhelms him. He sees or intuits too much, and, as such, is perhaps closer, though not approximate to, baroque vision. (Along with the aesthetic of Dutch painting, which has affinities with the non-centred nature of photography and early cinema, and the anti-perspectivalism of impressionism, the baroque offers an alternative way of seeing in Western culture.) That said, the film does not share this vision.[20]

Rather than focusing, as has been the dominant tradition, on the victim's neck / vampire's fangs or the victim's swooning body, the kill and temporary satisfaction, in keeping with the nominal point of view of the vampire, is written on the vampire, specifically the eyes — not on what they see, but on the actual eyes themselves. This is particularly evident in the kills of Lestat and Armand who, while feeding on different occasions, direct their intense gaze to their vampiric object of desire — Louis. The effect of the camera's fixation on the vampire's eye directs attention away from the body and imbues the vampire with control and aggression, so that the vampire's swoon is displaced onto the audience (and victim). Furthermore, it denies any status to the victim, who, again in line with splatter and body horror,[21] is seen as meat (blood).

Indeed, Lestat's detachment is beautifully registered in his ornate silver thumb cap or gruesome guitar pick, which is designed to pierce flesh, as well as in how he pours the warm blood of the rat, and later the prostitute (as a human pump), into a crystal wine goblet for Louis. If these images suggest the instrumental rationality with which he views (human) life, they also speak of display. This is most apparent in relation to the prostitute.

Though he praises Claudia after her first vampire feast for being efficient and not spilling a drop (of blood), Lestat, it would seem, delights in conspicuous consumption. After subtly exhausting one prostitute, he turns to her friend, whom he quickly sends into orgasmic delirium, until she realises that the dampness which she feels in her reach to prolong her sexual pleasure is her own blood; but this is only the beginning of her uncanny experience. Lestat's misogynist and highly sexual crime is at the same time his gift to her — not the gift of eternal life (temporal continuity) which he gives to Louis, but the fulfilment of her deepest (necessarily repressed) desire. This is death and loss of subjectivity (spatial and temporal continuity, beyond the boundaries of the self). Wearing her now blood-saturated ivory gown, he forces her into his coffin, which, though terrifying, is at the same time nothing but what Freud refers to as the fantasy which once was "filled with a certain lustful pleasure — the fantasy . . . of intra-uterine existence".[22] Sitting on the lid, he shouts to her that she should take pleasure in this rare opportunity. Louis, passive as ever, ironically placed in front of a portrait of a woman, looks on, protecting his own mortal sensibility rather than ending both her misery and his vampire thirst. After much sadistic taunting, Lestat finally finishes her off.

While this vulgar messiness, justified on the grounds that it is essential to Louis's education of what he is, lies uneasily with Rice's vampires, it makes sense within the film, not least because of the image's richness, black humour, and sensuality, as well as acting to stir up Louis's thirst, to which he yields when later that night he sees Claudia; but also because it visualises, if excessively, the power and coldness of Lestat in contrast to Louis. This contrast is also written throughout in terms of the palette and texture of their respective clothes. (Louis wears natural, soft earth tones against Lestat's mechanical electric blues and harsh greys.)

Notwithstanding the body count and the lack of interest or identification with the victims who, as noted, are never more than meat, the episode also links art and performance with vampirism. Here, as in a number of other kills — though not Louis's and Claudia's early kills — the vampires create a highly choreographed scenography of death. Consider Claudia's and Lestat's concerts, which she finishes with "sombre" music, Claudia's little orphan routine, and her presentation of the twins to Lestat.

Most obviously, the Parisian vampires perform their kill to the applause of an audience. After their short morality play, the real performance which, like that of Lestat's to Louis, is both brutal and misogynistic, begins. A young woman is brought on stage and greeted by the trickster "buffoon". She is then stripped and humiliated, in a way that goes beyond a critique of the dominant visual (and cinematic) practices of objectification of the woman, so that Jordan becomes complicit. Armand takes her life and hands her to the other vampires, who cover her with their cloaks like a litter of black shiny rats.

Despite the number of women victims — the beautiful Yvette; the primal evil grandmother, the widow St Clair, who has had her boy lover kill her husband; the sexually available waitress and prostitutes; the girl in the theatre — and children, much of the critical comment generated focused on the film as a homoerotic, if not homosexual, text. While this homoerotic aspect is undoubtedly present, particularly in the initial moments of the Lestat/Louis relationship, and perhaps when Armand catches Louis's eye during his "theatrical" performance, to view the film in such narrow terms is necessarily as limiting as to view it as an allegory on AIDS.[23] For the most part, the Lestat/Louis dynamic is played out as asexual familial bickering (of estranged husband and wife, or, father and son). Also, the vampires transcend sexuality and sexual preference in that all bodies (even non-human), regardless of age and gender, provide the potential for erotic engagement: the kill itself is erotic, with the warm blood sending the vampire into a swoon.

In summary, *Interview with the Vampire* is a rich and visually beautiful film which moreover is sensitive to the various cultural moments that it charts. However, though it explores the gothic or baroque world of sensuality and desire, it keeps this from engulfing the audience. Like the cinematic montage of sunrises that cannot harm Louis, we, too, are locked into the mediated experience which formally and visually keeps us at a safe distance from the vampires and their threat. Nevertheless, through Louis's attendance at the cinema from the 1920s to the 1980s, we are invited to enjoy a series of intertextual jokes: he views F.W. Murnau's classics, the germinal 1922 vampire film *Nosferatu*, made in Germany and originally to be called *Dracula* after Bram Stoker's novel, and his influential American film *Sunrise: A Song of Two Humans* (1927); the epic *Gone with the Wind* (1939), with its aside to Irish-America; the new all-American superhuman, *Superman* (1978); and on leaving the cinema after seeing *Tequila Sunrise* (Robert Towne, 1988). In the open-ended structure, at least at a narrative level, some threat is registered which ultimately serves, like so many horror films, to erase or damage the communal grammar of causal interaction. The vampires are out there — we might sit beside them in the cinema theatre — but then death might be preferable to becoming part of their dysfunctional family!

Notes

[1] Following *Company of Wolves*, which dealt with various myths around the werewolf, Angela Carter and Jordan thought of doing something similar with regard to the vampire. However, Carter died before any such project was developed. The Rice adaptation was suggested by Geffen (see Chapter Fifteen).

[2] The sense of sucking and biting or sucking the life out of the parent is powerfully evoked in the graveyard scene during which Louis be-

comes a vampire. Of course, the shared intimacy at this moment is not limited to mother–child relationships, but can become a metaphor for any obsessive or intense relationship, whether between father and son or between lovers.

3 See Moretti (1995: 157): "In one set of works (Poe, Hoffmann, Baudelaire: 'elite' culture) they are women. In another (Polidori, Stoker, the cinema: 'mass' culture) they are men."

4 Linda Williams (1984), "When the Woman Looks", in *Film Theory and Criticism: Introductory Readings*, Gerald Mast, Marshall Cohen, Leo Braudy, eds. (1992), fourth edition, New York/Oxford: Oxford University Press: 561–77.

5 A hallmark of Jordan's work is a love of the irrational and chance. In his commentary on the DVD edition of the film, he draws attention to the beauty of the "irrational" entrance of Lestat. He comes from nowhere and is without history. Indeed, he remains an enigmatic character throughout the film.

6 Jordan in his commentary on the DVD explained that to render Rice's "vampire vision" "would have been very difficult, perhaps probably a little corny".

7 The music, as ever, this time by Elliot Goldenthal, is beautifully complementary to the film's narrative. This is most especially the case here, and in the choice of the song which ends the film, but also in rendering the various historical periods with music that recalls and draws on these periods.

8 See Hillel Schwartz (1996), *The Culture of the Copy*, New York: Zone Books: "Advertisers this [the twentieth] century first exploited twins for their exponential powers"; their promise was to "double your pleasure" (p. 38 and passim).

9 Jordan, in his commentary on the DVD, indicates that it was Rice who rewrote this.

10 See Julia Stonehouse (1994), *Idols to Incubators: Reproductive Theory Through the Ages*, London: Scarlet Press. Another reading of this "family" is that Louis *is* the father — a disempowered father — while Lestat, figured as more effeminate, and who Jordan in his DVD commentary calls a "bitchy wife", is the transgressive mother, who must be punished. It is only when Louis finds a "real" mother for

Claudia (Madeleine) that Louis is accepted as "father"; but the Paris vampires cannot accept this nuclear family. Indeed, Lestat's retreat into the derelict mansion can be compared to Norma Desmond in *Sunset Boulevard* (Billy Wilder, 1950).

[11] See Martin F. Norden (1994), *The Cinema of Isolation: A History of Physical Disability in the Movies*, New Brunswick, NJ: Rutgers University Press.

[12] There is a sense that Europe is nothing but a tomb to these living dead. As Louis says on their arrival in Europe, "I wanted the waters to be blue, but they were black — night-time waters — and how I suffered then, straining to recall the colour that in my youth I had taken for granted."

[13] For a discussion of the various pleasures in viewing and screening out in horror cinema see: Dennis Giles (1984), "Conditions of Pleasure in Horror Cinema", in *Planks of Reason: Essays on the Horror Film*, Barry Keith Grant, ed., Metuchen, NJ, and London: Scarecrow: 38–52.

[14] The allusion is to Seltzer (1998) and his discussion of serial killers.

[15] Of course, such abnormal or "warped reflection[s]" (*Sunrise with Sea Monster*, 1994: 108) of families populate all of Jordan's work and include, amongst others, the triads of Sam, Donal and Rose in *Sunrise*; Sam, Jimmy and Renée in *The Miracle*; the various combinations of Claire, Vivian and, alternatively, Vivian's mother, and Claire's child/ child substitute, in *In Dreams*; and the Bradys in *The Butcher Boy*. It is interesting that, in both *Sunrise* and *Butcher Boy*, the father and son find their relationship improves when the father is seriously disabled or when his silence echoes the blank silence of God, which frustrates Bendrix in *The End of the Affair*. In *Sunrise*, the father becomes a "vegetable", while in the *Butcher Boy*, Benny dies but is treated by the son as if he were simply sick or resting. In both cases, the son discovers a new caring and open relationship with their "incapacitated" fathers.

[16] This image recalls a similar one in *We're No Angels*, when the Robert De Niro character looks through a window with desire on a young woman, with whom he later tries to recreate a nuclear family.

[17] Jordan on DVD commentary.

[18] Without discussing this in detail, it is clear that the film's camera is not approximate to Louis's experience. Indeed he is absent from sev-

eral key scenes, such as Claudia's attack on Lestat, and Madeleine's and Claudia's deaths.

[19] The superhuman speed with which he achieves this suggests, at least for science fiction fans, that Louis may have taken Gibberne's "new accelerator" serum; see H.G. Wells, "The New Accelerator" (1901) in *The Complete Short Stories of H.G. Wells*, John Hammond, ed. (1998) London: Dent.

[20] For a more complete consideration of these ideas, see Martin Jay, "Scopic Regimes of Modernity" (and the accompanying discussion) in *Vision and Visuality*, Hal Foster, ed., Seattle: Bay Press, 1988.

[21] See various essays in *Screen Special issue on Body Horror*, Vol. 27, No. 1, 1986; and Ken Gelder, ed. (2000), *The Horror Reader*, London: Routledge.

[22] Sigmund Freud, "The Uncanny" (1959), cited by Sue-Ellen Case in "Tracking the Vampire" (1991, extract), in Ken Gelder, ed. (2000), *The Horror Reader*, London: Routledge, 207. As well as this, and the fantasy of cannibalism in relation to the mother, intimately tied up with vampirism is the whole area of death and the taboo on the dead, which according to Freud arises "from the conscious pain and the unconscious satisfaction over the death that has occurred" (Freud, 1955 cited by Moretti, 1995: 155).

[23] Nevertheless, Jordan in his commentary when discussing the look of the vampires suggests that they should provoke the "strange feeling that [they] are of this world and yet not of this world" and that their paleness could pass in the night as that of "an AIDS victim".

Chapter Ten

Michael Collins (1996)

No figure in twentieth-century Irish history so towers over the Irish political landscape as Michael Collins, even if it is Eamon de Valera who *appears* to have dominated the Irish cultural and political vista from the early 1930s until the late 1950s and after (he retired as President in 1973). De Valera was certainly the man most responsible for moulding Ireland as an insular Catholic and morally repressive nation, run, according to Donal Gore, the central protagonist of *Sunrise with Sea Monster*, "on Euclidean principles" (Jordan, 1994: 170).[1] Nevertheless, as de Valera himself aptly put it in 1966: "It is my considered opinion that in the fullness of time history will record the greatness of Michael Collins, and it will be recorded at my expense." De Valera said this on the occasion when he refused relatives of Collins permission to erect a proper commemorative monument above Collins's grave in Glasnevin cemetery (Dublin). Following a rather negative depiction of de Valera in contrast to Collins, Jordan uses this comment as a justificatory coda to the film.

Michael Collins was born in 1890 at Woodfield, Clonakilty, County Cork, the son of a small farmer. At sixteen, he went to London, where he worked as a civil servant, and joined the Irish Republican Brotherhood (IRB) before returning to Ireland to fight during the 1916 Rising as part of the rebels' garrison in the General Post Office, Dublin. A little over six years later, he was dead, killed by some of his former colleagues at Béal na Bláth, County Cork on 22 August 1922, at the age of thirty-one.

During those six years, the span of Jordan's film, Collins rose to a position of senior leadership within the Irish independence movement, including as a member of the Supreme Council of the secret and powerful IRB. After the electoral gains by Sinn Féin in the 1918 general election, and the establishment of Dáil Éireann, Collins was appointed Minister for Home Affairs and later Minister for Finance, in which latter capacity he organised the successful Dáil Loans campaign.[2] He also arranged the supply of arms for the IRA as military activities began to intensify during 1919–21, while also successfully infiltrating the British military network at Dublin Castle with a sophisticated intelligence-gathering system that kept him informed of British plans against the IRA. Against his will, he was a member of the team which negotiated the Anglo-Irish Treaty of December 1921, supported its adoption by Dáil Éireann, became Commander-in-Chief of the Irish Free State army, and had largely neutralised the anti-Treaty forces by the time of his death. In carrying out these tasks with great courage and energy, he not only evaded capture but developed a reputation as a "Scarlet Pimpernel" who cycled around Dublin in a pinstripe suit without being detected, part of the Collins myth which is referred to in the opening of Jordan's film.

This latter characteristic is depicted also in the first feature film dealing with Collins, *Beloved Enemy* (H.C. Potter, 1936), which shows Brian Aherne as "Reardon" (Collins) who openly rides his bicycle around Dublin and takes Helen (Merle Oberon), daughter of a British diplomat and peace envoy, to the mountains. This relationship is based on Collins's "friendship" (often fantasised in the popular imagination as an affair) with Lady Lavery, the American-born wife of the painter Sir John Lavery. While this was given prominence in a script, *Mick*, about Collins written by Eoghan Harris, which was never made into a film, its absence from Jordan's film is explained by the fact that Jordan chose not to include any scenes set in London during the Treaty negotiations.

In *Beloved Enemy*, Helen/Lady Lavery is shown convincing Reardon to give up the gun, and indeed that film rather fancifully has the Collins and Lavery stand-ins happily reunited at the end.

Such a sleight-of-hand was allowed because within classical Hollywood narrative and its drive towards a positive and happy cinematic closure, the Collins story caused major difficulties because the hero is killed rather than lives on with the girl. Consequently, the producers shot two versions of the ending: in one, the Collins character dies in the historically correct way, even if the assassin shoots him in an urban setting; in the other, he is seen to survive the assassin's bullet and is being comforted by Helen. "It's all right darlin', I'm not going to die", Reardon tells Helen. "A good Irishman never does what's expected of him", he jokes in the film's final line. Sensibly, the producers confined distribution of the latter version to North America.

Warner Bros. were similarly concerned with Jordan's ending. Taking the advice of his friend, film director Stanley Kubrick, Jordan framed the film as a flashback. "You have to tell them at the start that he dies", Kubrick told him, "otherwise they'll think he goes on to become President of Ireland and will be disappointed." Producer David Geffen also felt that it was necessary to see Kitty learning about Collins's death. In the original version, the film cut from his death to a bridal wreath being placed on her head in the wedding shop; "in the great European tradition, emotion is implied rather than presented," Jordan commented. In order then to address the "blank page" of American audiences' knowledge of the story, the framing story — Collins's aide Joe O'Reilly (Ian Hart) in Kitty's bedroom talking about the dead Collins — and the scene where the young, tearful officer comes to tell her of his death, were added (Jordan, 1996: 62).

Jordan set the story within a conventional (and generally favoured by Jordan) narrative triangular relationship of Collins (Liam Neeson) and the other real people in his life, his close friend Harry Boland (Aidan Quinn) and his fiancée Kitty Kiernan (Julia Roberts), with whom Boland is also in love and initially had been romantically involved. As a result, what is seen is Jordan's clearest representation of his attitude to the relationship of the violent male world of the public sphere and how it impinges adversely on the private world of the domestic sphere. *Michael Collins* is, above all else, a story of love destroyed by violence, as is depicted in two of the film's key scenes, yet nevertheless it is also the oxymoron, or paradox of violence as love. Collins may be a murderer, but he hates himself for hating, and the British for making hating "necessary". In other words, Jordan's Collins is a man who kills so that love is possible. He is a typical Jordan character bound by the irony which has him killed on the eve of his attempt to "take the gun out of politics" by a young thug who uses the guerilla techniques, invented by Collins to frustrate the British, against him and the new Irish Free State.

This juxtaposition of love and violence is visually summed up in the "Jesus conversation piece". The face of Jesus (a statue in a church) fills the screen: He is looking down and His hands are posed in such a way as to suggest a blessing or forgiveness. The following shot has one of Collins's men praying beneath the statue. He gets up, leaves and on the street outside, kills with a single bullet one of the Dublin Castle policemen, saying as he does, "May the Lord have mercy on your soul". Elsewhere, such as in *We're No Angels*, *The Miracle* and *The Butcher Boy*, the (religious) statues are similarly allowed to "speak".

Collins discovers through his informants the names and addresses of the British intelligence officers known as the Cairo gang (named after the café in which they met), and sends out the Twelve Apostles (his most experienced and effective killers) to assassinate the agents. As these eleven killings are taking place (in bedrooms, a bathroom, in a park, on the street), in a cinematic style which recalls *The Godfather* (Francis Ford Coppola, 1972),[3] Collins and Kitty are hiding overnight in a bedroom in the Gresham Hotel. Even though the couple are clearly in love (a rose is dangled between them), Collins never makes his feelings clear, even though she tells him that she waited for his letter, but that Boland's arrived instead. He even asks Kitty never to care about him, but, of course, this is impossible for both of them. The scenes between the pair have an ethereal quality because here, as elsewhere in the film, they are shot predominately in blue.[4] Noticing Collins's obvious distraction and unease despite her romantic overtures, she asks him about his "boys" and what is the content of their "love letters".

She finds his response — "to leave us be" — "unromantic". However, he continues, they also say, "give us the future, we've had enough of your past. Give us our country back, to live in, to grow in, to love."

So, it would seem, there is love. The killings, while they are horrendous — though hardly more so than the torture of Broy (played by Stephen Rea, he is a composite character with the real name of one of Collins's informants) and the dumping of his bloodied face and body on the road — are necessary, painful bouquets that might allow "Irish" life to bloom. "Do you think they got the message?" she asks in the hope that the war will soon be over, but there is no response from Collins as this question ends the Gresham Hotel scene. The answer is supplied in the following scene, when the British armoured tanks enter Croke Park and randomly fire on the spectators and players. Collins is never so "generous" with his bullets, his targets carefully selected for maximum efficiency. He gives out to his men for "riddling" the G-men of Dublin Castle, all of whom, according to his instructions, are single.

At the end of the film, Collins and Joe are traveling in convoy in west Cork, ostensibly to meet de Valera. Collins jokes about the wedding list for his planned marriage to Kitty, saying that as part of "marital diplomacy" he should make de Valera best man and invite the British Prime Minister Lloyd George and his minister, Winston Churchill, as bridesmaids. Meanwhile, Kitty is choosing a wedding dress while Collins's final moments are intercut as he travels to Béal na Bláth in the military convoy. A third strand of parallel editing shows the anti-Treaty IRA group race towards the ridge at Béal na Bláth to fire down on Collins's motorcade. As the haunting voice of Sinéad O'Connor sings the Irish love song "She Moves Through the Fair", previously sung by Kitty in her family home when Collins and Boland were staying there, the sequence ends with the officer arriving to tell Kitty the news of Collins's death, but it is too painful for either of them to speak, and she cries uncontrollably.

Near the beginning of the film, Collins and Boland witness a wedding party at a railway station[5] and Collins comments that it is a "lovely picture", adding half-jokingly, "Maybe we should settle down." "Just the two of us," Boland responds. The homosocial relationship between them is made explicit on a number of occasions: when they stay at the Kiernans' and share a bed together, only to be woken up by Kitty the next morning; when Collins challenges Boland, "I'll wrestle you" for Kitty before the pair roll on the floor; and at the train station as Boland leaves for America, Kitty says: "He's leaving me", to which Collins replies, "Thought he was leaving me." Indeed, shortly after Collins returns from the Treaty negotiations, and believing the fighting is over, Kitty says to him that she has known them both for four years: "You've lived together, slept together, fought together. But your war's over now."

Perhaps most poignantly, the personal and political events are intertwined during the subsequent civil war. Collins stops at the old IRA headquarters, Vaughan's Hotel, now occupied by the anti-Treaty IRA, where he finds Boland and they go upstairs to a bedroom as Collins confirms he is engaged to Kitty. As they argue over the Treaty, "Collins grips Boland's head close to his, like a woman's" (to use Jordan's own description, 1996: 149) as Boland tells him to go, their relationship now ended because Collins has not only accepted the Treaty, but he is going to marry Kitty.

However, for Collins, his relationship with Boland is not finished. Later, when Collins comes across his dead body, he tries to have an intimate dialogue with the corpse, "What happened? Who closed your eyes?" and he takes his anger out on the Free State soldier who has just killed him. "You were meant to protect him", Collins shouts at the soldier, because he "was one of us".[6] As Jordan put it, "What I did like about the triangular thing was that it was almost like these two men were in love with each other."[7] In that, the relationship recalls that of Fergus and Jody in *The Crying Game*, though here it arises from their conflict.

There is, though, another homosocial triangle in the film: Collins, Boland and de Valera. One of the unexplained historical issues is why de Valera insisted that Boland accompany him to the USA on his year-long failed attempt to try to gain American government recognition of the Irish Republic. While the Collins/Boland team proved to be a formidable counter-weight to de Valera during his imprisonment in Lincoln Jail, Jordan represents de Valera's decision as rooted not just in political jealousy, but "also from unconscious resentment of Collins's intense and intimate relationship" with Boland (Butler Cullingford, 2001: 217), in the tradition of the strong male bonding found in *The Crying Game* and *Interview with the Vampire*.

De Valera, though, is represented not just as a jealous lover who breaks up the Collins/Boland couple, but in the escape from Lincoln Jail he is characterised as a prostitute. While he escaped wearing women's clothing using the cover of prostitutes seeking clients at the prison walls, Boland and Collins joke at his expense as they make their getaway, the latter saying, "Some died for Ireland, but Dev, he whored for Ireland." Such a witticism is particularly pointed in the context of de Valera's strict Catholic morality. In this scene, with de Valera dressed in women's clothing and sitting between the two men in the back of a commandeered taxi, there is a parody (or parallel) of the triangular relationship of Collins, Boland and Kitty. In fact, Collins's singing of the Irish-American lament "I'll Take You Home Again, Kathleen", which ends the scene, draws a parallel between de Valera and Kathleen/Kitty. (Indeed, de Valera's female dress code, fur coat and hat, is similar to Kitty's when she is with Boland and/or Collins on a number of occasions.)

There is a further scene which implies the exclusion of Kitty, with even de Valera sharing a bed with the other two men, perhaps a signal that the relationship with Kitty will never be consummated as the bonds between the men are too strong. This is also suggested in Jordan's intercutting of Broy packing up his things in Dublin Castle and Kitty being helped by Collins to gather her things in Vaughan's Hotel on the night of the planned "valentine" assassinations. The fate of all three is intertwined, so that Broy's torture and death casts a shadow on Kitty and Collins, both as a couple and individually.

The representation of de Valera goes to the heart of the film's politics, and it is crystal clear who the film's villain is, especially after the British leave. English actor Alan Rickman looks, acts and speaks with an uncanny resemblance to de Va-

lera (and, some would say, an uncanny resemblance to Dracula). De Valera is always something of an outsider: his name
evoking Latin connotations; his American birth saving him from
the firing squad after the 1916 Rising; and his reputation as a
mathematician making his most obtuse and abstract comments
seem "normal", at least for him. His association was with intel-
lectualism, and thus in cinematic narrative terms not the world
of action but of reflection, a suspiciously feminine activity. In
contrast, the muscular, toweringly physical Collins, the man of
action, is, paradoxically, never seen to fight (except for the
wrestling with Boland), a condition which bothered some reviewers of the film.

De Valera, though, is tight with his body, angular in his
movements even during public speeches, while when Collins is
speaking he is the target of physical assault. Despite his infamous
"rivers of [Irish] blood" speech of March 1922, regarded as en-
couraging the drift towards civil war, de Valera is not seen subsequently as a man of action, but rather, at the end of the film,
he is frozen, cowering and crying in a haystack, unable either to
make peace with Collins or stop the young insolent assassin
(Jonathan Rhys Myers) from setting the fatal trap for Collins.
Already feminised in women's clothes on his escape from jail,
where he had "allowed" himself to be detained rather than following Collins's path of action, he is now seen as ineffectual, and
suffering from the stereotypically feminine affliction of "nerves",
as Collins tells Boland. He is more interested in the symbolic, in
words and ideas rather than the reality of a free Ireland.

Thus, if Jordan's critique of de Valera fits within the post-
1960s secular and "modernising" impulse, which regards him as
the person most responsible for the inward-looking and pro-
tectionist Irish society from the 1930s to the late 1950s, by
which time the "moderniser" Sean Lemass became Taoiseach,
the film also explores issues around appearance, representation
and reality. Dynamic Michael Collins wants to effect real
change, and though cognisant of the importance of the flag and
of "words", equally he understands the need for compromise,
and refuses to go to war again and shed more Irish blood,
when, for the first time, they have managed to get something

from the British. De Valera, on the other hand, unable to come to terms, not with partition which he accepted, but with the symbolic Oath of Allegiance to Britain, was "prepared to wade through Irish blood". Consequently, de Valera, an anglophobe, fits into Jordan's character type who is unable to distinguish between representation (or ideology) and reality. As such, he becomes a political version of *Mona Lisa*'s George, who is also cast as a seeker of racial purity — in effect, a racist.

Indeed, de Valera's decision to visit America as the Republic's President, instead of "fighting" for it, or the grand but suicidal gesture of attacking the Customs House even though the IRA have no chance and lose nearly eighty men, all position him as being obsessed with an idea rather than as being anchored, like Collins, in reality. Likewise, in the scenes of the Pathé Gazette newsreels in the picture house, which seamlessly become "real", and in Broy's defiant, but pertinent, comment as he burns the papers in Vaughan's and for which he is killed, that they are only "words, just words", Jordan plays with the slippage between representation and reality. (In "reality", Colonel Eamonn Broy (1887–1972) lived to become an important police officer in the Irish Free State, rising in 1933 to Commissioner, or in overall administrative charge of the police, before retiring in 1938.)

Jordan's fashionable view of de Valera conveniently ignores not just the role the British played in the division of Ireland (there is no reference in the film, for example, to the Government of Ireland Act, 1920) but in Collins's role in upholding it, though, of course, in his defence, it is said that he supplied guns to the Northern Ireland IRA after the Treaty. However, as Jordan has said, what he wanted to highlight was the fact that the War of Independence was in many ways "really a war among Irish people; I mean most of the people Collins assassinates in the Castle are Irishmen working for the Empire" (McSwiney 1996: 12).

The representation of de Valera's principled defence of the republic recalls a not dissimilar cinematic representation, that of "Lenehan", the James Cagney character, at the end of *Shake Hands with the Devil* (1959). As the increasingly pathological anti-Treaty leader of an IRA unit, he is killed by one of his own men because he wants to continue to fight for the republic. For Jordan, this Manichean contrast is only a further layer to the black and white Irish/English-Northern Irish contrasts which had already been established, paradoxically, as a means of trying to draw parallels between the 1916–22 period and contemporary events in Ireland.

Luke Gibbons characterised as the "most obnoxious features" of de Valera's representation those which identify him with the post-colonial state: "the glacial impersonality required for an institutional and administrative takeover of power" (Gibbons, 1996b: 262–3). Instead of discrediting "the nation" or "the republic", Gibbons goes on to argue, the film throws "a shadow over the incomplete project of Irish *state* formation, a shadow that extends into the present". Since the nation is usually represented as the maternal or female body and the state in terms of patriarchy, "Collins's tragedy lies in his failure to make the transition between the two, to bring about a union between the state and the nation" (Gibbons, 1996b: 263).

Far from closing off the Civil War to the present, as many commentators suggested, the film left open the possibility of a happy ending. Utilising Fredric Jameson's work on national allegory, Gibbons reads the film as within the tradition of Vietnam War allegories such as *The Wild Bunch* (Sam Peckinpah, 1969), *Soldier Blue* (Ralph Nelson, 1970), and *Little Big Man* (Arthur Penn, 1970), which explored the painful events of the present through the western genre. In this way, *Michael Collins* can be read as an allegorical engagement with the unresolved issue of Northern Ireland's state formation, as indeed Jordan himself suggests in the emergence of the peace process — Gerry Adams and Martin McGuinness in London to discuss a resolution of the Northern conflict (McSwiney, 1996: 23).

Gibbons goes on to note that the conflation of the public and private — Collins and Boland vying for Kitty — explains in part the much-commented-on lack of depth to Kitty's character. While that is valid, Jordan has pointed out that she was not some "Rosa Luxembourg", a revolutionary. Consequently, her non-political status renders her somewhat irrelevant to the film, which though "about" the life of Collins is foremost a political exploration. Just as the film is not, nor ever could be, a historical document (unless it is read in loose terms as reflecting a 1990s cultural or political viewpoint), neither can it be made to serve some political feminist agenda, in which Kitty could be read as such a revolutionary. Additionally, Gibbons draws attention to the parallels between the film and W.B. Yeats's play *Cathleen ni Houlihan* in which "another Michael forgoes marriage to a real woman and sacrifices his life on the altar of Mother Ireland" (Gibbons, 1996b: 265). Thus, Kitty is never allowed to become a "real" woman — married with family, as in most Hollywood genres. With the effacement of the real woman, the public sphere is conceded, as noted above, to the homosocial world of the male triangular relationship. Thus, as Gibbons states, even in relation to the Gresham Hotel scene and the killings by the Twelve Apostles, "there is no hiding place from history" (Gibbons, 1996b: 267).

With the public/private split complete, the film can only end in tragedy. As Collins returns to west Cork where he was born, and visits the now ruined family home, he sings the ballad "Old Skibbereen", which he had recited previously in Kitty's home, in the semi-public sphere, the twilight arena of the pub:

> Suspended between the (private) maternal and the (public) paternal, with no possibility of return but unable to progress further, Collins's fate tragically allegorizes the incomplete narratives of the nation itself. (Gibbons, 1996b: 268)

As a result, Jordan's desire to present a new originary narrative of the Irish (Republican) nation-state was doomed to failure because of the incomplete nature of the nation-forming project which is most apparent in *Sunrise with Sea Monster* (Jordan 1994). The film's use of archival footage of Collins's funeral, while attempting to place the events in the past, only serves to emphasise the task still facing partitioned Ireland.

Predictably, much of the British Tory press attacked the film's depiction of the British security forces, while being alert to the modern parallels of the story, such as the protracted peace process; IRA leader Gerry Adams now a negotiator; the August 1921 and August 1994 ceasefires; the outbreak of civil war over the Treaty and the Canary Wharf bombing which ended the first IRA ceasefire. In an editorial, the *Daily Telegraph* even quoted Yeats's lines from "Easter 1916": "Did that play of mine [*Cathleen ni Houlihan*] send out/Certain men the English shot", as if Jordan's film could motivate militant republicans in a similar way.[8]

Historians hostile to republicanism attacked the film, sometimes sight unseen, including Roy Foster, who spent an uncomfortable few minutes on RTE Radio's *Morning Ireland* as he tried to defend his attack on the film while Jordan poured scorn on him as a historian who had not seen the still-unfinished film. Another historian, Ruth Dudley Edwards, with a political agenda close to the Ulster Unionists, claimed the kicking of the wounded James Connolly did not happen, while "revisionist" Paul Bew objected to the scene in which the Northern Irish detective declares that what was needed was "a bit of Belfast efficiency" before he is killed in a car bomb.[9] As others also pointed out, such car bombs were only introduced by the IRA in the 1970s, and thus the modern parallels were potentially dangerous, while the (cinematically very effective) use of an armoured car during the Black and Tans attack at Croke Park on the afternoon of the Cairo gang assassinations, was not historically correct, even if twelve people were killed there by other means. Elsewhere, Bew argued that Britain would have (paternalistically) conceded Irish independence anyway — another spin of the revisionist history merry-go-round as it sought to denigrate all armed resistance to the colonial power.[10]

The most sustained and vocal attacks on the film came not from the British press or academia, but from the *Irish Times* columnist Kevin Myers and writer and broadcaster Eoghan Harris, who relentlessly portrayed the film as neo-fascist in the tradition of Nazi filmmaker Leni Riefenstahl. The film's depiction of the "Brits as bastards" was "racist", according to Harris.[11] What Harris had in mind was that, with the exception of the smooth-talking and suave Soames (Charles Dance), there is no depth to any British character. However, there are many positive portrayals of British military and police forces in Ireland, such as the G-Man being killed as he leaves church; one of the British agents praying "The Lord is my shepherd" before being killed in the park; and Soames[12] being described by his maid Rosie as a "gentleman". Significantly, McSwiney (1996: 10) notes that the British press were pleased that "they got off so lightly" in the film.

Nevertheless, the Black and Tans are shown, as is established beyond doubt, that they used state-sanctioned terror against civilians. Harris's attacks on the film stung Jordan (1996b) into writing a mocking commentary on Harris's own script for a Collins film. Entitled "Tally Ho! Mr Harris", he drew attention to Harris's shallow version of the period and his elevation of the Collins/Lavery "affair" to a central feature. Harris replied in kind, drawing attention to the inaccuracy of the events depicted in Jordan's film.[13]

One of the great ironies of the right-wing British press and Irish "revisionist" attacks on the film, which in part was fuelled by the Sinn Féin/IRA newspaper *An Phoblacht* welcoming of it, was that what Collins represented — partition, the Irish Free State, even the Oath of Allegiance — were the most detested features in the republican credo. Indeed, the Provisional IRA saw itself in the lineage of the anti-Treaty IRA which killed Collins, and in a sense they might be expected to object to the caricature of de Valera, though he outlawed the IRA in 1936. The issue for the "revisionist" camp was that history should have been safely confined to the past and the very ordinary nature of Collins's task — running a war like an efficient business — was too close to recent events in Northern Ireland.

The Irish popular response to the film, whatever its limitations as a Hollywood "epic" or as "history", clearly demonstrated that there was welcome for this most painful and suppressed period of Irish history being brought to the surface. Taking over €5 million at the Irish box office, it was the most popular film yet to have been released in Ireland.

Notes

¹ Jordan depicts de Valera in the background in his short story "A Love" in which his funeral forms the backdrop; in *The Past*; and in *Sunrise*.

² For an account of the Dáil Loans film featuring Collins, see Rockett (1987: 24).

³ The use of *The Godfather* is a two-edged sword here, because its theme — the controlling but "clean-hands" manipulator — emerged after that film's release as a powerful ideological tool used by the British government against the IRA, the "Godfathers" of terrorism, manipulating young innocents, being engaged in crime, not politics, etc. Contrasting views on Jordan's use of *The Godfather* are offered by Gibbons (1997b: 51) and Butler Cullingford (2001: 91).

⁴ Jordan commented that, in order "to achieve a kind of elegiac realism . . . with bursts of violence and long bursts of discussion . . . [there are] sequences of very rapid editing and sequences that are quite languorous and quite operatic and more open". In order to realise this, they "needed a very graphic kind of dramatic quality to the image, and as well to highlight the kind of documentary base in which it's set. We used a process called ENR, which is a process . . . which basically introduces a slight element of black and white dye into the printing that desaturates the colours very slightly and builds up the contrasts which would enhance that silhouette feeling, the contrasts between light and dark" (McSwiney, 1996: 15–16).

⁵ The image of a moving train is used a number of times throughout the film. For example, the train puffing smoke, rushing three-quarter frontal towards the viewer, the popular representation of early cinema, echoes the smoke and flames of the burning barracks in the background, compositionally linking violence and the future. Later, Collins meets Broy at another train bridge. As the train rushes past, Collins tells him: "I love trains . . . They make me think of places I know I'll never see." It is from a train station that Boland leaves for America and he tells Collins and Kitty of a sighting in Clare of a green, white and orange butterfly. It flies the night the three of them go dancing, which is also the night that they learn of the truce. But, as Collins said at the station, where he stole his first kiss from Kitty, the problem with butterflies is that they last only a day.

6 This is a fictitious representation of Boland's death. For an account of his killing by National Army troops at the Grand Hotel, Skerries, County Dublin on the night of 31 July / 1 August 1922, see Eugene Coyle, "Film failed to do justice to drama surrounding death of Harry Boland", *Irish Times*, 5 August 1997: 4. Collins was killed three weeks later.

7 *Sunday Business Post*, 27 October 1996.

8 *Daily Telegraph*, 15 October 1996: 23; see also Toby Harnden, "Collins Film 'Is Insult to Murdered RUC Officers'", ibid., 22 October 1996.

9 Paul Bew, *Daily Telegraph*, 14 October 1996.

10 Paul Bew, *Sunday Independent*, 29 September 1996; "When Jordan Shot Collins", *Sunday Times*, 10 November 1996: Section three: 6.

11 Eoghan Harris, *Sunday Times*, 10 November 1996.

12 In a typical layering of irony, or a further critique of de Valera's New Ireland, Jordan names the feminine-voiced intelligence-gatherer for the Free State who works in Dublin Castle in *Sunrise*, Mr Soames. It is to him that Donal has to report his acts of personal and political "betrayal".

13 Eoghan Harris, "Tally Ho: Not so Funny, Mr Jordan", *Irish Times*, 26 October 1996: 8.

Chapter Eleven

The Butcher Boy (1997)

In all of Jordan's work, there is a richness and texture that is rare within Irish cinema. This is especially true of *The Butcher Boy*. However, for all its electric and sumptuous aural and visual sensibility, it displays measured understatement — for example special effects do not draw attention to themselves[1] — and is, like *The Miracle* and a number of his "smaller" films, narratively tight.

What is remarkable is that, to achieve this, Jordan sacrificed very little of Patrick McCabe's award-winning 1992 bittersweet novel on which it is based. Indeed, unlike the stage play, *Frank Pig Says Hello* (also written by McCabe) the film (co-scripted by Jordan and McCabe) is an extremely close relation of the novel, but though it captures the transgressive border wonderland between sanity and insanity, and optimism and despair, it is arguably also less complex and ambiguous, particularly with regard to the representation of women, and specifically Francie Brady's relationship to Mrs Nugent (but then the film is more interested in the father–son dyad).

Absent is one of the novel's most uncompromising images, which occurs when Francie imagines inserting himself into the Nugent family. Knowing his fantasy, Mrs Nugent "slowly unbuttoned her blouse and took out her breast", but such an explicit action forces him to acknowledge the shame of betraying his own mother — he is no better than the butcher boy and the lying "bastards" that "let you down" (McCabe, 1992: 215) —

while it also registers the sexual nature of the mother–son relationship, so that his desire becomes repulsion, "I thought I was
going to choke on the fat lukewarm flesh" (McCabe, 1992: 60).

The film prefers to position Mrs Nugent as a monster, approximate to the alien or nuclear threat, and not someone
that, if things were different, he could love (as is the case in the
novel). In short, Mrs Nugent is never Jimmy's seductive Renée
(*The Miracle*), who also suffers a kind of death through her son,
even if the bogman's song "The Butcher Boy" and Francie's
identification of himself as the eponymous errant lover, may
suggest something more. Yet, ultimately, this role aligns him
with his father, of whom, by the end of the film, wearing an Al
Capone coat, he has become a version.

However, in contrast to his father, who tries through alco-
hol to repress his past, but in which he remains trapped in a
repetitive cycle of violence and abuse so that his own family is
destroyed, the older Francie has learned to keep his difference
secret. In this respect, he is like other Jordan characters, including Danny (*Angel*), Simone (*Mona Lisa*), Renée (*The Miracle*),
the beast (*The Dream of a Beast*) and Dil (*The Crying Game*). All
of these characters understand that, in order to survive within
a divisive society which operates according to the limiting categories of cultural and biological identity (e.g. intellectual/mental,
physical, racial, sexual, national, political, and socio-economic),
simulation of normality is the simplest option. If, finally, the
beast and Dil are allowed to find love not despite but because
they are "monstrous", in both cases, they do so beyond the
confines of society: the beast reunites with his wife in an imaginary space where boundaries dissolve — a place of "hope
eternal" (Jordan, 1993a: 174); while Dil and Fergus continue
their relationship in prison (see Rogers, 1997).

Though in the novel Francie may give up on love and the
beautiful things, only to have another inmate share with him his
negative understanding under the "orange sky", which, like the
snowdrop, becomes a symbol for such things, Jordan's ending is
simultaneously promising and hopeless, refusing Francie any
human companionship or solidarity. He remains alone, with
only Our Lady to comfort him. The divine consolatory snow-

drop that She gives him, while it keeps alive his belief in beauty and the non-rational aspects of reality, also marks the end of his public embracing of this seeming unreality. By accepting, in the film's closing scene, the psychiatrist's comment that he picked the flower, for the first time, Francie chooses to keep private his "unreasonable" joy (Jordan, 1993 (1983): 100), and like Sarah Gilmartin who finally marries in order to give her daughter a name (*December Bride*, Thaddeus O'Sullivan, 1990) makes everything "smooth to the eye".

The Butcher Boy is essentially about how a young boy violently and logically, if insanely, reacts to the loss of the possibility of love and the "beautiful things" by destroying what stands in for perfection and aspiration: the quasi-bourgeois Mrs Nugent. The film has much to say about the nature of the family and dysfunctional or damaged small-town communities, and the universal themes of love, loss, and longing. However, it also raises a number of issues more specific to Ireland of the late 1950s / early 1960s which remain, or have become even more, relevant today, not least the role of the church; the treatment of children; sexual abuse; cultural identity, aspiration and representation; modernisation; globalisation; and Ireland's relationship to Britain (more correctly, England), which balances an ideological (post-colonial) resentment of England with it as a place to realise economic and social ambition through emigration there. Indeed, its representation of emigration is two-edged. At one level, it is the place of material success, which can be seen through the wealth and attitude of the Nugent family, who have recently returned home from England, and the respect that the townspeople have for Alo (Ian Hart), who has ten men under him in England. At the same time, it is a place of loss, which is clear in Alo's homecoming party. He has a nice red handkerchief that "wifey" irons, but it is at the expense of the home, community, and most of all, the girl he loves, Mary.[2]

The film is at once a continuation of the political project of *Michael Collins* in its critique of Eamon de Valera's ideal Catholic Ireland of the cosy homesteads with their nuclear happy families,[3] as it is of *Angel* in its understanding of the irrational compulsion towards violence, or his (broadly) "fantasy" films, including *We're No Angels* in its interest in faith and religion, *High Spirits* in its play with stereotypes of Irishness and the gothic imagination, or indeed, *Company of Wolves* or *Interview with the Vampire* in its child killer who chooses (or is forced to choose) to operate beyond the confines of society and morality.

But, if *Interview*, which also revelled in dark humour, promises the point of view of the vampire, *Butcher Boy* delivers such a viewpoint. Throughout, we are trapped in Francie Brady's world, with only him and his older self to guide us. We are in a place where often there is a disjunction between what we see and hear, so that, as Rosaleen points out in *Company*, seeing is not believing (or understanding). As McLoone observes, by keeping intact the first person narration of the novel — through Francie's idiomatic and playful speech, both as an on-screen character and as an older/inner voiceover, and through the visualisation, without cinematic "inverted commas", of his fantastic, though culturally derivative, hallucinations — we are denied any reality anchor: there is "no point of reference for the bewildered viewer" (McLoone, 1998: 33).

The film begins with a contextualising comic-strip credits sequence, over which an instrumental version of Kurt Weill and Bertolt Brecht's Jack the Ripper song "Mack the Knife" plays. As with Francie's imagination, one cartoon seamlessly bleeds into the next — cowboys giving way to superheroes, to outer space, rockets and astronauts with guns, to war images and soldiers fighting the Commies, until finally, the black-lined and orange-hued images appropriately end on what becomes the first image of the film: Francie completely covered in bandages with Sergeant Sausage (Sean McGinley) and Leddy (Peter Gowen), the pig man, by his bedside.

The film, like the book, begins as a confessional narrative with the voiceover of the older Francie (Stephen Rea) telling us the whole town were after him on account of what he "done on Mrs Nugent", and we presume that is the reason why he is now in hospital. From this reality, we descend into his comic-tragic childhood world of fantasy and adventure, and to a moment when twelve-year-old Francie Brady (wonderfully played by newcomer Eamonn Owens from Killeshandra, County Cavan) enjoys happiness with his best friend Joe Purcell (Alan Boyle). Together, they run wild as Sitting Bull and Geronimo — Irish injuns in a white man's colonial world — in a too-perfect lusciously green countryside, shout to each other from atop mountains which frame an azure lake below, and, in an aside to the novel where Francie's father Benny and his dad's brother Alo rob apples from the presbytery orchard (McCabe, 1992: 32), the two rob the Nugents' "Garden of Eden", located behind the church. They then try to swap the apples for nerdish Philip Nugent's (Andrew Fullerton) comics, until Mrs Nugent (Fiona Shaw), like Dorothy's malicious neighbour who becomes the Wicked Witch of the West (*The Wizard Of Oz*, Victor Fleming and King Vidor, 1939) interferes. She calls around to the Bradys, and as Francie hides in his bedroom, she stands at the door of their back-lane terraced house and berates his silent mother Annie (Aisling O'Sullivan), insultingly dismissing the father Benny (Stephen Rea again)[4], and thereby the family, as pigs, before wiggling, in a walk worthy of John Cleese, down the squalid lane in her tight green clothes, brushing against a typically drunk Benny Brady. He responds to Annie's distress by beating Francie.

In classic Jordan fashion, the camera, in ironic counterpoint, moves away from the familial violence and focuses instead on the television screen, on which there is an image of nuclear destruction accompanied by the comment: "Man has realised his dream, now he must control it." Against this equation of global or political violence with the domestic, or the negative effect of the former on the latter — an informing motif in *Angel* and *Michael Collins* — we see Annie desperately fidget with her small bottle of mind-numbing tablets.

However, Annie in her soft blue dress and floral apron, with memories of childbirth and the young Francie as a five-pound infant, and in her suffering and isolation, which causes her to die for love, is no more real than the woman of "The Butcher Boy" song, with whom she over-identifies. As such, though differently, she is like Mrs Nugent, Francie's nemesis. Figured as the harsh vitriolic devouring alien mother, she appropriately only wears green, and must be murdered to allow Francie and the community to live (and love?).[5] Put another way, Annie and Mrs Nugent are products of Francie's (and Jordan's rather than McCabe's) imagination, in which the woman becomes important only in her symbolic functions, which are rigorously separated into good (the comforting Virgin Mary, and the Mother-Ireland figured as de Valera's harp-playing colleen in the kitsch tourist ornament) and the bad Mrs Nugent. Despite this, there are sufficient slippages to problematise such a division. Mrs Nugent is obsessively a cake woman like Francie's mother, while the two women decorate their houses with representations of the Virgin and John F. Kennedy. More telling is that both the Virgin and the Irish colleen, though they provide comforting fictions, nonetheless bring to Francie further pain and trauma, not least because they are symbols of the utopian, *ergo* impossible, national vision. (That these two ideals are played by Sinéad O'Connor and speak in a colloquial language, often interspersed with swear words, only emphasises their problematic relation to the public imagination and the everyday lives of ordinary people.)

After Francie interrupts his mother's attempted suicide, she is taken into the "garage", the first mention, in a linguistic play, of the many institutions that support the broken community and come to structure Francie's life. That her absence, at least on the surface of things, does not radically change their lives says more about her representation than the male culture of cowboys, from which women are excluded, and through which father and son bond. Together, they watch the Lone Ranger on television, with Benny providing musical accompaniment until that, too, is ruined by his violence. Frustrated by the bad television reception, Benny tries to fix it, but only succeeds in putting his foot through it and, in so doing, partly denies Francie the release from the monotony and misery of his reality. Thereafter, he can only numb his pain and enjoy an alternative existence through watching (from outside the house) Mrs Nugent's television, reading comics, and his single visit to the cinema in Dublin, all of which fuel his doomed relationship with Joe, through whom he has access to love and normality. Of course, his imagination or insanity become his final escape when these more mundane avenues of release are insufficient to his needs.

What sustains him most, and remains when Joe does not, is religion. If McCabe acknowledges Francie's intimate relationship with the Virgin, his love of religious ritual, and the sensuousness of the church, he nevertheless notes Francie's irreverence — "I was supposed to say *Et clamor meus ad te veniat. Et fucky wucky ticky tocky that was what I said instead*" (McCabe, 1992: 76). In contrast, Jordan refuses to make any such qualification, even if he does have Francie, like Jimmy (*The Miracle*), abuse the statues when he is taken to the "school for pigs". (However, this is of a different order, as it never undermines the statues' reality or validity.)

This coupling of television (or sensory/spectacular popular culture) and religion, both of which are seen to offer consolation and liberation, yet also emptiness and illusionary surface, is a recurring trope within many of Jordan's films (most obviously *We're No Angels*, *The Miracle* and *The End of the Affair*). It is here explicit when Our Lady appears on the broken television to Francie following his escape from the mental asylum, and in the person of Mickey Traynor, "the holy telly man" (McCabe, 1992: 100), who sells holy pictures and televisions. It is unsurprising then that, just as Mickey sells dud television sets, his daughter, who sees an apparition of the Virgin Mary, offers a dud message. Like Queen Victoria, who never bothers to show up and appreciate the town's fountain erected in her honour, the Queen of Heaven fails to appear and save the town from the end of the world.[6] The miracle on this occasion turns out, like other Jordan miracles, to be a secular one, with the Virgin Mary being replaced by Francie.

Butler Cullingford has argued that Jordan's engagement with Catholicism and organised and institutional religion is not uncritical. This is obvious in the casting as the Virgin Mary of singer Sinéad O'Connor, who is known for her controversial and very public relationship with the Catholic Church, which, she argues, is guilty of abusing its power. (In a later ironic twist, O'Connor, subsequent to the making and release of *The Butcher Boy*, was ordained a priest.) An equally pertinent factor in her casting is aesthetic. As with *Angel*'s Veronica Quilligan, in whom Jordan observed a similarity to Velázquez's Virgin Mary,

O'Connor has a facial structure similar to the dominant images of Our Lady (see Butler Cullingford, 2001; and McLoone, 1998: 35; 2000: 218–19).

The Virgin gives "out-of-date" or mis-information to Francie which causes him to learn of his unhappy origins in Bundoran, which is also where Joe disowns him, while her visitations lead to Father Sullivan's (Tiddly's) interest in him and, later, to electric shock treatment, as Butler Cullingford (2001: 253) observes. Religion itself, how it is practised and organised, are also found wanting. Despite the ubiquity of religious imagery — statues, holy pictures and crucifixes — within and without the home (consider the Bradys', Nugents' and Purcells' houses; the psychiatrist's office; the Catholic institution for young boys; the town's procession and spectacle laid on for the Virgin, complete with singing girls in their First Communion dresses; and the local priest's public prayer for the soul of the murderous Francie), there is little evidence of any Christian ethos or practical help given by the church or the (Catholic) community to Francie (and his family).

It is this more insidious neglect and abuse of power that is highlighted, rather than the sexual abuse at the hands of Father Sullivan (Milo O'Shea). Even if it is not required of the film in terms of some realist agenda, it is clear that his actions do not reflect the reality and extent of abuse and corruption within Ireland's various industrial and reform schools at the time. Firstly, Sullivan, obsessed with the image of his mother in bonnets and the great Mother of God, never seems to go beyond masturbation; and, secondly, the whole episode is treated in a light comic fashion. Sullivan's abuse has no detrimental effect on Francie — or, at least, through humour which belies his deeper hurt, Francie contains or manages the abuse and exploitation — until, that is, the priest forces him to remember his mother and how he killed her.

Instead, Francie's special status (and his relationship with Tiddly) works to his advantage: he is freed from the routine of work and rewarded with sweets by Tiddly, while Father Bubbles (Brendan Gleeson), who has Tiddly sent off to his sister in Dublin "moryah", gives him custard creams and the "Francie Brady

Not a Bad Bastard Anymore Diploma" to ensure his silence on the matter. Interestingly, the gardener (Tom Hickey) who is critical of the priests — the "effing sky pilots" — but who refuses to stand up to them, writes off the abuse as the effect of what the "Balubas"[7] did to him. *Dancing at Lughnasa* makes a similar statement through the priest who returns from the missions as someone who enjoys paganism and sensuality of the body, but in that case there is no suggestion of abuse. Therefore, Tiddly becomes an aberration within the church rather than, as Butler Cullingford suggests, a metaphor for the church's abuse of power where his playing with Francie is the sexual equivalent of his (colonising) missionary work in Africa.[8] That said, the embarrassed explanation, Francie's detention in the boiler house, and Tiddly's enforced departure, reflects how the church covered up incidents of sexual abuse whereby the cleric was simply (re)moved and was free to and invariably did, re-offend.

This is supported in the recent scandals of child abuse concerning the Catholic Church in Ireland (and elsewhere, notably, the USA, Australia and Canada) documented in Mary Raftery's and Eoin O'Sullivan's disturbing study *Suffer the Little Children* (1999), a number of television documentaries including the seminal *Dear Daughter* (Louis Lentin, 1996), the three-part *States of Fear* (Mary Raftery, RTE, 1999), and *Saints and Sinners* (Orla Walsh, 2001).

Before any of these were made, the formally rich and provocative *Our Boys* (Cathal Black, 1981) was produced, in which interviews, actuality footage and dramatisation mingle to produce a snapshot which, while retaining some degree of sympathy for the Christian Brothers and the closing of their school, exposes their system as (physically) abusive and controlling. Despite RTE, the national public service broadcaster, supporting the film financially, they refused to screen it for ten years fearing it would offend the still dominant Church.

A decade further on, though, following the screening of RTE's *Cardinal Secrets* (Mary Raftery, 2002), there were calls for the resignation of the head of the Dublin Archdiocese, Cardinal Desmond Connell, who colluded in the cover-up and protection of paedophile Catholic priests, and who refused to fully co-operate with the civil authorities in the prosecution of clerical child abusers. By then, the moral authority of the church had been shattered.

Nevertheless, the related issues of management and practice within "orphanages" and educational/industrial/reform institutions is somewhat distorted in The Butcher Boy. They were largely funded by the state (and not as charity as is commonly presumed), were run predominantly by Christian Brothers (in the case of boys) and the Sisters of Mercy (for boys under ten, and girls) and not, as is the case in The Butcher Boy, by priests, while the prevailing culture was that of oppression, violence, neglect and exploitation, something which is explored in The Magdalene Sisters (Peter Mullan, 2002), in which the brutal treatment by nuns of unmarried mothers is depicted.

While these elements are hinted at in the turf-cutting scenes, the dining hall and, in the absence of formal learning, it is overshadowed by the warm if tough friendship that Bubbles seems to offer not just to Francie, but to the four bogmen "protection" group, and the more generalised culture of violence that exists within the community. This is evident in Sergeant Sausage's comment when he leaves Francie at the school, "If he were one of mine, I'd break every bone in his body."

However, considering that such widescale abuse was perpetrated by the Catholic Church — which in Ireland held the "moral monopoly" — remains problematic. That they were effectively supported by the State, despite a growing awareness, certainly from the 1940s, that such a "care" system was inadequate and counterproductive to the needs of children, speaks volumes of the uncritical power the church exercised, and the mutually beneficial financial arrangements for church, state (and, ultimately, middle-class Irish society). As Austin Clarke writes in his poem "Corporal Punishment" (1955),[9] which represents the state as complicit with the church in this enterprise, "all enquiry is boxed in office". Put crudely, in the short term, "the institutional model for the processing of children into adulthood by religious orders was undoubtedly the cheapest option available" (Raftery and O'Sullivan, 1999: 15), even though it was counter to the official ideology of the primacy of the family.

It is of note that Mrs Nugent (out of anger and disgust) and the gossiping women (out of idle sympathy) understand Francie's behaviour as the result of an unhappy and dysfunctional family. (Nevertheless, they all fear Francie.) When Francie is good it is because he wants to position himself within a loving family. He "saves" his mother from suicide, watches television with his dad, cleans the house for him when his mother is in hospital, brings her home a gift after he has run away, though the bitter irony is that she has already killed herself, and provides for and cares for his father when he returns from the industrial "school". In fact, Benny tells Francie when he visits him at the "school for pigs" that he and Alo were in an industrial school just after the Second World War, thus hinting at the incompleteness or inadequacy of their family as Benny seeks to bond with his son. This father–son fantasy continues after Benny dies at home. In a wonderfully gothic moment, Francie knocks the flies from his "sleeping" face and protects him from "Dracula". (Francie's relationship with Joe is also about love and family. He is not just a friend who comes from, at least in an Irish Catholic context, an equally incomplete family — he is, as Philip seems to be, an only child — but he is Francie's blood brother. It is Joe, not Francie, who makes them blood brothers, and Joe cries when he ends their friendship.)

To expect a realist representation of the industrial school, however, is to miss the point, for this is Francie's world. Furthermore, it must be remembered that the institution offers Francie an alternative identity to that proposed by Mrs Nugent. For the first time, he is free not to be a pig, but can unlock "something precious" and be divine, by becoming one with the images and religio-mystical stories he finds there. A photograph of altar boys motivates Francie to be one; Fr Sullivan's sermon about the three children to whom Mary appears allows him to see himself as worthy; while the school's ethos of inherent goodness delivers him of his previous guilt and responsibility to the extent that he can ask his father, "What did I do [wrong]?"

Put another way, Francie, like the schizophrenic who cannot define the limits of himself and shares too close a proximity with his surroundings, is nothing more than a reflection of his physical and emotional environment. He is mad or dysfunctional only in so far as the society is. As such he is a cultural projection of Ireland of the late 1950s and early 1960s, caught between Catholic oppression and state control (the rational) and superstition and mysticism (the irrational). Or, on the one hand, between tradition, cultural protectionism, and economic poverty and stagnation, and, on the other hand, modernity and (non-Irish) bourgeois values.

It is of note that the young Philip Nugent plays "Fur Elise" and not music from *Emerald Gems of Ireland* (as in the case of McCabe's novel). That said, there is an eclectic mix of music — which goes beyond the confines of Irish music — not only on the soundtrack, but played during Alo's party and the trumpet performances. Indeed, music is central to the understanding and rendering of Francie's world, as it is more generally in the work of both McCabe and Jordan. In the case of Jordan, not only is the figure of the (jazz) musician employed, but the film's musical accompaniment is carefully selected from the popular cultural repertoire which, like Baz Luhrmann in *Moulin Rouge* (2002) or Umberto Eco's ironic gesture,[10] gives renewed meaning to the original as it contributes to and condenses the film's theme.

It is no accident that "Night in Tunisia", *Mona Lisa*, *The Crying Game*, and *In Dreams* take their titles from musical compositions. This is also the case with *The Butcher Boy*, in which the eponymous song is central to both the novel's and the film's narrative. It mirrors the tragedy of Annie's unhappy condition, brought about, the song suggests, by a pregnancy out of wedlock and Benny's resentment of her and his own past. As such, it positions both Benny and Francie as butcher boys who let the woman down. While Jordan uses the song most effectively when she and Benny fight — "I wish I was a maid again" plays on the soundtrack — he draws on an additional musical commentary by giving Francie another theme or identity through the song "Where are You?", even if Francie himself does not consciously adopt it. Francie is not simply a (double) murderer, but the lover who has been removed from paradise: love (as innocence) is lost. In a sense then, just as he is a reality of the contradictory aspects of Ireland's culture (McLoone, 1998: 36; 2000: 221–2) he also occupies the contradictory positions of butcher boy (the father) and spurned lover (mother).

The melancholic "Where are You?", lusciously performed by Frank Sinatra, opens the film's magic-photo-realist centre-piece, and succinctly sums up Francie's sense of loss and isola-tion. Having survived the industrial school, Francie returns to the town, to Joe and his father, and it would appear, to happy times, only better because with his job at Leddy's he can buy a million trillion flash bars, and provide for his dad and Joe, but things have moved on. Two new boys "own" the fountain now, while Joe, following another altercation they have with Mrs Nugent's thuggish brothers, disowns him which, after Francie having told him of Father Tiddly, seems inevitable, and his fa-ther is sick (with tuberculosis?).

When his father dies (in the armchair), Francie denies the reality. But then there is little difference save a few flies be-tween Benny's corpse and his former drunken stupors. Francie continues his now nurturing housewifely relationship with him, tells him of his problem with the Nugents and that he loves him, while he provides their entertainment — the radio which offers music and yet another programme on American politics and the 1962 Cuban missile crisis. In a typical Jordan gesture, Francie, for the first time, plays his father's trumpet.

However, this domestic scene is destroyed when the suspi-cious doctor and sergeant call around. It is they, not Joe as the Irish colleen tells Francie, who peer through the window at the dead Benny, before they break in and sedate Francie, who screams for his da to help. As the instrumental opening music of "Where are You?" plays, soft white petals gently fall over Francie, then Benny. We are outside, and Francie is lying down on the grass amid snowdrops. Disconcerted, he wakes up, but in answer to Sinatra's croon, "Where are you? Where have you gone without me, I thought you cared about me. Where are you?", Joe's head pops into frame and says, "There you are, I was looking for you."

Together again, and in an echo of the opening scene, they are on the mountaintop looking down at the grey lake from which suddenly erupts a huge nuclear explosion mushroom cloud. This is a loaded image. At its most basic, this is Francie's personal end of the world — his parents are dead — and an intimate imagining of the real nuclear threat which throughout the film is signalled in the unremitting references to the Cuban missile crisis and the 1961 "Bay of *Pigs* incident" by the media (television and radio), particularly when Francie breaks into Mrs Nugent's home and looks at "the duck and cover" documentary on television; the gossiping townswomen; the various people he encounters on his travels; and, indirectly, the portraits of President John F. Kennedy, Ireland's answer to royalty, which are always juxtaposed against religious images.

At another level, the explosion can be read as a metaphor for the cultural and economic bomb of transformation, modernisation and globalisation which McLoone, perhaps too narrowly, but nonetheless relevantly, reads in terms of the establishment in 1962 of Ireland's first national television station — the Trojan horse in the home for foreign popular culture. (Cinema, music and comics also shape Francie's life, as does official Irish culture albeit, in the ornament he buys in Dublin, transformed into a piece of sentimental commercial kitsch celebrating the simple rural ideal — the colleen, the turf, and the limewashed cottage.) To this end, McLoone cites the station's inauguration speech given by Ireland's President, Eamon de Valera: "Like atomic energy, it can be used for incalculable good but it can also do irreparable harm" (McLoone, 2000: 217).

In terms of representation, the explosion is, as McLoone suggests, one of the most subversive images within Irish cinema. In that single moment, the dominant representation of the Irish landscape is destroyed and its mythic and constructed nature revealed.[11] This is not simply an anti-pastoral statement, but an engagement with the landscape and its representation. As such, it serves the same purpose as the fake backdrop of sublime nature in *The Quiet Man*, when Sean Thornton stands on the bridge and looks towards the equally unreal, though physically present and comforting maternal home, "White O'Morn" (its dream status undercut by its derelict condition).

That said, the explosion is not seen as a special effect, but as real. Accordingly, it goes beyond John Ford, and becomes approximate to David Lynch's *Blue Velvet*. It takes pleasure in its very perfection and stylisation, but, nonetheless, suggests a blackness, a disease or a violence at its core, which reflects paradise lost and the encroachment of civilisation and history (see Leo Marx, 1964). With the death of his parents, the pastoral ideal, bound to the idea of origins and the notion of plentitude — the semi-primitivist place of supernatural perfection, "'between', yet in a transcendent relation to, the opposing forces of civilization [culture] and nature" (Marx, 1964: 23) — is no longer possible. (However, a version of it, complete with snowdrops and Our Lady, even if it is tinged with loss, is re-imagined in the final scene of the film, when he is finally released from the mental institution and during which plays "Where are You?".)

Grene (2000) makes a similar point in an analysis of Martin McDonagh's *The Beauty Queen of Leenane*, Frank McCourt's *Angela's Ashes* (which also deals with an "abused" childhood), and Jordan's *The Butcher Boy*, in which he argues that the 1990s in Ireland saw a new engagement with the landscape, which he sums up as "black pastoral". These works "self-consciously invert or flout the earlier convention of the form" (Grene, 2000: 68), reworking the dominant tropes related to the pastoral (the mother, childhood, emigration) so that the very desire to return to origins is mocked. Though this magic realist perfection is also common to the numerous heritage-type films that were produced during the 1980s and 1990s, it is clearly of a different order, with the latter privileging nostalgia over ironic or critical engagement. (Of course, critical engagement with representations of landscape and the pastoral has been one of the features of Irish cinema, particularly during, but also since the 1970s and 1980s, With few exceptions — including *Korea* and *December Bride* — this has also meant a sacrificing of the picturesque and beauty in favour of presenting an invisible, unremarkable or ugly

[handwritten margin note: the same theory can be applied to Rice's book.]

landscape.) Following his separation from his father, Francie's need of Joe becomes even more pronounced. The two — the last survivors on earth — walk through the decimated town which still burns and where charred pigs and disembodied voices take the place of the various townspeople. Suddenly, in a marriage of the western and science-fiction, they are confronted by a bug-eyed alien on horseback. It is none other than Tiddly. Francie and Joe run.

"And you say the alien looked like?" asks the psychiatrist, who for a moment appears like the alien of his vision. The session with the ineffectual psychiatrist (played after all by Sean Hughes, a comedian!) is then interrupted when a picture of Our Lady (next to one of Kennedy) winks at him. Off he is sent for electric shock treatment — rendered as a visceral trip into hyperspace — before he escapes (disgusted at the other mad men and how they treat mass as a football game) from yet another institution inappropriate to his needs and once again returns home. Yet, there is no home, no ma, da, Alo or Joe. The Virgin appears on the screen of the broken television, comfortingly telling him that Joe is his friend and could not be gone, before she sings "Beautiful Bundoran", the second rendition of the song, the first being during the party for Alo. This gives him the idea of returning to his origins — as Francie says, "where it all began" and the honeymoon location of his parents, the maternal nostalgic playground. It is also there that Joe is at boarding school.

Happy at last that he is part of something good, he cycles along the busy seafront (a familiar trope of Jordan's — *Night in Tunisia* collection, *Dream of the Beast*, *The Past*, *Mona Lisa*, *The Miracle*, *The Crying Game* and *The Good Thief*). When he finds a photograph of his parents posing as Tarzan and Jane — the same one as he saw at Alo's party — hanging on the wall of the Over the Waves hotel, it promises to make real his father's fantasy of lying with Annie on the bed listening to the waves, playing the trumpet, and saying the rosary on the rocks.

The photographs, both this and the one that sits on their piano, in which they stand windswept by a car amidst a wild Irish traditional landscape, as documentary evidence, is clearly a

Jordan contribution, not just because there is no such photograph of them in the novel — the guesthouse owner wants to
forget them — but because it is a device used elsewhere in
Jordan's work, notably *The Past*, *Mona Lisa*, and *The Miracle*.
However, like the picture of Dil (*The Crying Game*) which only
describes the surface, the honeymoon image is nothing but a
visual lie which only brings bitter disappointment to Francie, of
whom there is no photograph. (He is literally denied a fixed
identity.) The hotel owner, realising who the "love birds" were,
tells Francie in an echo of Mrs Nugent, that his father was no
better than a pig. The photograph, like the lake, explodes.

Unable to deal with the truth of the unhappy origins of his
drunk father who always treated his mother badly, he runs out
of the hotel with a bottle of whiskey and, like Benny, gets
drunk on the beach. There he kicks the same Tarzan and Jane
cutout, which earlier, reliving the mother's and father's happiness, he had enjoyed popping his head into, and yelling: "Who
wants to be Mr and Mrs Monkey anyhow?" Francie and his family, it would seem, are trapped in the identity of pigs.

Both images — pigs and monkeys — are equally loaded
within Irish culture, and, like the figure of the unruly, irrational
and willful child, have been made to function as metaphors or
symbols of the Irish. Unsurprisingly, given Ireland's post-
colonial relationship with Britain, these stereotypes of the Irish
as monkeys, or the pig as part of the Irish family, predominantly
have had a British currency, most especially in the pages of
Punch, which was responding to the rise of militant Fenianism at
the same time as an increase in Irish migration to England occasioned by the Great Famine. However, these images also circulated within American popular culture.[12] An early series of films
produced by Thomas Edison's film production company features Casey, a negatively stereotyped Irish man, who is represented as impetuous, stupid and drunk. In one of these, *Casey's
Twins* (1903), a pig (dressed in clothes) and infant share the
same crib and fight on the floor over a bottle.

If the image of the monkey was not confined to the Irish
(consider British representations of the French as apes), but
became so through repeated use, the pig, while not having a

quasi-scientific basis like the monkey, which suggested the Irish as an evolutionary missing link, was more rooted in the Irish experience. The pig was in fact an important animal for many poor Irish families. It lived on their slops, but provided them with income or a valued source of meat. Put another way, the smelly pig in the kitchen (noisily and vulgarly eating) transformed waste into capital. If from an urban or modern perspective the pig by its proximity degraded humans, from a British one, it was yet another instance of Irish independence and self-sufficiency: the pig was a domestic animal and served the family rather than the Empire.

To be a pig then is not just to be uncouth; it is to be too Irish and too rooted in the past, and not like Mrs Nugent with her modern "sophistication" borrowed from the English — although more in line with the new social and economic smugness of the Lemassite era. Indeed, the title of Cathal Black's 1984 film *Pigs* refers to the *marginalised outsiders* who squat in a derelict Georgian house in Dublin. Francie, through the neglect of his family and the state, is clearly one such outsider, and not the first Irish pig to turn into a murderous wild boar (see Foster, 1993: 186).[13]

Believing that at least he can have Joe, Francie rides off to his final disappointment. He arrives after "lights out" at the boarding school, a swisher version of the school for pigs, and makes a scene in one of the dormitories, which attracts Joe's attention. After Joe rejects his friendship and the chance to "ride out" with him, the priests physically drag Francie out and one of them, who subsequently is revealed to be one of the large-headed, green bug-eyed aliens, ironically tells him to go home. Though Francie acknowledges Joe's rejection, he cannot accept that it was actually his old friend. The only explanation is fantastic: the aliens (or Mrs Nugent who stands in for them as she does for communism or Britons), like in the film he saw in Dublin, *The Brain from Planet Arous* (Nathan Juran, 1958), or in Don Siegel's *The Invasion of the Body Snatchers* (1956) must have taken him over. A final mushroom cloud — clearly a television image — explodes.

He returns to his hometown where the whole community, even the village drunk, Jimmy the Skite (played by author Pat McCabe), is preparing for the appearance of Our Lady. Complete with welcoming banners to the Queen of Heaven, they want it to seem as if it is the holiest, brightest, happiest town in the whole of Ireland.[14] While the villagers carry statues and pictures of the Sacred Heart, Francie pushes his butcher tools and barrow across the diamond to Mrs Nugent's house. In a logical reply to his personal apocalypse, he delivers with his pig gun his end of the world message to Mrs Nugent as he tells her she won the Purcell-Brady-Nugent battle. We (as Mrs Nugent, like the victims in Michael Powell's *Peeping Tom*, 1960) see the murder in the mirror. Frenzied, he chops down on her with a large cleaver as he recites the childhood nursery-rhyme, "This little piggy went to the market . . ." while the hymn "Sweet Heart of Jesus" is sung on the soundtrack.

Though this recalls Stanley Kubrick's *A Clockwork Orange* (1971, the "Singin' in the Rain" scene) and his later *The Shining* (1980), given its double quotation suggesting innocence, purity and sensual or spiritual beauty, and the fact that Francie is a child, it is more powerful. This juxtaposition is visually echoed in the image of the rising and falling cleaver and the blood slashing across a statue of Our Lady, and also in the "reaction" shot from another statue in the town diamond which looks to heaven[15] while the townspeople punch in time waiting for Our Lady, gossiping, drinking tea, oblivious to what has happened.

Francie then wheels her body through the diamond, exchanging pleasantries with the women folk, and dumps her cut-up body into the brock heap (the pigs' food) behind Leddy's. Mrs Coyle (Anita Reeves) is left to find the murder scene where all over the walls the word "PIG" smeared in blood, in a gruesome echo of his earlier lipstick effort, when he broke into her house for the first time and defecated in her sitting room. (This writing on the wall is repeated in *In Dreams*.)

When Mrs Coyle runs horrified from the house, the crowd believe she has seen the promised spectacle, and that Traynor's daughter was right after all. That another child from the same village claims to have seen the Virgin and discusses with her the end of the world, is further evidence that Francie only reflects "the paranoia and mysticism" that Jordan speaks of which prevailed in Ireland during this time. Just as the moving statue phenomenon in 1980s' Ireland suggests a culture in transition, where Catholicism and the general suppression of the body was being challenged by a more secular, global liberal materialism, so, too, do such incidents indicate a moment of crisis.[16]

Culturally speaking, the end of the world did come, or at least an end to a certain type of insular Ireland bound by de Valera's vision of the idealised frugal, simple peasant and athletic youth (Francie's boney-arsed bogmen), which is epitomised in Francie's present to his mother. Ironically, this romantic rural ideal was only ever a product of the urban (Dublin) middle-class imagination and did not reflect Irish reality, where the cottage had already become associated with backwardness.[17] Consequently, it is fitting that he should buy it in Dublin, where in a further irony it serves capitalism (and modernity): it is nothing more than a cheap mass-produced tourist image.

Indeed, that he misses his mother there and seeks a type of ideological shelter echoes the experience of the majority of country people who worked in Dublin but, like Francie, they couldn't take their mothers with them and retreated to the country at weekends. Even if the small-town rural community could be critiqued, as it is even in heritage films, it nonetheless remained an essential escape-valve from the city and modernity, as is seen in the television feature adaptation of Maeve Binchy's novel *The Lilac Bus* (Giles Foster, 1990). Regardless of its ideological significance, the souvenir makes aesthetic sense and is typical of the mass-produced standardised ornaments that decorated working- and lower-middle-class homes of the time, tourist-cultural artifacts which Belfast artist John Kindness in a number of his sculptures literally incorporates and reworks.[18]

The interlinking of the two shows — Our Lady's non-appearance and Francie's over-appearance — inevitably alters their meaning. Arguably, it gives Mrs Nugent's murder the status of a (secular) miracle (with Our Lady as complicit or powerless) and points to the emptiness and theatricality of religion despite all its sensuous props and sound system — the singing, statues, pictures and burning candles — or at least points to the hypocrisy and fickleness of the Christian crowd, summed up in the various comments (and behaviour) of Jimmy the Skite.

In this, Jordan not only returns to *We're No Angels* and *The Miracle*, but also to Fellini's poetic masterpiece *La Strada*. During a religious procession, Fellini shows us the cardboard backing of the holy images as well as the images themselves. As Millicent Marcus observes, this has the effect of "suggesting that the ecclesiastical world is as guilty of showmanship and illusionism as is Il Matto who, in the very next scene, has his own apotheosis on the high wire connecting the *church façade* to the *tavern* across the street" (emphasis added).[19] That film's phenomenological realism — favouring the individual, mysticism and spirituality over, but located within, if transcendent to, raw reality — is also common to *The Butcher Boy*, but also to Jordan's work generally, both in his writing and filmmaking.

Francie is brought off to jail, where, in yet another slippage of identity, he is disturbed that hanging has been outlawed.[20] He then makes his escape by leading the guards to the supposed burial site of the body, but instead he takes them to the chicken coop, where earlier he had taken Philip and which brought down on him the wrath of Mrs Nugent and her brothers as well as Joe's disapproval. Inside the expressionistically lit coop — the fan interrupts the light so that it is a frenetic place of energy and violence — he finds the chain with which he beat Philip and swings it at the police. He slides down the runway to freedom. While they search for him, he takes refuge in his (and Joe's) hideout by the river, where he reads the imaginary narrative of his own escape in which *The Fugitive*'s Richard Kimble is quoted as taking his hat off to the young Francie, the last of a number of references to the popular television series.

Before he sets fire to his own house, to the diegetic musical accompaniment (he turns on the record) of Rossini and the Lone Ranger theme from the *William Tell* overture, he sends off the two boy guardians of the fountain to the brock heap, where he promises they will find a million trillion flash bars. Instead, they find Mrs Nugent's mutilated and rotting body parts. Their subsequent reactions of repulsion and fascination, respectively, put into context Francie's behaviour, but also problematise the notion of child innocence.

Though the boys' unsavoury interest in the body has gone unmentioned, the child as killer was the focus of a number of reviews. In the British context, reference has been made to the murder of Jamie Bulger[21] by two pre-teenage boys, while in America, reviewers alluded to the Jonesboro High School killings. Such attempts to find real-life analogies to Francie are ultimately less rewarding than the allegorical reading of McLoone and his understanding of Francie as a metaphor for a damaged and abused nation, who is driven to violently respond to that abuse; or, to see Francie as a register of the cultural effect of Ireland's linguistic crisis and (subsequent) indebtedness to British and American popular culture;[22] or, more simply and inclusively, a snapshot of Ireland in transition: for Francie's story, like Rosaleen's dreams (*The Company of Wolves*) or the confessional narrative of *Usual Suspects* (Bryan Singer, 1995) is nothing but a fantastic patchwork quilt of meaningful and deliberate quotation and linguistic somersaults where simile and metaphor become literal.

Notes

[1] The use of special effects to create a new or enhanced reality that otherwise could not be physically rendered or filmed was used to great effect by Rob Legato in *Interview with the Vampire*. It is a testimony to his work that much of it is invisible.

[2] Patrick McCabe debunks the myth of Alo's success and reveals that he is in fact a lowly worker. This underside of the emigration success story is explored cinematically in Thaddeus O'Sullivan's *A Pint Of Plain* (1977), where a version of a delusional Alo dreams of returning home. Jordan also, in *Mona Lisa*, presented an all-too realistic image of a young Irish girl of fifteen who is "on the game" in King's Cross. Of course this constant haemorrhage of the Irish to Britain also made a joke of Ireland's policy of self-sufficiency.

3 The much-quoted 1943 St. Patrick's Day speech by de Valera out-lines his vision for Ireland, where people would be satisfied with "fru-gal comfort . . . devote their leisure to things of the spirit"; a country of "cosy homesteads, . . . sturdy children, . . . athletic youths, . . . comely maidens", and people gathered around the fireside (*Irish Press*, 18 March 1943: 1, cited in Brown, 1981, and elsewhere; see also But-ler Cullingford, 2001: 251).

4 It is significant that Rea plays the older Francie, and as such provides the voice-over to the young Francie's imagination and his perception of events, as well as playing Francie's father, Benny. This has the effect of recontextualising Benny and his own dysfunctional upbringing and exclusion from the nuclear family ideal.

5 Unlike McCabe, Jordan does not have her cry, which causes the young Francie to feel sorry for her.

6 There is no mention of Queen Victoria in the film; see McCabe, (1992: 103).

7 The Balubas are an important Congolese tribe, mainly based in the province of Katanga, who entered the Irish lexicon in the early 1960s when a number of Irish soldiers on United Nations peacekeeping duty were killed by them as the Balubas sought to assert Congolese na-tional unity in the wake of the departure of the Belgian colonial power and the attempts to secede Katanga from the state. The term became a familiar one in Irish schoolyards as a means of threatening or pour-ing abuse on another.

8 Generally it was the case that the younger and more engaged clergy went to the missions, thereby leaving the more conservative and tradi-tional clergy behind. See Austin Clarke's poem, "Flight to Africa", in *The Collected Poems of Austin Clarke*, Dublin: Dolmen Press, 1974: 252–4.

9 Ibid., p. 271.

10 See Umberto Eco (1985), "Postmodernism, Irony, the Enjoyable", in *Reflections on "The Name of the Rose"*, trans. William Weaver, London: Secker and Warburg, 67–72.

11 A similar image is presented in Sean Hillen's montage *Collecting Me-teorites at Knowth, Irelantis*, in which he reimagines John Hinde's classic postcard of two red-headed children gathering turf and loading it into

a donkey's panniers. In Hillen's piece, they gather meteorites while a huge nuclear power plant looms in the background. John Kindness has also reworked Hinde's original but to a different end by substituting drugs and syringe needles for the turf.

12 See image reproduced in L.P. Curtis (1971) of "American Gold" (1882) drawn by Frederick Opper, which appeared in *Puck*, vol. 11, no. 272, p. 194. It shows in one section a ragged family of ape-like Irish surrounded by pigs and an empty whiskey bottle.

13 In RTE television's adaptation by Louis Lentin of Eugene McCabe's *Roma*, transmitted on 29 November 1979, Mick Lally plays a character with the same name as Francie's father, Benny Brady, or colloquially, Benny the Blind and Benny the Brock, the latter a reference to his task early in the film of feeding pigs. The parallel with *The Butcher Boy* does not stop there, because Benny has a fascination with the Virgin Mary, to whom he prays intensively, and with Maria, the teenage daughter of Italian immigrants who run the town's Roma café. Benny is in love with Maria, thinking that she is as pure as the Virgin. When Maria disabuses him of this notion after she finds a love letter to her written on the reverse side of a painting of Our Lady, the Beckett-like demeanour of devout Benny is shattered, and before leaving town he goes to the priest to confess that he has lost hope. Benny has already revealed to Maria that his father, like Patrick McCabe's Mrs Brady, had spent time in a mental hospital. Additionally, Benny's friend is named Joe, though unlike twelve-year-old Joe in Jordan's film, he is an adult, and is more akin to the drunkard Jimmy the Skite. The television film ends with Benny alone, standing still on a deserted rural road, a bleak landscape not unlike ones evident in Samuel Beckett's work. While Benny is no Francie Brady (he does not kill, but internalises his oppression), the depiction of Benny as from a dysfunctional family, the use of the Virgin Mary, and, more generally, the pathology which is generated in small-town Ireland, has prescient parallels to McCabe's text.

14 This scene has some interesting parallels to another small-town Irish film, *Saints and Sinners* (Leslie Arliss, 1949), from a script by Paul Vincent Carroll, a controversial Catholic priest. In this film, Ma Murnaghan (Maire O'Neill), whose predictions have often come true, upsets the local Canon with her prediction of the end of the world.

15 There are similar "reaction shots" of religious statues in *Mona Lisa*, *We're No Angels*, *The Miracle*, *Michael Collins* and *The End of the Affair*.

16 For a discussion of how Irish society responded to the "modern" world with belief in apparitions of the Virgin Mary and "moving statues", see Tim Ryan and Jurek Krakowsky (1985), *Ballinspittle: Moving Statues and Faith*, Cork/Dublin: The Mercier Press; and Colm Toibin, ed. (1985), *Seeing is Believing: Moving Statues in Ireland*, Laois: Pilgrim Press.

17 See Brian Kennedy (1993), "The Traditional Irish Thatched House: Image and Reality, 1973–1993", in *Visualizing Ireland*, Adele M. Dalsimer, ed., Boston/London: Faber and Faber.

18 See essay, "Precious Ornaments", by John Carson, in *Kindness* [Exhibition Catalogue], Dublin: Douglas Hyde Gallery, 1990, unpaginated.

19 Marcus, Millicent (1986), *Italian Film in the Light of Neorealism*, New Jersey: Princeton University Press, 149.

20 For an exploration of the theme of capital punishment in Ireland, see Brendan Behan's 1956 play, *The Quare Fellow*, which was directed for the screen in 1962 by Arthur Dreifuss.

21 At the time, the media was implicated, with the suggestion that the killers were motivated after being exposed to the horror film *Child's Play 3* (Jack Bender, 1991); it transpired later that this had not been the case. (See David Buckingham (1996), *Moving Images*, Manchester: Manchester University Press.) However, in Francie's case, he does suffer from an over-identification with everything around him. For example, it is only after he hears Tiddly's sermon of Mary's apparition to the three children that she appears to him. That said, his murder is provoked by his tragic circumstances. He would have been happy to continue with his cowboys and injuns fantasy had events not overtaken him.

22 See Kevin Rockett, *The Los Angelesation of Ireland* (forthcoming).

Chapter Twelve

In Dreams (1999)

Even though *In Dreams* was less than enthusiastically received by both critics and audiences, it represents Jordan at his cinematic, if not narrative, best.[1] Notwithstanding its dark gothic sensibility, where literally the sins of the parents haunt the child, it is a beautiful piece of visual poetry that looks to the past and to the best of European art cinema, while, at the same time, to Hollywood and American popular culture. After all, it is a veritable catalogue of cinematic references and horror riffs,[2] but not in the superior tongue-in-check surfaceness of most contemporary horror or, more generally, postmodern cinema. *In Dreams* takes itself and the fantastic seriously, and locates us in a mythic and primal world of the unconscious, of oedipal desire and sin, and of fairytales.

Accordingly, *In Dreams* is more than a story about a serial killer whose victims are little girls or the killer's possession of the mother of one such victim. Indeed, in its exploration of the nuclear family, and through a complex merging of love and jealousy, victim and killer, child and adult, sanity and insanity and, most explicitly, dream and reality, *In Dreams* is concerned with problematising such (rational) ways of perceiving the world. As Jordan has said, "I just like stories that go to points that are beyond explanation". This interest in the fantastic or the supernatural may be understood, as Jordan himself does, within the context of a specifically Irish cultural tradition of "striving unrealism", which includes such writers as James Stephens,

Bram Stoker and Flann O'Brien (Byrne, 1999: 23). Certainly, this aesthetic is palpable in Synge's description of the Aran islanders as a superstitious people (*Riders to the Sea, Aran Islands*)[3] and has been cinematically explored in the surreal *By Accident* (J.N.G. Davidson, 1930), the occult short films of Hilton Edwards and Michael MacLiammóir (*Return to Glennascaul*, 1951, *From Time to Time*, 1953), *The Kinkisha* (Tommy McArdle, 1977), and, more recently in the comedy which suggests an affinity between the Irish and the aborigines, *On the Nose* (David Caffrey, 2000).

Similarly, the family can be seen as an Irish preoccupation. Even in the Irish Constitution, the family is recognised as the basic unit of the state, while it has been one of the staples of Irish cinema,[4] particularly since the 1970s, where it has been dissected and challenged. Like *Psycho*, these films, including *Traveller, The Field,* and *The Butcher Boy*, as already discussed, largely view the family as a psychosexual quagmire of repression and violence.

Nevertheless, *In Dreams* remains clearly an American film. While this owes in part to its production — it was made for DreamWorks — the largely American cast, and that it is set in New England, the film's interest in the pastoral ideal (figured as the unnatural lake, the forest, the orchard/cider factory)[5] give it a particular American resonance. As Leo Marx has observed, the pastoral ideal "has been used to define the meaning of America ever since the age of discovery" (Marx, 1964: 3). In other words, the striving for the utopian landscape is simultaneously a striving for origins and a coherent narrative: in short, a search for the perfect family. However, as Francie (in *The Butcher Boy*) discovers and Vivian in *In Dreams* knows, even though he tries to believe otherwise and wears the cider factory's logo — "The Good Apple" — on his coat, Eden's apple is already rotten, or, in fairytale terms, poison and "death the germ within it".[6] That said, death here, as in fairytales, does not really mean finality. It is clear that Rebecca does not simply cease to exist, but waits for her mother to resolve her own oedipal conflicts before she can join her beyond the looking glass (arguably Rebecca had always been there) and (re)enter the original home. Therefore, Claire's suicidal drive into the lake, which would release her from the various emotional obstacles and from the killer Vivian, whom she haunts as he does her, is doomed to fail. It is only by negotiating these and rejecting the bad mother (Vivian's, and Snow White's) that she can pass (without her phallic stiletto heels) to another (higher) version of being and embrace her daughter again. This poetic and romantic underwater image is the fairytale's happy ending.

Unfortunately, it is not the film's only ending. Like *Company of Wolves*, a second ending is given in which an imprisoned Vivian, having been found guilty but insane, is haunted by Claire. In a reprise of Mary Plunkett in *High Spirits*, she appears in a mirror from which she reaches out, though unlike the angel Mary, she delivers punishment and smashes his head against it. While this provides the visceral twist reminiscent of *Candyman* (Bernard Rose, 1992), and fits the ideologically problematic, though often commercially driven, open ending of recent horror, this final "jump" is delivered at the expense of the film's integrity. In *Candyman*, it allows Helen to become one with the monster who represents the uncanny underside of society and the world of the irrational, myth and transgressed borders. Why Claire *still* haunts his dreams after she has found peace with her daughter is a puzzle. In *The Sixth Sense* (M. Night Shyamalan) and the darker and ultimately finer *Stir of Echoes* (David Koepp) which were also released in 1999 and explore similar territory, the visions or waking dreams stop once justice or equilibrium has been restored: Heaven offers the ultimate release. However, in a too-clever gesture that favours irony, postmodern playfulness and, it must be admitted, fairytale logic where punishment fits the crime, Claire violently returns from her happy-ever-after to terrify Vivian.

As with much of Jordan's work, particularly in *The Butcher Boy*, the "images come with startling immediacy" and "lushness is overwhelming."[7] This is immediately apparent in the opening underwater sequence[8] which is one of the finest and most beautiful visual moments in cinematic history while at the same time succinctly encapsulating the film's narrative and thematic concerns. It is 1965 and Northfield, New England, is being flooded by two billion gallons of water in order to create a reservoir. Following the opening image (drained of colour and light) of water seeping into a diner (recalling the blood which spills from the escalator in *The Shining*), the unanchored and fluid camera, so typical of Jordan, passes into a church. There, amidst the pews, a dismounted crucified Christ floats. Dramatically, the church window explodes inwards (the same window as that of the young Vivian's bedroom) and a gush of water which now flows with images of childhood — abandoned and abused toys[9] — violently pours into the church. The effect is disturbing and serves to condense the film's confusion and celebration of crossed boundaries (as was the case with the shattered window in *The Company of Wolves*).

We are seamlessly in the present, and through the drowned *ghost* town, which clearly represents a repressed past and the unconscious, swim two divers with searchlights (pre-empting the light which is later shone into Claire's eye in the hospital and, like an eye, see or illuminate only partially).[10] If the threat that lurks there is registered from the beginning, like in de Chirico's metaphysical paintings, through the absence of people within an unnatural human landscape, as it is by the toys, the large crucifix and the symbolic "rape" of the church, its gothic aspect is overt in the credits — white, scrawling, intense handwritten script — which are overlaid on the images photographed with a dark green-grey-blue palette. It is also suggested by the nest of eels that the divers disturb; and Jordan's focus on the church, its statues and its graveyard. The divers rise, following the line of the church spire (the journey of Vivian). It transpires that they were searching the reservoir for the body of a child, abducted by a serial killer.

At the water's edge, there lies a forest from which Claire (Annette Bening) and her daughter Rebecca (Katie Sagona) emerge rehearsing the lines of *Snow White*: Rebecca as the enchanted mirror and Claire as the wicked and vain stepmother who insists that Rebecca *is* Snow White, the fairest of them all. After Claire nervously looks to the artificial lake (the reservoir of the unconscious) she suggests they run home to greet Paul (Aidan Quinn), her husband and Rebecca's father. Consequently, a connection is made between the repressed and the happy family. Claire is like other Jordan characters — such as Francie (*Butcher Boy*), Renée (*Miracle*) and Rosaleen (*Company*) — who suffers from a maddening over-identification with her environment (theatre and popular culture) and creates from the reality a pastiche narrative or identity.[11]

Once at home, she begins to sketch with her charcoal pencil in bold and manic strokes, a predatory dog. As she tells her husband, it is, like all the other drawings on the table, which he had presumed were illustrations for Red Riding Hood, an attempt to render (bring to life rather than exorcise) her recurring nightmares which seem to be linked to the missing child. In retrospect, she is imagining and thereby creating a future using the structure and motifs of the fairytale through which she comes to terms with her own critique of the nuclear family and her relationship to Rebecca.[12] The beastly canine is not Red Riding Hood's big bad wolf (see *The Company of Wolves*), but is no other than their much-loved pet Dobie who later gruesomely feeds on the murdered Paul.

Therefore, the drawings (as the dreams) can be seen as a way of working through her own role within the oedipal triangular scenario (where she is both the arrested child and the mother who refuses to let her own child grow up), as well as her conflicting feelings towards Paul and Rebecca. To her frustration, Paul remains independent and refuses to be grounded (after all he flies Boeing 747s) or bonded exclusively to her. It is clear, for example, that it is Rebecca who is the apple of his eye and who is likewise "in love" with him. Dressed in his uniform jacket, she delivers to Claire Paul's betrayal of her — explicitly in the love letter from his Australian (girl)friend, but also by telling her, behind the screen provided by the gauze wings, that Snow White is more beautiful than she. Furthermore, Rebecca, like him, and enabled by him and her school, has learnt to fly. Her dad brings her back a present of a model airplane which she flies, though, according to Claire, the gift comes *too early*, while both at home and for the school play she wears angel's wings. It is these wings that Claire (so as not to damage them) and her killer (to keep her as a child without the power to

make little miracles — she makes the rain stop with her magic
wand) remove.

Later that night, Paul gives Claire a present, a red flowing
kimono: she becomes Little Red Riding Hood. However, as he
wraps her in it and they make love, like in *Stir of Echoes*, the
nightmare visions intrude. For his touch, there is a dream counterpart: as Paul takes her by the hand, a killer's hand leads a
child — her's though she does not see this — through an orchard. (The resonances to serial killer Peter Lorre in *M* (Fritz
Lang, 1931) holding the young girl's hand as he entices her to
her death, or the haunting reality of the dead young girl in *Don't
Look Now* (Nicholas Roeg, 1973) are unmistakable here.) The
reality and dream blend so that at once she is his victim, the
innocent child afraid of sex, and his creative partner. She knows
that the child (her and her daughter) is being brought to a terrible place, yet foreknowledge necessarily makes her complicit
in this act. This link or empathy with the killer also happens
when she stares out of her bedroom window in a trance-like
state when Paul leaves her to get his present for her. (The evil
outside is suggested by the camera's unanchored point-of-view
and the dog's barking.)

The next day, Paul goes to the police station to report
Claire's psychic hallucinations and orchard tip, but he is dismissed by the detective who tells him that they already found
the body. Instead of simply imparting this information and focusing on the interaction between the two men, the scene,
photographed in tones of greys and blues, does much more. As
is the spirit of the film, the camera invites us to look beyond
the two silhouetted figures to the action in the background.
This is not an avant-gardist reference to early cinema or indeed
to a (postmodern) Lyotardian "acinema" which privileges the
image over the rational linear narrative,[13] but more akin to Polanski in *Rosemary's Baby* (1968) when he frustrates the viewer
by an off-centred camera. Put simply, it is a stylish visualisation
of the film's obsession with sight as partial, even when it is supernatural or *Claire*voyant[14] while nonetheless hinting that
there is something more interesting or of narrative significance
beyond the range of normal vision. This is repeated elsewhere

in the film to unsettling effect, such as when Paul and Mary look for Dobie.

Just as *Destry Rides Again* is central to *The Miracle*, so, too, is "Snow White" to *In Dreams*. Unlike "Red Riding Hood" which is reworked in *Company*, as it is in *In Dreams*, both of these complementary narratives are presented as straight, if sumptuous, theatrical performances, and are the screen against which the films' characters play out. *Snow White* is never just a children's performance, albeit beyond any school production, or a set piece within the film, but is the source narrative around which the film weaves. Complete with magnificent detailed costumes, the show takes place at night in the real forest lit by soft golden lanterns and filmed in the predominant rich palette of reds and orange-yellows contrasted against greens and black, it enters the magical world of aesthetic perfection and superrealism. Like all fairytales the story is known in many versions, but the most popular is that of the Brothers Grimm. As it is their tales that Claire illustrates in her book, it is their's that we will outline (Grimm, 1982: 74–82; see also Bettelheim, 1978: 194–215).

Once upon a time, a queen sitting by an ebony window pricked her finger from which fell three drops of blood. She thought to herself that she would like a child as white as the snow on which the blood had dropped, as red as the blood itself, and as black as the window frame. Sometime later a child was born with black hair, red cheeks, and white skin, after which the queen died. The king took a new wife who was as vain as she was beautiful, and who would satisfy her insecurity by consulting a magic mirror that always truthfully told her that she was the fairest of all. However, on the princess' seventh birthday, the mirror tells her: "My lady queen is fair to see, but Snow White is fairer than she" (Grimm, 1982: 75). Jealous, she instructs her huntsman to kill the girl, but he takes pity on her and kills an animal in her place so that he can present to the queen its lungs and liver as Snow White's.

Alone in the forest with the wild beasts who do not harm her,[15] Snow White finds shelter in a little cottage owned by the seven dwarfs who allow her to stay on the condition that she

works for them. The queen, having eaten what she believes are
the lungs and liver of Snow White, is content, but the mirror
tells her that the child lives with the dwarfs and is still fairer
than her. Disguised as a peddler woman, she visits Snow White
and invites her to try on some of her laces (corsets). The
queen laces her up so tightly that she collapses. The dwarfs
return and bring her back to life. The queen reappears, this
time with a poison comb, but again the dwarfs save Snow
White. Finally, she comes back with an apple, the red half of
which has been poisoned. Snow White refuses the apple but
when the queen cuts it and eats the white half, Snow White is
tempted. The queen gives her the other deadly half so that
stepmother and daughter share the apple.

This time the dwarfs are helpless and place her in a glass
coffin over which they keep watch. A prince passes and falls in
love with her. As his servants move the coffin they stumble,
causing the apple to dislodge from her throat, and she comes
to life and agrees to marry the young prince. The queen is invited to their wedding feast, unaware that the bride is Snow
White. Dressed in all her finery, the queen stands in front of
her enchanted mirror only to be told that the young princess is
fairer than she. Furious, she attends the ball, and is frozen by
terror and fright when she sees Snow White. She is then given
red-hot shoes and dances until she literally expires.

Jordan's use of the story is not limited to the children's play
which is incomplete and fragmented. It does offer key moments: Snow White communing with nature (figured as Disney's rather than Grimms'); the hunter showing mercy (not
because of Snow White's entreaties but the twelve good fairies
of "Sleeping Beauty"); the dwarfs' guarding of the coffin and the
arrival of the prince who falls in love with the sleeping Snow
White; and the mirror scene, wherein Rebecca speaks of Snow
White's beauty and enrages the black-dressed queen, who
throws herself on the floor in a childish tantrum (despite her
age, the queen wishes to remain a beautiful young girl rather
than to be a mother and take pleasure in her stepdaughter's
beauty). However, the pivotal apple scene is absent, but Jordan
returns to this repeatedly in Claire's dreams and her daytime

(hallucinatory?) experience. The image of the *red* apple, and all it symbolises (sex, blood, knowledge) haunts her as the image of the pig does Francie.

Following the play and Paul's departure, Claire looks for Rebecca. Panic overtakes her as she towers over the diaphanously clad winged fairy angels that demonically run around her and whose squeals of delight threaten something sinister. She lifts up the mask of one such child, only to have a bemused impish smile mock and verify her distress. Rebecca is missing. Claire's frenetic run into the forest confirms this when she finds her angel wings, caught on a briar, abandoned. Snow White, it would seem, to the distress of the little theatrical troupe, including even the wicked queen on whom the camera lingers, is beyond the reach of the thousand police search lights and she has been killed by the huntsman.

However, like in "Cinderella" or "Hansel and Gretel" (the front cover illustration of Claire's *Grimm's Fairy Tales*) if it is the bad (step)mother who wishes the child(ren) dead, ultimately and by default the father, through his abdication of parental responsibility, is also guilty. In this way, Murphy is right when she suggests that it is "as though her dad's going has literally wiped Rebecca out, 'disappeared' her" (Murphy, 1999: 15). It is not just his leaving that puts her at risk, but his favouring of her over the mother, and his gift which has brought her to maturity and independence too early. Like Little Red Riding Hood, she is too little and perishes.

While the police still hope they can find Rebecca, Claire is hysterical, because she knows from her visions that Rebecca is dead. As they try to fetter her and give her a sedating injection, like Francie when his dead father is discovered, she and the camera enter another space. She sees her terrified child with mountains of red apples all around her. As the killer approaches, Rebecca drops an apple from her hand that he squashes underfoot. She is dead. If this allows Claire to witness the tragedy, it also forces her to realise that her dreams give her glimpses of the future, not the past or the present. Put another way, it highlights her problem with tenses, one that she shares with the schizophrenic (whom Frederic Jameson regards as an apt metaphor for the postmodern condition).[16]

The following day the police search the river, and in the unholy graveyard, caught in a tree, they find her body. Unable to cope with her death (or with Paul?), she drives the *red* BMW into the reservoir as the police haul Rebecca's body out. As her daughter emerges, her mother descends. Underwater, the child reaches for Claire to tell her that she is no longer afraid. The camera focuses on Claire's eye before floating to the beautiful dabbling-lit drowned town. We pass through a broken window into a bedroom where, scrawled on the wall, is the rhyme which is whispered on the soundtrack — "My daddy was a dollar, I wrote it on the fence, My daddy was a dollar, not worth a hundred cents."[17] We see her eye again and a light shines into it. Claire is in hospital, where she has been for six weeks, and is coming to. She returns to the subconscious space to see a boy chained to the same bed; the room is flooding and he struggles to free himself. The water breaks through his window (and the church's window). She wakes briefly and returns to the apple room, where the same voice sings the popular song, "Don't Sit under the Apple Tree".[18]

Dressed in black and with her hair cut short (reminiscent of the wicked Queen?) she returns home with Paul. She cannot bear to look into Rebecca's room and her magic mirror and falls to the floor where Paul comforts her. Disembodied, she walks in her dream with the killer who tells her as he draws her near that he knows she's been dreaming about him. As his kiss turns into a bite, she identifies with him and delivers her/his vampire's kiss to Paul, who is lying with her on their bed. In a carefully composed scene where Jordan, through a long mirror, plays with appearances, reality and reflection, and disorients the viewer's sense of space, she tries to tell an angry and frustrated Paul that she didn't bite his lip, but that it was the killer who is in her head. The more she protests, the more he thinks that she is crazy. Only Claire and her alter ego Vivian (Robert Downey, Jr) know she is not mad (he is not *literally* in her head) but that she is the sensitive little girl of her own "Snow White" fairytale.

The following day, Paul leaves an apparently stable Claire, both of them wearing dark glasses,[19] under the care of their housekeeper. In her absence, Vivian continues to torment her. Working on an image of an apple on the computer, she knocks over a bottle of red ink — the blood that must spill. She is disturbed by a child's laughter, but when she looks to the swing in the garden, it is empty, but it is still moving and the dog is barking at it. She goes down, only to find a single apple on the seat and a tape playing the song "Don't Sit under the Apple Tree".

In a panic — visually rendered in the camera's frenetic movements and editing — she runs into the forest, calling for Dobie. Instead of Dobie or the ominous presence, she discovers the detective in charge of her daughter's case, thus implicitly critiquing the law. She returns to the house, where apples have invaded her kitchen, and in a nod to horror cinema and the terror of the everyday, as she shoves the apples down the sink's internal "muncher", it violent rejects them, spewing out a gush of reddish-brown sludge. Upstairs, the killer becomes the "ghost in the machine" by invading her computer: her words of abuse to the killer appear simultaneously as an echo in his voice and as type on the screen. This pairing of rational technology with art, imagination and the irrational is further explored in *The Good Thief*. Like Francie Brady, with red ink (blood) she smears all over the house the nursery rhyme and Rebecca's name, before slitting her wrists.

She is brought to the hospital, where she undergoes various tests and has a session with psychiatrist Dr Silverman (Stephen Rea), to whom she tells her dreams. That night, Dobie appears outside her window. She climbs out the window, only to cause a major pile-up of trucks and cars when she tries to cross the road after him. Her husband reluctantly agrees to have her committed to a hospital for the mentally ill.

The image morphs and she walks to the Carlton Hotel in the quiet seaside town of Hamlyn (perhaps a reference to another fairytale, that of the pied piper leading the children to their doom). This time, the dream is rendered with the colour bleached but for her vivid red kimono, which flutters in the breeze though all else remains still.[20] Like Jack Torrance of *The*

Shining, she opens a room of desire and dread: inside room 401, she sees her dog tied to a bed, feeding on the face of her husband.

Disturbed, she paces her padded cell, but is restrained by unsympathetic staff. The image of her looking out the padded cell through the glass door down the corridor and to Paul is a powerful one that captures the pain and isolation of her condition. Helpless, as she was when Rebecca was killed, she tries to tell Silverman her dream so that he can warn Paul. However, the psychiatrist refuses to accept her visions at face value and tries to give them symbolic meaning. Consequently, she attacks him. This is intercut with the killer, clearly Claire, attacking Paul. Fittingly, in the dream Claire stabs him in the eye, the punishment that Oedipus gave himself for not being able to see.

She then settles down to institutional life with her roommate Ethel (Pamela Payton-Wright), who makes explicit for the audience that Claire is considered to be a schizophrenic with "people in [her] head", rather than a clairvoyant. Nevertheless, *In Dreams*, like so many recent films, including *The Sixth Sense*, *Twelve Monkeys* (Terry Gilliam, 1995), and *Terminator 1* and *2* (James Cameron, 1984 and 1991) refuses to see madness as a mental disability or as an invalid way to understand the world, it is simply a different, more subtle, and heightened form of perception, or, as is the case with Jordan's Danny (*Angel*), Francie (*The Butcher Boy*), or Vivian, a logical response to an insane and abusive environment. Because the camera affirms what she sees, never are we allowed to share the official (or institutional) perception of Claire as mad, unless we, too, are mad.

Instead, we are invited to see the institution as not just incompatible with the needs of patients, few of which, as Ethel reminds us, are actually mad, but as a sadistic and aggressive regime which instead of listening to the patients, break them by confinement, violence and sedation. (The cinematic parallel here is to Anatole Litvak's *The Snake Pit*, 1948, the seminal critique of the American mental hospital regime.) If Francie has to wait to make a billion trillion baskets before his imagination, and his will to be different, is sufficiently dampened so that he can be released back into the "real" world, Claire escapes by following her vision. She tears away the peeling yellowy wallpaper in her cell to discover the verse of her dream etched on the black wall. It is signed not Red, the name she has given to him, but Vivian Thompson. It becomes clear to her that Vivian, who had earlier occupied her room, is attempting to possess her so that she can help him stop the murders. She tells a disbelieving Silverman that she must surrender to Vivian. Back in her cell covered with her red blanket, she dreams until a wall air-grid falls on her face.

She follows a teenage red-haired feminine Vivian (Geoff Wigdor) through the building's internal duct. Past and present, dream and reality merge, as his and her escape are intercut (as they are interchangeable). Having passed through the hospital, the boy, dressed as a nurse provocatively stands in the car park showing his knee and accepts a lift from a policeman. Likewise, Claire as nurse Vivienne gets a ride from a policeman. Their respective journeys and conversations mirror one another, with both nurses (sexually) teasing their two aroused males in a move that problematises gender and desire far in excess of *The Crying Game*. However, while Vivian brings his "lover" to the Northfield look-out, where he shoots him, Claire pulls the gun on the policeman and instructs him to go back to the hospital and to tell Silverman, who, having found Thompson's file, now believes her, to check out the Carlton. She then drives to the lookout, where Vivian meets her and he takes her to his "enchanted castle", where Ruby, who will be their new daughter, waits for them.

Once he gets her gun, which he knows she had taken from the guard, he dances with her to the dreamily sung "Ebb Tide" (performed by the Righteous Brothers). This mismatch of the song with his violence, and the monstrous perverted family which he seeks, puts nostalgia into the service of terror. The past, just as was the case in *The Butcher Boy*, is refigured, not as a place to safely return to, but as already rotten. As they dance, he tells her all he wants is a family, a dreamer like himself, like her. Indeed, he represents his killing of Rebecca as a "normal" domestic event. She "cried and hollered and I punished her, *like any dad would*, and she was lying quiet, beautiful, but like a doll now" (emphasis added). What he assumes as normal is, of course, a reflection of his own abusive childhood and his being abandoned by his useless father "not worth a hundred cents" and his sadistic mother who beat him. It also displays his regressive gender politics which understand the woman as a doll (see Chapter Nine).

The imprisoned Ruby (Krystal Benn), delighted that Claire is no longer a ghost, just "plain old Claire", brings her to Vivian's special place where he keeps his mother (or a dummy with her clothes on) and his various toys. Claire tries to escape with Ruby, but the child calls to Vivian, who punishes "mommy" the way his mommy used to punish him. He dresses her in bad mommy's clothes, binds her and seals her mouth. Later, still tied, the three sleep together in the ultimate parody of the nuclear family, while Vivian dreams away. Frightened, he tells Claire that he dreamt his mother drowned, but that she had Claire's face. After Claire frees Ruby (who functions for Claire as a second Rebecca) she, too, tries to escape, but as police SWAT teams enter the apple house, he has already chased her to the bridge over the reservoir. A sniper in a police helicopter fires, but she and he dive below in a replay of his dream. He survives.

In summary, *In Dreams* is a simple but formally complex and rich narrative, tightly directed by Jordan and wonderfully filmed by Darius Khondji, who was the cinematographer for *Delicatessen* (Jean-Pierre Jeunet, Marc Caro, 1991), *Se7en* (David Fincher, 1995), and *Alien Resurrection* (Jean-Pierre Jeunet, 1997). Jordan succeeds in immersing the audience in a sumptuous visual world of the unconscious, as well as delivering one of the few recent horror films that intelligently engages with American culture, its desire to return to a perfect place, yet the reality of which is impossible, and has become even more so in the wake of 11 September 2001. Just as *The Butcher Boy* suggests salvation is partially possible, it is only by accepting the mirror — the secret underside of life — that we can grow. That, of course, is the cop-out that David Lynch makes in *Blue Velvet* with which it shares much, not least the Roy Orbison song "In Dreams", when he restores love, harmony and normality, even though the robin is clearly mechanical.

Jordan's message seems to be consistent in challenging the status quo and in exploring borders. *In Dreams,* the psychological gothic fairytale supernatural thriller, does precisely that, and, like *Jeepers Creepers* (Victor Salva, 2001), or indeed other Jordan films, suggests that seeing is not analogous to understanding or that it can facilitate empowerment. As Eve in Wood's novel points out, her "talent" should not be called "power", because it implies control (Wood, 1993: 15). Claire and Vivian see, but they are helpless to stop their dream-realities.

Notes

¹ Despite the almost universally negative reception the film received, this is a positive reading of the film. Nevertheless, Jordan has said that he has to "agree with the critics", explaining that "it was one of those intractable stories that wasn't really my own. I found the premise fascinating and the roots of it [clearly the image of an underwater "unconscious" appealed to him], but the development of it went into this black hole . . . I sort of relished sending it there" (Neil Jordan in Hugh Linehan, 2000).

The script is loosely based on *Doll's Eyes*, written by Bari Wood (1993) who, with Jack Gleasland, co-authored *Twins*, which was filmed by David Cronenberg as *Dead Ringers* (1989). The script makes several important departures from the novel, not least that the central female clairvoyant character survives while the psychopathic serial killer, who kills women rather than children, does not, and that there is no underwater city. However, the key characters, if nuanced and named differently, are present; so, too, are extremely subtle references to the fairytale ("Snow White" and "Frog Prince") in that Eve (in the film she is named Claire) seems to fall in love with the Frog/Beast monster whom she understands is an abused child. His stepmother, whom he believed to have been his actual mother, sadistically abused him to the point of near castration, with the result that he lost the ability to love or feel any emotion. Unlike Claire, whose "gift" is never explained or contextualised, Eve understands that it has been handed down the maternal line of her family. Like Claire, Eve regards her seeing, which is more focused and "regular" than Claire's, as something of a curse.

2 The cinematic quotations are numerous and include most obviously *Psycho* (Alfred Hitchcock, 1960), *Blue Velvet* (David Lynch, 1986), *The Shining* (Stanley Kubrick, 1980), *The Silence of the Lambs* (Jonathan Demme, 1991), *The Innocents* (Jack Clayton, 1961), but above all, in terms of a psychic link between the killer and his victim/lover, the *Nightmare on Elm Street* series, which began in 1984 with Wes Craven directing. Of course, similar scenarios had been conceived of in *Eyes of Laura Mars* (Irvin Kershner, 1978), *Dreamscape* (Joseph Ruben, 1984), *Blink* (Michael Apted, 1994), *Hideaway* (Brett Leonard, 1995), *The Stendhal Syndrome* (Dario Argento, 1996), and *Paperhouse* (Bernard Rose, 1988). Comparison can also be made to *The Cell* (Tarsem Singh, 2000), which is equally dark, gothic and visually detailed, but which is ultimately uncinematic, as well as to *The Sixth Sense* and *Stir of Echoes*, both of which are discussed in the text.

3 See John Millington Synge (1941), *Plays, Poems and Prose*, London/ Melbourne: Dent; introduction by Micheal MacLiammóir, 1958 edition.

4 Even in a number of British films which focus on the political question and the republican nationalist campaign such as *The Gentle Gunman*, or *Odd Man Out*, the family is central. It is used as a way to show, as did playwright Sean O'Casey, the negative effects of political violence on the domestic, but also how violence is passed down from father to son and brother to brother.

5 Nevertheless, all these "natural" images of the pastoral are shown to be fake or to have been tainted by civilisation or culture — the reservoir is manmade, the orchard is not real, but a cider factory, while the forest is where the children's drama is performed.

6 Patrick Kavanagh, "A Childhood Christmas" (poem), *A Soul for Sale*, 1947.

7 Armond White (1999), *NY Press Arts and Listings*, 27 January – 2 February: 10.

8 "The vast underwater set was built in the same Mexican tank that housed sunken-ship scenery for *Titanic* [James Cameron, 1997]" (Janet Maslin (1999), "Want to Share Dreams? Be Careful; It's Murder", *New York Times*, 15 January, E14).

Laure Marsac is stripped and is about to be murdered by the vampires led by Antonio Banderas as the theatre audience watch her humiliation and death as another performance in *Interview with the Vampire*.

Jimmy (Niall Byrne) with his friend Rose (Lorraine Pilkington) interrogates his mother/lover, the *Destry*-performing Renée (Beverly D'Angelo) before inviting her to his own musical performance in *The Miracle*.

In *The Butcher Boy*, Mrs Nugent (Fiona Shaw) is forced to confront her own image by the murderous Francie (Eamonn Owens) as the Virgin Mary passively ignores proceedings and fails to turn up for the townspeople praying outside.

In *Company of Wolves*, Sarah Patterson's Rosaleen discovers, high in a tree, the nest of femininity complete with mirror, rouge and marble babies.

Transvestite Dil (Jaye Davidson) performs *The Crying Game*'s title song at the Metro bar.

Femme fatale Miranda Richardson seeks to assert her fragmented image in *The Crying Game*, having earlier appeared as the cheap girl on the pull, and the Aran sweater-wearing Jude.

In *The Butcher Boy*, Sinead O'Connor plays the Virgin Mary, who here appears to the adult Francie (Stephen Rea). They make a pact that she remains for him a secret joy and she reminds him that the beautiful things are still there.

In a sumptuous Catholic Church, a familiar refuge for Neil Jordan's characters, Bendrix (Ralph Fiennes) returns his ex-lover, Sarah's (Julianne Moore's) stolen diary in *The End of the Affair*.

In *Angel*, saxophonist Stephen Rea's Danny seeks inspiration from the lit Wishing Tree, which has to compete with alternative symbols of magical reality: the advertising signs (right) and the Dreamland ballroom, similarly lit with white bulbs.

Stephen Rea seeks solace from the shiny, blue-suited seventh son of a seventh son in *Angel*, before he returns to the burnt out dancehall to conclude his dreamlike, though violent, adventure.

In *The End of the Affair*, Ralph Fiennes and Julianne Moore celebrate the resumption of their affair at Brighton's fairground, where they make plans to marry and have children.

In *Mona Lisa*, Bob Hoskins's George is comforted by Cathy Tyson's Simone after his violent realisation that she will never be his lover and that he sold out for a "couple of dykes".

At the ubiquitous seaside in *The Miracle*, Lorraine Pilkington and her friend Niall Byrne watch "specimens" about whom they create narratives.

In a dream, another form of artistic creation Jimmy imagines his mother (Beverly D'Angelo), with whom he is romantically involved, and his father (Donal McCann) as elephant trainers on the seafront, though the film's real elephant trainer becomes the lover of Jimmy's friend Rose.

Friends Bob (Nick Nolte, right), his young acolyte Paulo (Said Taghmaoui, centre), and his old friend Raoul (Gerard Darmon, left) plan the robbery of the casino at Monte Carlo in *The Good Thief*.

In *The Good Thief*, Bob restores his fortunes at the Riviera casino with his lucky muse Anne (Nutsa Kukhianidze) who, on this special night, has already turned eighteen.

9 The intimate relationship of children and toys with the latter, most particularly dolls, often serving as a metaphor for, or as a projection of, the child, means that discarded toys are necessarily potent and horrific images. The damaged doll is nothing less than damaged innocence (and childhood). Cf. *Company of Wolves* and *Interview with the Vampire*.

10 Just as in *Company*, Jordan returns to the problem of sight. While Claire is "psychic", she suffers partial sight and needs an interpreter, but even interpreters only see when it is too late. As Vivian tells her, dreams are always right, but they are always wrong. Indeed, as if to emphasise the problem of seeing, which here is linked to tense — she thinks she sees the past/present, not the future — the composition frustrates vision, such as in the police station at the beginning, but even before that in the curtained windows blocking out the light and garden when Paul explains that being psychic is the ability to see through things.

11 She is a schizophrenic, who, in Jean Baudrillard's words, suffers "too great a proximity of everything . . . not even [her] own body to protect [her] anymore . . . can longer produce the limits of [her] own being . . . [S]he is now only a pure screen, a switching center for all the networks of influence." in "The Ecstasy of Communication" in *The Anti-Aesthetic*, Hal Foster, ed. (1983), Seattle: Bay Press, 132–3.

12 See Kathleen Murphy (1999) who also highlights Jordan's use of the fairytale.

13 Jean Francois Lyotard, "Acinema", in *The Lyotard Reader*, A. Benjamin, ed. (1989), Oxford: Basil Blackwell, 169–80.

14 If Wood's names Eve and Adam carry a particular over-determined meaning, the names of their film counterparts are no less so. Claire is Claire because she is clairvoyant, while Vivian recalls Tennyson: Vivien is Tennyson's name for the Lady of the Lake.

15 Like in *Company*, the beasts are less harmful than incomplete humans.

16 Jameson discusses the "second basic feature of postmodernism . . . its peculiar way with time" in relation to current theories of schizophrenia. See for example, "Postmodernism and Consumer Society", pp. 118–23 in Hal Foster, op cit.

[17] The nursery rhyme can be read literally as the father being a "dollar" "not worth a hundred cents". In other words, as a client of his mother's, as such, it is an attack on the mother. She tells him that like his father, he is useless.

[18] While the song is appropriate on a number of levels — the reference to the apples, love and jealousy — it is also the dead Pete's song in Patrick McCabe's *The Butcher Boy*.

[19] This is another reference to seeing and reflective (rather than translucent) surfaces, but more than that it suggests glass as separation. Later the sense of isolation and alienation is figured in Claire, and subsequently Vivian, looking out of the glass-panelled door in their respective cells.

[20] Each dream is treated or filmed differently.

Chapter Thirteen

The End of the Affair (1999)

Belief in God, even the exploration of it from sceptical, rationalist or atheistic perspectives, is not fashionable within either contemporary cinema or western secular society in general, even if a number of millennium films such as *Stigmata* (Rupert Wainwright, 1999) and *End of Days* (Peter Hyams, 1999) foregrounded religion and the spectacle, and brought a hitherto quiet sub-genre to a mainstream audience. Arguably, interest in the "supernatural" has tended, generally speaking, to focus on the forces of "evil" rather than of "good", or darkness, not light.[1]

Certainly, Neil Jordan had displayed an interest in the non-rational and that which hovers beyond the surface or ordinary perception of objects in much if not all of his work made prior to *The End of the Affair*. This was most explicit in the body-horror, comic-gothic, vampire, and psychological-horror-fairytale genres. Nevertheless, the subject of God and faith remained beyond his direct engagement, notwithstanding *We're No Angels* and, indeed, the prayers for miracles or references to them elsewhere (such as in *The Miracle* and *Sunrise with Sea Monster*).

In *End of the Affair*, Jordan maintained on the one hand his interests in the relationship between the real world (war-time Britain and its immediate aftermath, in this case) and the other-world, or Divine intervention in the real. As with *Angel*, *Michael Collins*, or *Sunrise*, the broader politics become intertwined with and subsumed in the personal intimate narrative in much the same way as the "realist" narrative of the "pre-tale" or intro-

duction of the fairytale world gives way to fantasy. Put differently, *The End of the Affair* marries both Jordan's interest in the
materiality of sensuality with an exploration of spirituality, and
the world of everyday surfaces and logic with the imagination
and irrationality. In that process, Jordan retains sympathy for the
protagonists caught between the pull of both worlds — the
world of flesh, desire and human love — and the all-seeing, all-
powerful Divine to whose Will one of the protagonists surren-
ders. In short, Jordan brings us into his world of faith and invites
us to take the imaginative leap in perception and meaning.

By the time his novel *The End of the Affair* was published in
1951, Graham Greene (1904–91) was already established as the
foremost chronicler (with, perhaps, Somerset Maugham) not just
of his native England, but through his extensive travels, of humanity's place in the twentieth century. Brought up a Protestant, he
converted to Catholicism in 1926 at the age of twenty-two. Unsurprisingly, an important strand within his subsequent writings is
a concern with the nature of religious belief in the modern
world, as is evident in *The End of the Affair* which is often regarded as his finest, most complex and most autobiographical
novel. The events depicted in Greene's novel, which are set
against the dark days of the London Blitz, were based on the
volatile combination of the widely known affair between Greene
(who was married) and the American-born Catherine Walston,
wife of wealthy farmer and aspiring Labour Party politician Harry
Walston. Interestingly, Greene did not try to disguise the book's
origins, dedicating the novel to Catherine. Its popularity in the
1950s is reflected in the fact that a somewhat tame Hollywood
adaptation of the book, directed by Edward Dmytryk, was released in 1955, and of which Jordan has been critical.[2]

It is easy to see why Jordan was attracted to the novel, not
just in terms of the irrational, but most especially because one of
the central protagonists, Maurice Bendrix, is a writer. For both
Greene and Jordan, this is explored as a way into the narrative
and becomes a means through which the characters are filtered
and shaped. Indeed, Greene opens the book with a modernist
meditation on storytelling: "A story has no beginning or end:
arbitrarily one chooses that moment of experience from which

to look back or from which to look ahead", while Jordan chooses to begin and end the film with Bendrix (Ralph Fiennes) at his typewriter attempting to understand, from the vantage point of 1946, what had happened between himself and his lover, Sarah Miles (Julianne Moore), when their affair ended abruptly two years earlier. Thus, Bendrix is reconstructing his own life, one of the features of the novel which attracted Jordan.

In this, Jordan revisits the trope of writer as detective, or as one who sees and (re)interprets the world around him/her, which he explored in *Mona Lisa* through Thomas and George, in *The Miracle* through Rose and Jimmy, and in *Sunrise with Sea Monster* through Mouse and Donal, amongst others. However, if in those earlier instances the "writing" allows access to and frames the characters, here it not only limits them, but the process of writing, or of fixing the image which refuses to be fixed, and which becomes a metaphor for detection, cinema and the (dis)pleasures of the voyeur, *is* the narrative. No amount of writing or analysis, it would seem, can contain the multiple viewpoints available.

Jordan retains a romantic attachment to writing (indeed, to the pre-computer ribbon typewriter), as he started his artistic career in this way. (In fact, he continued to write in "longhand" in school copybooks, some of which are amongst his papers at the National Library of Ireland.) In the film, he saw himself as giving life to type, giving it back its former glory (as he puts it in his commentary on the DVD edition of the film). The meditation on writing recurs in the film. For example, during the restaurant scene after the pair renew contact, Sarah enquires whether he is working on a new book; she expects him to be writing about their relationship. He replies that a book is "too hard work for revenge", though, clearly, their relationship is both his novel's and the film's concern.

Through Bendrix, Greene speaks succinctly about the practice of writing: "One sits down sterile and dispirited at the desk, and suddenly the words come as though from the air: the situations that seemed blocked in a hopeless impasse move forward: the work has been done while one slept or shopped or talked with friends" (Greene, 2001: 19–20; orig. 1951). To that Jordan might add, while one looked. Nevertheless, such looking, as both Bendrix and detective Parkis discover, can be deceiving.

After Bendrix meets Sarah and her husband Henry (Stephen Rea) at their home in 1939 during the course of his research for a novel in which a civil servant, Henry's profession, features, Sarah presents her husband as a perfect model for Bendrix's fictional character with whom he seems to share so much. Following this flirting with the *mise-en-abyme* of fiction and reality, Sarah comments unfavourably on his last book, but takes up his invitation to see a screen adaptation of one of his works. That only Sarah is able to go sets in train the possibility of the affair.

At the cinema, Bendrix colludes with Sarah in denigrating the adaptation (in a further piece of trickery by Jordan, the film being screened is *Twenty-One Days* (Basil Dean, 1940),[3] an adaptation *by* Greene of John Galsworthy's *The First and the Last*). As Greene records in the novel through Bendrix (and which reflects his own more public attitude to the film): It "was not a good film, and at moments it was acutely painful to see situations that had been so real to me twisted into the stock clichés of the screen" (Greene, 1951: 43). In Jordan's version, Bendrix tells Sarah that the words spoken were not even his, perhaps an ironic comment in relation to Galsworthy. Nevertheless, Sarah suggests the "onion" scene was clearly his and the two re-enact his transcribed fiction so that his fiction becomes their reality and theatrical conceit of their affair. Her eating of onions, like her fictional counterpart's, is done in order to please the lover and frustrate the husband who does not like onions.

Cinema as a central feature of peoples' lives is seen at a number of points throughout the film, most especially when a cinema newsreel is screened of the VE Day celebrations in June 1945 following the Allied victory in the war, and the jingoistic audience cheer when Winston Churchill appears. Sarah seems alone and distressed in the theatre, greeting the end of the war as the death of her soul and an end to her love affair with Bendrix, which had been made possible through the war. This suggests that the cinema's presentation is problematic, or at least is used to reiterate the public/private[4] relationship. This binary, moreover figured in terms of conflict, is typical Jordan and, though most clearly manifest in his "political" texts such as *Angel*, *Michael Collins* or in *Sunrise*, is present throughout his work. Furthermore, the cinema is also dismissed culturally, not worthy of consideration, as is noted when Henry tells Bendrix that Sarah never goes to the cinema, while the front door being closed at another point is explained by the fact that the *maid* is returning from the pictures. Although it was certainly true that working-class patrons constituted a majority of cinemagoers in the 1940s, the snobbish disdain for the cinema audience which is seen in both novel and film perhaps tells its own story.

Indeed, in the lead-up to one of the film's key scenes, the confrontation in the small church between the estranged lovers, Bendrix follows Sarah by car, alighting when she enters a cinema, but she leaves by a rear exit into a laneway when Bendrix appears. Following her, he finds her in a small, sumptuous Catholic church. To enter the realm of the spiritual, it is necessary, the film seems to be suggesting, to leave the cinema behind. Yet, equally, it might be argued that she goes through the cinema as if it were a magical looking-glass. Only through it can she enter the other non-material/irrational world of desire (albeit of a different order to that of cinematic eroticism). In short, there is a conflation of the two places where ritual, spectacle and love are of primary importance. This notion of the church and the performance of mass as a comforting "entertainment" is explored in *Sunrise*, *The Butcher Boy* and, to a lesser extent, in *The Miracle*. That we follow her into her world of the church and leave the "male" space of the cinema (or at least male in so far as it is generally accepted that the dominant voice or "look" within Classical or Hollywood cinema is male and the subject of cinema is the elusive woman who is finally contained by the text's end) indicates the interesting gendering within the film, which distinguishes it from the standard realist text.

In cinema, subjective shots, as well as various narrative techniques, are used to privilege a character's viewpoint. For example, the use of flashbacks and voiceovers (common within *film noir*) give credence to the veracity or authenticity of a protagonist's point-of-view. Through this hierarchy of voices and looks, the viewer of the film comes to know the film's reality by identifying with a character, usually figured as a male. *The End of the Affair* complicates this formula and can be read as akin to those subversive *noir* films, including *The Dark Corner* (Henry Hathaway, 1946)[5] and *Sunset Boulevard* (Billy Wilder, 1950) where the male's central position of control and authority is eroded and is seen to be illusory. The detective/writer's quest ends in a realisation of his own vulnerability or incompleteness, even if the female comes to be punished or killed. Sarah, too, suffers such a fate, but her death is figured in the non-violent terms of British cinema. Like films such as *Brief Encounter* (David Lean, 1945) with which it has at least a stylistic similarity, transgression is not punished by death (as in *noir* films such as *The Postman Always Rings Twice*, Tay Garnett, 1946), but death is slow through illness, a metaphor, perhaps, for the repression at the end of such films as *Brief Encounter* where the transgressive woman returns to her boring and unemotional husband.

In this way, *The End of the Affair* adopts some of the narrative features of both American and British cinemas of the period. Thus, from the opening shot of the film, Bendrix at his typewriter in his flat, allied with his voiceover, implicates the viewer in this protagonist's point-of-view. However, his novel, or his making sense of events, helped by Parkis (Ian Hart) as novelist/ detective, whose stealing of Sarah's private journal ironically undermines Bendrix's version of reality, comes to be contaminated by Sarah's narrative. Though initially Bendrix reads the journal, thus mediating her voice, her point-of-view is allowed to emerge, and scenes which had been seen already from Bendrix's point-of-view, are re-presented from hers. Moreover, it is her understanding or narrative that wins out. Bendrix comes to accept, though not embrace, her God and her faith.

However, though her story achieves prominence, she remains the subject of investigation and as such is mediated. Interestingly, the representation of their lovemaking, despite the camera's refusal of clichéd choreographed impossibilities, further undermines the narrative "progressive" gendering. Her opened mouth remains the visual shorthand for their orgasmic pleasure, or put differently, it is written on the passive woman's body.

This fugal arrangement of narrative is further layered through Jordan's play with time. Past and present seamlessly interweave so that borders and categories dissolve. Such fracturing of vision only further distances Jordan's *Affair* from classical texts and allows comparison to be made with such other multi-layered texts as *Citizen Kane* (Orson Welles, 1941), *Rashomon* (Akira Kurosawa, 1950), and *Last Year at Marienbad* (Alain Resnais, 1961). Indeed, Jordan has also made reference in his DVD commentary accompanying the film to Samuel Beckett's 1949 play *Waiting for Godot* in which, like *Affair*, *nothing happens twice*. Fittingly, Julianne Moore (who plays Sarah) has since appeared in Jordan's version of *Not I* in the Beckett on Film project (see discussion of *Not I* on pages 274–5).

In short, *The End of the Affair* is a multi-layered meditation on love and jealousy fuelled by the erotic intensity between the adulterous lovers and the cold formality of the husband towards his wife. To this mix is added the search for belief in God. As already noted, this complex and highly unusual range of themes is anchored by the triangular relationship, but rather than being a straightforward account of a tragic love affair, the book is a reconstruction of the relationship two years after the affair has ended from the points-of-view of the two lovers.

Henry is the stereotypical civil servant, working in Widows' Pensions and being promoted to the Ministry of Home Security. His distance and unemotional life centres on his work, while Sarah reports that on a trip she and her husband slept "side by side night after night like figures on tombs" (Greene, 2001: 99). This information is recorded in Sarah's personal journal, which is acquired by Bendrix two years after their affair ended abruptly following his injury during an air raid as they were making love at his flat.

While the novel gives a sexually explicit account of the affair, something which is also a feature of Jordan's film, like *The Crying Game*, which contains a very different type of triangular affair, novel and film share with the earlier film a "big secret". In the case of *The End of the Affair*, Bendrix is bewildered following the air raid in which he is temporarily knocked out, as Sarah leaves his bomb-damaged flat in a hurry, never to return. It is only when Sarah's diary is stolen by private detective Parkis, employed by Bendrix, that it is revealed she believed him to be dead from the bomb.

The way in which the scene is photographed, together with his description of the peace and serenity of the moment, goes some way to suggest a vaguely spiritual moment, or something which might approximate to an out-of-body experience. His voiceover records, "My mind for a few moments was clear of everything except a sense of tiredness as though I had been on a long journey. I had no memory at all of Sarah and I was completely free from anxiety, jealousy, insecurity, hate: my mind was a blank sheet on which somebody had just been on the point of writing a message of happiness. I felt sure that when my memory came back, the writing would continue and that I should be happy" (Greene, 2001: 71). The moment of implosion of the window, which visually recalls that in *In Dreams*, is followed by an almost static distanced photographic series of images taken from a height above the body.

During the moments while Bendrix is knocked out, Sarah, an unbeliever, though, we discover, baptised a Catholic, prays to God that Bendrix should not be killed, or even that he be restored to life, since she believes him to be dead. In return for the favour granted, she promises to end the affair. Surprised when Bendrix reappears upstairs, she is caught between her pact with God, which she believes has produced a miracle, and Bendrix's offhand, phlegmatic attitude to death and God.

Rushing from the house, she begins her spiritual search to reconcile her newfound belief in God and a continuing disregard for religion. In the process, as her diary records, she comes to hate God because her free will is urging her to reject the pact. When Sarah's point-of-view of Bendrix's apparent death is presented, she says that she loves him and "will do anything if you'll make him alive. I'll give him up for ever, only let him be alive with a chance." She adds, in lines delivered in the film as she sees Bendrix for the last time at the bomb-damaged flat, "People can love without seeing each other, can't they? They love You all their lives without seeing You." She concludes with his reappearance and notes in her journal: "I thought now the agony of being without him starts, and I wished he was safely back dead again under the door" (Greene, 2001: 95).

While she severs her relationship with Maurice Bendrix, in the novel she continues her promiscuous life with a brief tryst with Henry's superior, Dunstan. She also tries to come to terms with her pact with God. As a result, she goes to see Smythe, a rationalist, who does not believe in God, and whom she saw speak publicly. At his house, which he shares with his sister, she seeks to bolster her disbelieving side and find the strength to break her vow. While Smythe provides her with rationalist arguments "proving" that God does not exist, Sarah is not convinced. As a result, her troubled self leads her to a Catholic church, where she comes under the influence of Father Crompton, but the nature of their conversations are not recorded in the journal or by "Greene" as primary narrator.

Maurice's continuing jealousy of Sarah leads him to trick Henry into having the private detective find out whom Sarah visits surreptitiously. At this point and elsewhere, the novel, and the film's interpretation of it, contain layers of irony — for example, the idea of Henry asking his wife's (former) lover to find out with whom she is currently liaising. As Greene, through Henry, puts it in the novel: "One can't spy on one's wife through a friend — and that friend pretend to be her lover" (Greene, 2001: 17).

In the film, Jordan conflates the Smythe and Crompton characters, transforming the scenes at the Smythes into those featuring a Catholic priest, Fr Smythe (Jason Isaacs), and his sister (Deborah Findlay), thus ensuring that the secular rationalist and the priest will be as one, carrying the contradictions at their most acute. As a consequence, while in the novel both Smythe and Crompton make appearances following Sarah's death, in the film only Fr Smythe can visit the house. Maurice, accompanied by Lance (Samuel Bould), Parkis's son, uses the excuse of a fake illness to enter Smythe's home, but is further hurt when he discovers that she appears to be involved with a priest. It is only when the diary is stolen that the nature of the relationship is revealed.

The latter part of the film was considerably changed by Jordan from what happens in the novel. For example, in the novel, the relationship between Maurice and Sarah is not resumed, but Jordan has them go to Brighton, which becomes for Jordan the ubiquitous place of magical possibilities, but invariably mocks that desire in its dullness and seediness, like it does at the end of *Mona Lisa*. This is a completely new scene, as the novel is exclusively set in London. At Brighton, the couple enjoy each other's company again while visually the scenes echo *Mona Lisa* with scenes at Brighton Pier and at a hotel similar to where the shoot-out in that film happened, but also, as is familiar from a number of Jordan's films, use is made of a fairground to echo childhood joy and exhilaration, or innocence. It is here that Maurice joyously tells her he wants children, while at the hotel, Sarah recalls a dream she had in which sea-water comes in through the window and fills their room, while a child rests between them.[6]

Following their disappearance to Brighton, Parkis turns up again, this time employed by Henry (something which is clearly not in the novel). Believing he has finally detached Sarah from Henry, Maurice is stunned to discover from Henry that Sarah has only six months to live and as a result a divorce is out of the question. While both Maurice and Henry have benefited from Parkis's surveillance of Sarah, these activities are given greater prominence in the film than in the book, with, for example, use made of photography by Parkis and an explicit conversation after Maurice sees Parkis in Brighton, in which the detective is invited to photograph the pair *in flagrante* to help speed up the divorce being planned by Maurice. Indeed, the choice of Brighton for such scenes cannot have been unconnected with the town's use for the unpleasant side of divorce proceedings and as the main location for the seedy adaptation of Greene's novel *Brighton Rock* (John Boulting, 1947).

Another significant difference to the novel is the more developed relationship between Maurice and Henry. Henry is not just the stereotypical civil servant who plays the cuckolded husband, but his whole physique is stiff and unemotional, leading him to admit to Maurice that he has not had sex with Sarah for years. (Nevertheless, the film's end presents another, more caring Henry.) As a result, there is a form of tolerance by Henry towards her lovers (as, indeed, there had been between Walston and Greene, a family friend, even when the lovers travelled abroad together),[7] including Maurice, when he discovers that he was once her lover. Thus, when Sarah dies from, it would appear, some form of consumption (though, of course, the illness is not exactly physical), Henry invites Maurice to move into the house. While this relationship does not have the same homosocial resonances as in earlier Jordan films, Maurice nevertheless serves as the stay-at-home "wife", working on his latest book (they have a maid so housework is not part of his responsibilities), he waits, sometimes anxiously, for Henry to arrive home from work so that they can go together to the pub. Jordan places Maurice in the house earlier, while Sarah is ill, and he spends time at her bedside. This also allows, after Sarah's death, for a comforting hug between the two men, both of whom love her and try to understand her or capture something of her essence.

The novel contains five "books", or sections. In the first of these, Bendrix recalls with bitterness and intense jealousy the course of the affair: "This is a diary of hate" are the film's first words, typed by Bendrix. In book two, he resumes contact with Sarah at the same time as hiring a detective to identify whom he imagines is her current lover, thus signalling the central obsessions of love, hate and jealousy, and, indeed, the problem of seeing and understanding. Book three records Sarah's point-of-view through extracts from her diary which detail the course of the affair, her intense love for Bendrix, her continuing love for Henry; provide, most importantly, the "revelation" of her pact with God; and chronicle her visits to the atheistic Smythe. The fourth book, the shortest of the five (only two chapters), includes the disbeliever Maurice's first, begrudging acknowledgement of the existence of God and Henry's phone call to Bendrix telling him of Sarah's death. Finally, book five focuses on the grief of both men, Sarah's cremation, and Henry's concern that she may have been a Catholic and thus should have a church ceremony. Sarah, it is revealed by her mother who attends her funeral, was indeed baptised a Catholic, even though her father was Jewish. Thus, a Catholic burial is what is pleaded for by her mother and by Fr Crompton.

Maurice, though, remains fixed in his rejection and resentment of her faith and religion generally. He returns to the theme of hate that begins both book and film. Now, he says (in the novel), "I found the one prayer that seemed to serve the winter mood: O God, You've done enough, You've robbed me of enough, I'm too tired and old to learn to love, leave me alone for ever" (Greene, 2001: 192). This ambiguously atheistic plea is made more direct by Jordan who has Maurice say just before Sarah dies, "So You are taking her, but You haven't got me yet. I don't want Your peace and Your love. I wanted Sarah for a lifetime. And You're taking her from me. So, I hate You God. I hate You as though you existed." As Jordan puts it towards the end of his voiceover to the DVD edition of the film, "How can you hate so much the thing that is not there? It comes into existence by hatred." Through this act he becomes a truly oedipal child who desires his mother. His competitor, fleshed out from the imagination and his jealousy, turns out to be no less than the all-powerful father — God — and though Bendrix's transgressive love for Sarah, like Donal's love for Rose (in *Sunrise*), or Jimmy for Renée (*The Miracle*), is consummated, it must be returned to the father, and in that sense is already doomed. It is a love that only has meaning within the triangular structure of the family.

When Sarah's viewpoint on jealousy is articulated, she comments that "He is jealous of the past and the present and the future. His love is like a medieval chastity belt: only when he is there, with me, in me, does he feel safe. If only I could make him feel secure, then we could love peacefully, happily, not savagely, inordinately, and the desert would recede out of sight. For a lifetime perhaps." She adds, "If one could believe in God, would he fill the desert?" (Greene, 2001: 91).

Central to Sarah's belief in God is the view that through divine intervention Maurice was saved, or restored to life, resurrected, after his "death" in the air-raid. As a result, she believes it was a miracle and thus she cannot break her vow to God. (As the Father, He had already given him life.) After her death, Maurice is confronted by two "miracles" in the novel, the first of which is treated somewhat differently in the film, while the second — in which Parkis's prayers to Sarah for the recovery of his ill son in the presence of some of her books are answered — is absent (Greene, 2001: 178). When Sarah goes to see Smythe (in the novel), she notices that he is pock-marked or diseased on one cheek. On one occasion, after Smythe abandons his professional distance from her and declares his love for her, offering to abandon his rationalist beliefs, she sympathetically kisses his cheek, even though hitherto she had found it repulsive. After her death, Smythe turns up at Henry's house to offer his condolences and while there tells Maurice how his cheek has cleared up following Sarah's kiss. This "miracle" is dismissed by Maurice, who is angry at his intrusion at this intimate moment. In the film, this experience is transferred to Lance,[8] who has a prominent birthmark covering one side of his face. While observing Sarah's visits to the priest, he falls asleep but is woken and comforted by her after she leaves the house. She gives the boy money and touches his "affliction". Lance, who has taken a liking to Sarah, and Parkis both believe, as Parkis tells Maurice, that it was Sarah's touch that caused the birthmark to vanish. Her voiceover in which she wishes the boy's affliction away confirms the possibility of Divine intervention.

If the trajectory of the doomed Sarah–Bendrix relationship is ultimately determined by God's miracle, it is facilitated and made worse by Bendrix's obsessive jealousy, which destroys Sarah and kills their love. His fault is that he cannot believe that she loves him; faith, not in God, but more generally in Sarah, comes too late. As such it is a melodramatic ghost story in which the lover who survives is forced to relive his past until he comes to understand it. Resolution can therefore never be achieved; only acceptance, retrospectively. Referring metaphorically to quantum physics, and Heisenberg,[9] Jordan has commented on such obsession in relation to the necessary destruction of pleasure: "If you observe a particle you've already disturbed it" (McCarthy, 2000b:15). More simply, "analysing pleasure, or beauty," as film theorist Laura Mulvey has written, "destroys it".[10]

The style of the film subtly shifts from wartime to post-war and as the film progresses these two different times merge such that the viewer is sometimes unsure in which period the scene is set. For this, Jordan was inspired by Japanese erotic prints from the early twentieth century, which have "that same haunting quality, because in a way the characters are haunted. When we meet them at the start of the story, they're almost dead in a way" (Jordan in Linehan, 2000). As such, it is a kind of ghost story. With the film's dual point-of-view structure, scenes are re-shown from the two perspectives. Prior to the film being made, Jordan watched *Rashomon* because it contains multiple points-of-view in its exploration of the truth behind a woman's rape. Thus, in *End of the Affair* present and past are interplayed until the two merge. While the film begins and ends very definitely with Maurice's point-of-view as he writes his account of the affair, in the intervening time a shift occurs from his to Sarah's viewpoint, which is highlighted and sympathetically endorsed. This is reinforced through camera movements where slow, languorous tracks are used to convey her perception of events. In this regard, Jordan screened two films for his crew prior to shooting the film: Robert Bresson's *La Dame du Bois de Boulogne* (1946), in which a woman exacts revenge on her ex-lover, and Max Ophuls's *Letter from an Unknown Woman* (1948). *Letter* is told from the woman's (tragic) point-of-view, where the idealised male lover only receives the letter as she is dying, and while the story is reconstructed from her perceptive, her love is a hopeless and forlorn one. [11]

Thus, *End of the Affair* develops such points-of-view by giving somewhat equal treatment to both lovers. Though she too will die, Sarah has both a highly physical relationship with her lover and a spiritual peace at the end. However, each time she wishes to return to her former lover, a "coincidence" occurs, thus preventing her "regression" to bodily desire. Indeed, in the novel, while she has an "affair" (perhaps unconsummated) with Dunstan, in the film, it first appears she has one also (seedily observed by Parkis's son), but later it turns out (when her version is presented through the diary), that she is being examined by her doctor. This then explains why her blouse is removed and her comment which metaphorically describes her illness: "There is a stone in my heart". By the film's end, Henry's point-of-view is also established. As a result, our earlier dismissal of him as a boring, asexual husband has been transformed through his unselfish act of inviting Maurice to stay at the house.

The End of the Affair is a detective story where the quest is not so much to establish who is sleeping with whom, but for a form of metaphysical truth; or, in other words, it is a metaphorical detective ghost story which seeks to examine the very means and validity of detection, or of writing. Most of all, it offers an invitation to see differently, to come to accept faith through a celebration of the non-rational and non-linear.

In short, it speaks to the imaginative possibilities which Jordan believes are played with in the Irish psyche. In *Sunrise with Sea Monster*, Donal explains to his German captor that in Ireland "each statement [has] two meanings, its apparent meaning and its actual one". After he warns him not to accept the "surface of things" he offers himself as an "interpreter, or to be more precise, diviner of facts, the hidden meanings, the hidden landscapes which [lie] behind the apparent ones" (*Sunrise*, p. 75). It is this work as an interpreter in which Jordan excels.

Notes

[1] However, recently there have emerged a number of films, notably by writer-director M. Night Shyamalan (*The Sixth Sense* (1999), *Unbreakable* (2000), and *Signs* (2002)) which have invited the audience to believe in something beyond the rational, in myth, faith and the afterlife, as something more powerful and ultimately more real than seeming material reality.

[2] As mentioned during Jordan's commentary on the DVD edition of the film.

[3] Though made in 1937, it was not released until 1940, putting a question mark over Jordan's use of the film in 1939.

ᵃᵃᵃ9

ᵃᵃᵃᵃ

[4] "The news [of the war] from Europe passed us by, seemed monstrous, but somehow less intimate than the monstrosities we had accomplished" (*Sunrise*, p. 165).

[5] See Frank Krutnik (1991), *In a Lonely Street: Film Noir, Genre, Masculinity*, London/New York: Routledge.

[6] This powerful symbolic water-laden image recurs elsewhere in Jordan, including the collection of stories in *Night in Tunisia*, *Dream of a Beast*, the proposed ending of *Company of Wolves*, *The Miracle*, *Sunrise With Sea Monster*, and, most notably, *In Dreams*.

[7] Amongst the places they stayed was Achill, Count Mayo, where Catherine owned a cottage. Another of her lovers was the Irish Jesuit priest, Father Donal O'Sullivan, later Chairman of the Irish Arts Council. See Michael Sheridan, "The truth behind *End of the Affair*", *Sunday Independent*, 23 January 2000: 19; Richard Brooks, "Graham Greene's secret 'bigamy'", *Sunday Times*, 16 January 2000: 7.

[8] In another aside on understanding, Parkis reveals that Lance has been named after the great Lancelot of Arthurian Legend, whom he believes found the Holy Grail. Bendrix cruelly and matter-of-factly informs him that Lance did nothing so noble but ran away with Arthur's wife. If the joke is on working-class ignorance and the ineptitude of the detective who earlier had mistaken Sarah and Bendrix as (active) lovers, it also calls attention to the act of naming, and perception. As a detective's helper, of course, the boy's "holy grail" becomes the woman, as he vicariously follows the scent of desire.

[9] Jordan makes reference to quantum physics in *Sunrise with Sea Monster*, where it is used as a key to a coded language between Donal and the German. The two discuss the Irish proclivity for believing the impossible possible.

[10] Laura Mulvey (orig. 1975), "Visual Pleasure and Narrative Cinema", in *Film Theory and Criticism: Introductory Readings*, Gerald Mast, Marshall Cohen, Leo Braudy, eds., fourth edition, New York/Oxford: Oxford University Press, 748.

[11] *Letter* also contains a discourse on cinema, including in the "Hale's Tours" section, where the couple watch changing mountain scenery from a stationary railway carriage.

Chapter Fourteen

The Good Thief (2002)[1]

"Isn't beauty always mysterious?"
— Anne (Nutsa Kukhianidze)

Unsurprisingly, one of the major features of early cinema was the craving for narrative. Within that unregulated institution, this meant that much of the product was heavily plagiarised, if not always an exact replica of earlier and indeed contemporaneous films. So successful was European cinema in the American market that often even major companies such as Edison would copy the films of its European competitors.[2] In addition, early cinema saw the extensive plundering of popular culture, as demand for filmed narrative increased during the 1900s.

Nevertheless, historical cultural amnesia presents the "remake" and quotation as a peculiarly and particularly postmodern phenomenon. However, if certain theorists, including most notably Fredric Jameson, have derided this aesthetic practice and, in the context of film, economic strategy, as a form of lazy cultural cannibalism, Neil Jordan's latest film presents an argument to the contrary. In short, *The Good Thief* (2002) is not a nostalgic "remake" of the beautifully constructed and complete, if slight, 1955 film *Bob le Flambeur* (Bob the Gambler) by French director Jean-Pierre Melville. Although *The Good Thief* manages to "bear an affectionate relationship"[3] to Melville's film in terms of the dialogue, many of the character names, and general scenario, as well as particular vignettes such as Anne accepting a motorbike ride from a client/boyfriend, it is a radical reworking of it. Before further discussing Jordan, or Melville, the historical and generic context of the heist movie will be considered.

The origins of the modern heist film lie in John Huston's *The Asphalt Jungle* (1950). The genre's staple gang, brought together by master criminal Doc Riedenschneider (Sam Jaffe), embarks on a jewel robbery. The consequence of the robbery is failure, with the various gang members succumbing to death — directly or indirectly through suicide — or capture. It has been remade on three occasions, first as a western, *The Badlanders* (Delmer Daves, 1958), then by Wolf Rilla, as *Cairo* (1963) with the booty figured as Egyptian treasure, and finally as *Cool Breeze* (Barry Pollack, 1972) in which the diamond robbery is designed to set up a black people's bank. *The Asphalt Jungle* has also served as the prototype for such popular films as the crime comedy *Ocean's Eleven* (Lewis Milestone, 1960), in which Frank Sinatra led the "Rat Pack" (Dean Martin, Peter Lawford, Sammy Davis, Jr, and others) to rob simultaneously five Las Vegas casinos. This film was remade by Steven Soderbergh in 2001 with George Clooney as Danny Ocean, amongst a star-studded cast including Matt Damon, Brad Pitt and Andy Garcia. However, despite the illustrious line-up, that film is unsatisfactory and somewhat pedantic, if at times beautiful to look at.

Ironically, Warner Bros.' involvement with *Ocean's Eleven* (2001) led to their withdrawal from the Jordan project which, unlike Soderbergh's film, does not boast of bankable Hollywood *stars* — although Nick Nolte in the lead serves this function to some degree — but of fine multi-ethnic international *actors* such as France's popular Tcheky Karyo as Bob's detective friend Roger; *La Haine*'s Said Taghmaoui as Bob's surrogate son Paulo; award-winning independent film director, writer, actor and musician, Sarajevo-born Emir Kusturica, who plays the "mad" genius Vladimir; and the spectacular newcomer Nutsa Kukhianidze as Anne, whom Jordan and Woolley rightly rank alongside their other "discoveries", Cathy Tyson (*Mona Lisa*) and Jaye Davidson (*The Crying Game*).[4] The cast also includes other key French entertainers and actors (Marc Lavoine, Gerard Darmon), Ouassini Embarek of Algerian descent, American actors (Mark and Michael Polish who, respectively, wrote and directed the award-winning *Twin Falls, Idaho* (1999)), and English actors (Sarah Bridges, who plays the transsexual body-builder afraid of spiders — an archetypical negative representation of female sexuality — and Ralph Fiennes as an art dealer whose *modus operandi* belies his name, Tony Angel).

Unquestionably, Jordan's film delivers a more considered and richly textured piece of cinema than does Soderbergh's. But then, Jordan's casting, even in *Interview* (where Tom Cruise and Brad Pitt played Lestat and Louis respectively) has always — and most notably with Stephen Rea in eight of Jordan's films, Julianne Moore in *End of the Affair*, and, in this instance, Nick Nolte — tended to make the actor invisible, or at least work to the advantage of the screen character. Nolte does not become so much invisible as approximate with Bob. It is as if Nolte's history and maverick persona of reformed hellraiser, always part outsider, finds a ready echo in and affinity with Bob, the rugged romantic who lives life to the full. As Jordan comments, "just as the character began to get its own energy and life on the page, so Nick is so much more like the character than I could ever have imagined".[5]

Just as the production contexts of *Ocean's Eleven* and *The Good Thief* intertwined, so, too, is there a connection between Melville's *Bob le Flambeur* and Huston's *The Asphalt Jungle*, though here the result was a textual reconceptualisation of the former in the wake of the success of Huston's germinal film. Melville originally drafted it as a "serious" heist film, but the same year, 1950, *The Asphalt Jungle* was released. Subsequently, he decided to reshape the script "completely and turn it into a light-hearted film", and thus he made "a comedy of manners".[6]

Bob le Flambeur tells of Bob Montagné (Roger Duchesne), an ageing and morally upright gambler (despite previous and future involvement with crime) who, down on his luck, decides to mastermind a raid on the casino at Deauville, on the northern coast of France. Like in *Asphalt Jungle*, a gang is assembled. In this instances, it includes Bob's friend, safecracker Roger (André Garrett), Bob's young acolyte Paulo (Daniel Cauchy), son of a former criminal partner, and an ex-con Jean (Claude

Cerval) who is now reformed by his hen-pecking greedy wife Suzanne (Colette Fleury) and works in the casino.

As the night of the robbery approaches, Suzanne (having bullied Jean into telling her of the robbery and then into accepting that he has been underpaid for his crucial role in the heist) looks for a greater share of the take. When she fails to get it, she informs on the gang to the police. Additionally, Bob has befriended a young *bon vivante* Anne (Isabelle Corey), who with Bob's encouragement has developed a relationship with Paulo. She finds his devotion a little tiresome and sleeps with pimp and police informant Marc (Gérard Buhr), to whom she innocently tells of the planned robbery. Realising her betrayal, she tells Bob. It is somewhat ironic that Paulo's pillow talk should jeopardise the heist, given that he had been warned against such indiscretion by Bob while he himself had characterised loose talk as a negative feminine trait. In order to make amends and acting out of passion, unseen, he shoots Marc as he is speaking with Inspector Lehru (Guy Decomble). That Lehru and Bob, notwithstanding their opposing professions, are old companions is partially because Bob saved Lehru's life.

On the night of the robbery, Lehru tries to stop the theft (and save Bob), but Bob, going ahead of the gang, starts gambling at the Deauville casino. Seeing his luck turn, he forgets about the robbery and begins to win huge amounts of money — the 800 million francs they were going to steal. Meanwhile, the gang drives into a police ambush in which Paulo is shot dead (a fitting punishment for his own killing of Marc) and the rest of them are captured. As Bob emerges from the casino, he is arrested for criminal intent and his legal winnings are put in the boot of the police car. During the subsequent friendly exchanges between Lehru, Bob and Roger, it is clear that he will possibly serve a short prison sentence, be set free, or even receive damages for wrongful arrest.

Conceivably, Jordan was attracted by the film's ironic twists, which celebrate the beauty of the absurd and the futility of (rational) effort, something that is clearly also found in Huston, and discussed by Melville.[7] After all, Jordan explored similar territory in *High Spirits*, when the central character fails to market, with the aid of fake and amateurish theatricals, his ancestral home as haunted. When he becomes resigned to his fate, the real ghosts and hauntings begin in earnest. However, it is Melville's European tradition which more obviously appealed to Jordan, who views such a cinema as a way out of the American-Anglophone cultural stranglehold. As Jordan put it in an interview at the time of the film's release, "I'm tired of the dominance of American movies over everything, every facet of filmmaking and cinema-going." He went on, "I just think it's time to make a move back to Europe. It's time European directors made films with reach, punch and intellectual ambition."[8] While *The Good Thief* certainly achieves this European "punch", it is not a "pure" project in the sense of being non-American, just as the films of Melville or other directors of the French New Wave are not. Like these films, it occupies the cultural interstices and rides the contradictions as well as recognising the complementary aspects of both cinemas. Using predominantly Canadian (corporate) money, Jordan created a European movie produced both in reaction to and as homage to American cinema. (His attempt to repeat this critical, though highly marketable, cinema has been less successful so far in achieving his ambition to make a film about the Borgias (see Chapter Fifteen).)

The Good Thief uses the basic premise of *Bob le Flambeur*, and, while retaining Melville's lightness, adds further layers of irony, as well as exploring themes of obsession, addiction, and the joy of visceral or intense engagement, and remodels and transforms it into a more self-conscious and reflective film. Put another way, Jordan's film delivers a more complex narrative that delights in its own conceit of the mirror or the double, both formally and thematically, for *The Good Thief* is nothing less than an exploration of deception, duplicity, doubling, and the surfaceness of appearances — in that reference can be made to Jean Baudrillard's theoretical work on the simulacrum.[9] Though Jordan plays with this very postmodern trope of multiple imitation and mirroring, unlike Baudrillard, he still holds to the modernist notion of the original. The film also presents a consideration of art and technology; or celebrates the non-alignment of beauty, luck and the irrational with science and rationality. In the film's press book, Jordan comments that when "a gambler plays with mathematics, chance and the laws of probability . . . the result will always be a mismatch".[10]

However, most of all, *The Good Thief*, which can be seen, like the equally cinematically stylish Mike Figgis's superb dark love story *Leaving Las Vegas* (1995), as a poem on addiction and love, belongs to the Jordanesque world of the imagination. As is the case with so much of Jordan, it operates within the twilight romantic sphere where sexual, national, moral and other more abstract borders, such as reality and fantasy, merge; meaning is open; the impossible is possible; and for the first time, the father — the beast and not the son — gets the young girl. In this, it reverses the pattern set by "A Love", *The Miracle* and *Sunrise with Sea Monster*, although in these texts, the son's victory is questionable.

Despite this, Bob (who inhabits, yet transcends, a seedy or gritty underworld), and the film in general, are never merely poetic or imaginary abstractions, but fit the film's time and place. Like Melville, who filters American cinema and genre through his own particular (French) form of filmmaking to create a world firmly anchored in its time and place, Jordan presents a world that combines elements from American and European filmmaking and makes homage to the past, while simultaneously rooting it in the present, particularly as shaped in Nice and Monte Carlo. If the "shifty, shady underworld of Nice and the gaudy opulence of Monte Carlo"[11] together with its Riviera Casino provide an optimum contrast, they are also essential to updating Melville's film, where the locations are Pigalle and the surrounding environs of Montmartre, and the casino at Deauville. While Melville's chosen area in Paris has, to a large extent, been taken over and tamed by the tourist, the setting of the Casino at Monte Carlo works because so many Americans have made their home along the Côte d'Azur.[12] Nevertheless, Melville's Pigalle (or his Casino at Deauville) even allowing for the barrier of time, offers a less visceral and less immediate access to the underworld of seediness, sex and gambling. But then, Melville always remains at an ironic and safe distance, preferring simple storytelling and humour rather than

dealing with drugs and the issue of addiction, which remain unexplored.

Furthermore, Jordan's Anne, unlike Melville's, is a young
East European whose passport is stolen by her would-be pimp,
nightclub owner Remi, which reflects a darker aspect of the
current criminal situation along the Côte d'Azur and the activities of the Russian Mafia, drug-dealing and the luring with promises of employment of such girls into prostitution.

The Good Thief follows the planned heist of the casino by
ageing American gambler Bob who is addicted to a heightened
engagement with reality as manufactured by gambling[13] and
drugs. Though down on his luck, he remains a romantic, a
storyteller — one of the many who populate Jordan's fiction —
who tries to weave a new reality for others (Paulo, Anne,
Yvonne) as he reconstructs his own past and identity.

We see Bob shooting up with heroin (we see the needle go
in) and meeting seventeen-year-old Anne to whom he ab-
stractly explains prime numbers (recalling the mathematical-
philosophical discourse in Sunrise with Sea Monster). He then
saves the life of detective Roger,[14] a friend going back to his
criminal days, when a young Algerian illegal immigrant and drug-
dealer — candyman Said — holds a gun to his head. Later,
Roger warns Bob to remain straight, but Bob responds by asking him to look out for Anne (who, moreover, is accompanied
on the soundtrack, as Renée is in The Miracle, by sultry sax music). Bob returns home where he sleeps under his most prized
possession, a Picasso, thus introducing the subject of art.

The next night, Bob's moral "crusade" continues as he
saves Anne from prostitution: he contrives a fight following a
card game with the nightclub owner/pimp Remi in order to
steal back from him her passport. Bob gives her money, but the
following day finds her walking the street again. In a typical Jordan image, the backdrop is the beach. He takes her to his
apartment and introduces her to his "son" Paulo, who falls in
love with her. While the young couple enjoy each other's company, Bob departs to the racetrack. He bets his last 70,000
francs on Prince of Orange,[15] but the horse is beaten.

Instead of returning home, his friend Raoul comforts him by taking him to nearby Monte Carlo and the Riviera Casino, which he hopes to rob with Bob's help. In a departure from Melville, rather than going after the cash in the safe, which seems impossible, Raoul suggests that the casino's art collection, assembled by a Japanese bank during the art boom of the 1980s, should be stolen. The ruse is that the paintings, on display in order to attract a middle-class clientele and signify respectability, are only copies,[16] while the originals by Van Gogh, Cézanne, Modigliani and others are kept in the underground vault of a villa a short distance from the casino, which is protected by a highly sophisticated security system. Art, Raoul tells him, is worth more than money.

Though strung out on drugs, Bob determines to go clean in order to plan the robbery, and with Anne's (and Paulo's) help, he achieves "cold turkey" within three days, by which time he has already conceived of a plan: the two robberies, one fake and one real. This doubling of the bet, or the idea of a two-part heist,[17] is only one instance of Jordan's multiplying of the narrative strands and actors of *Bob le Flambeur*. In yet another layer of irony, the fake robbery (of the money) becomes a reality carried out by casino security guard Albert, his twin Bertram and Paulo (Albert having spotted Paulo photographing the artwork in the casino — or in Jordan's linguistic play "burning" the image). With Raoul, Bob visits Russian security expert Vladimir, who had installed the system in the villa where the paintings are housed. He agrees to join their team and help them overcome his unbreakable security system. To this end, during a maintenance visit to the villa the following week, he installs a neutralising bug. The guards that check him as he enters are unequal to the new invisible and highly sophisticated technology.

In Vladimir, the figure of the double is evoked as Melville's "insider" is now necessarily split into two. The twins Albert and Bertram function as one insider (even if they themselves number two and rely on the misperception of others to misread their surface identity as their true identity) and enable the decoy (though nonetheless real) robbery, while Vladimir becomes the second insider for what is conceived of as the real robbery.

At one level, his name allows for Jordan to play with language, in that his family are stuck in Vladivostok, but at the same time, their being trapped there allows for the more serious issue of suggesting how an ordinary moral person can go to extraordinary lengths for personal or familial reasons. Like Said, he is trapped by circumstances and is not robbing for the sake of money but for the freedom that it will afford his family. At another level, the name inevitably conjures up the famous vampire, who like Vladimir is intimately involved in infecting systems. (The twins also recall the vampire's spiralling doubling or reproduction as well as returning us to Jordan's only other set of twins, the young boys that deliver the poisoned blood to Lestat in *Interview with the Vampire*.)

Through Vladimir, Jordan is not simply playing with opposites — the security engineer as thief, which has been used elsewhere as a narrative device, most recently in David Fincher's *Panic Room* (2002). Neither is he merely enjoying regional accents and exploring comic turns of language such as in Vladimir's confusion between "bugs" and "beetles", and to which Jordan returns in the scenes involving the reluctant casino manager paying Bob his winnings, or even the twins with their Dublin (Irish) accents. Instead, or in addition to these, Vladimir clearly draws attention to, or is the filter through which the film examines the interrelationship between art and technology, or music and mathematics.

Jordan does this by using a set of established and recognisable, though logically contradictory, tropes of the (rock/modern) musician-artist as creative and anarchic romantic genius[18] and that of the mad scientist, who, generally figured as European, uses his knowledge for evil or megalomaniac ends. Of course, though Bob and his gang are criminals, Bob is nonetheless a "good" thief, an ordinary decent criminal,[19] so to speak. As such, the film contrasts corporate capitalism, as figured in the giant and vulgar Japanese organisation that uses art to acquire respectability while trading on the dreams of the small man, whom Jordan clearly figures as one who enjoys the riddles of mathematics and probabilities as much as the imaginative leaps of romanticism and optimism. In this pairing, the casino can hardly be regarded as a "victim", or Vladimir or Bob as evil.

Additionally, Vladimir's character allows for the expression of the current obsession with technology as potentially liberating and as a tool for creative talent, as well as allowing Jordan to partake in its somewhat fetishistic representation, common within contemporary cinema, ranging from *The Terminator* and other cyborg movies to those concerned with genetic modification and virtual reality. If 007 seems to be anachronistic in many ways, his gadgets and technology, like Vladimir's, more than fit current tastes.[20] Through Vladimir and his multimedia security/laser performances, Jordan attempts to render (post)modern technology's libidinal power. While the distant representation of technology as visual or artistic spectacle is initially given precedence (such as during his first meeting with the gang), later in the scenes featuring Vladimir's camera-pen, when he introduces the bug into the security system, this is complemented by the immersive and subjective view through technology.

If such a strategy facilitates a first-person cinema of identification and recalls the look of the fuzzy and often frenetic or "*emotional*" hand-held camera, Jordan does not use it in a critical manner to challenge notions around realism, representation and ideology, but to celebrate visual difference and alter the film's palette and texture, a task in which he is amply aided by experienced cinematographer Chris Menges.[21] This celebration of the image, which is a key feature of Jordan's cinema, while generally not unrelated to the requirements of the narrative and, as such, cannot be seen as explicitly challenging rationality and narrative, is clearly palpable in this film. It is simply that Jordan is aware of the visual canvas and just as he invites us to take conceptual leaps or to *think* differently, so, too, does he literally force us to *look* differently and to see reality filtered through heightened colour; a prolonged or lingering look (as, for example, when Anne erotically dances over a restrained Bob on his bed);[22] a strangely angled camera; a monochrome greenish camera-pen lens; frozen as a still; slowed or otherwise manipulated through post-production techniques; fractured and repeated in compositionally similar shots (such as the three shots of the various

characters descending staircases on the night of the robbery);
or lit in a highly theatrical or staged manner, which may produce
alternatively a silhouetted image of black on red, as in the developing room, or more naturalistic silhouettes in shades of
blues and greys. These techniques are most visible in the nightclub scenes and at the horse-racing track.

Even if, ultimately, it is the sensuality of the images which is
of greatest importance to Jordan, he never loses sight of the
problem of vision or surfaceness. Both Bob (in his education of
Anne on gambling) and Paulo comment on the importance of
looking good, or of creating the illusion of appearance: Paulo tells
the twins, "gel is essential when things get complicated", while
Vladimir's disarming of the security system relies on making the
camera lie. Of course, this is a common cinematic device — used
most explicitly in *Speed* (Jan de Bont, 1994), where it enables the
film's successful resolution — and is a technological updating of
the straying human eye which fails to read the closed-circuit
camera, as in *Coma* (Michael Crichton, 1978), which otherwise
"celebrates" the ubiquity of modern invasive technology.

Nevertheless, though perception and appearance are undoubtedly explored, in these instances, as in the twins and more
generally through the works of art — the casino's and Bob's
Picasso, which is scientifically revealed to be a fake — Jordan
sees within this imaginative and positive possibilities.[23] Put in
other terms, he suggests that technology, rationality, or vision
as approximate with knowledge, let you down; art does not.

Meanwhile, returning to the plot, under threat of deporta-
tion, Said becomes a police informant and seeks to get information from Anne about Bob and his associates. If Melville's
informer is given a certain independence of function, Jordan has
Bob conscious of, and thereby to a degree in control of, the inevitability of betrayal which any planned heist will involve and
accordingly incorporates it into his scheme. (Such an understanding of betrayal is also explored in *Sunrise with Sea Monster*.)
However, as with everything in the film, the Judas figure becomes split or doubled, with the one favoured as Judas — illegal Algerian immigrant Said — never, as Bob had counted on,
posing a real threat to the robbery, as he remains unaware of

the nature of the real robbery. Paulo, less analytical, confuses appearance with reality and facilities the real Judas, Remi, while negating the fake or chosen traitor.

In order to raise money for the art theft, Bob convinces corrupt art dealer Tony Angel to buy his treasured Picasso, which he claims to have won from the artist, but when this turns out to be a fake, Angel cuts up the canvas and threatens that unless the one and a half million paid is returned within a few days, his "heavies" will give to his face a similar "new aesthetic without an anaesthetic". In an amusing aside, akin to the comment on the deranged Irish man (Stoker) in *Interview with the Vampire*, Angel asks whether it was not Picasso's Irish cousin, Paddy, who gave Bob the piece. That he goes on to make reference to Paul Keating is of note, in that it calls to mind two key Irish representational painters: Paul Henry, who developed a distinct school of Irish landscape (and in particular the representation of the West), and Sean Keating, who "sums up the 'discovery' of the West of Ireland as a source for patriotic, heroic, almost propagandist subject matter which seems to have been adopted by the [Irish] independence movement to straight-jacket Irish art into nationalist terms".[24]

Though the planning and training go ahead, with the addition of Albert and Bertram's robbery, which Bob welcomes as a bonus diversion to the art theft, Roger is increasingly putting pressure on Bob and continually tails him. Such journeys include going to an addiction recovery meeting, out of which Bob immediately walks after reciting the trite aphorism and confession. More interestingly, there are "red herring" trips to the countryside, where he suggests, in a flourish of storytelling, that he is seeking his origins and his mother's home, and to a Catholic church — which if narratively surprising is, nonetheless, a familiar trope in Jordan's films — where Bob, on the pretext that he is going to pray to his dead mother in a side chapel, gives Roger the slip. He tells Roger that his mother was French; she met an American GI during the war, but he left her for another woman and took Bob as a young child to America. If these serve to mislead Roger, and are yet another layer of falsehood or creative reinterpretation of reality, they are also part of the narrative thread that binds the two men. For Bob, he and Roger are co-dependents, with Roger caught up in Bob's imagined identity as much as Bob himself is.[25] By the film's end, Bob clearly no longer needs to search for his lost mother, having found Anne, and so the narrative he spins to her is inevitably radically different: his father and mother, he tells her, were performers.

However, it is not Roger who poses a threat to the heist, but chance and passion. Remi discovers, through a drugged Anne, Paulo and Bob's plan to rob the casino and subsequently accidentally finds negatives/contact sheets of the pictures to be robbed. Fittingly, he finds the "evidence" behind Paulo's bathroom mirror, as he is posing as her protector — the flipside of his protector role as pimp. He then confronts Paulo, telling him that Anne and Said are lovers, and that she has told Said everything about the plan. In an irrational outburst of passion, Paulo tracks down Said and shoots him while the (ignorant) informant speaks with Roger, leaving the real traitor free to do the damage.

Bob advises Paulo to cross the Italian border at San Remo to escape arrest, but he turns back to join with the twins and, as their "triplet", gets ready to rob the casino's safe. Meanwhile, Anne realises, as she puts it, that "everyone wants a piece of me". This epiphany leads her back to Bob's protection. He decides to educate her in the world of gambling and the two get ready for the big night. Looking handsome and beautiful, the couple discover the magic of chance and, to his astonishment and the dismay of the casino's management, he wins.

That this should be the outcome is written not so much by Melville, but is already visible in Anne's unusual eyes, one of which is green and the other brown, and to which attention is drawn by Bob. Unlike in *Chinatown* (Roman Polanski, 1974) where the eyes of Faye Dunaway's character serve as one of the film's many metaphors for vision and knowledge, it is important to note that her iris is flawed. This physical mark embodies the film's tragedy and suggests the inevitability of her own and the film's tragic end. Anne's eyes are not seen as flawed but as possessing magical difference; they are, in Bob's terms, "lucky". These eyes, together with her maturation into womanhood have already written the happy ending: she is no longer a prime (a number only divisible by itself) on the all-important night during which she, as otherworldly muse, persuades Bob to back even numbers, thus triggering his winning streak.

The corollary of Bob's success is the failure of the scientifically and militarily precise plan. Working in the gothic Napoleonic sewers, the transsexual Philippa is paralysed by her fear of spiders that crawl over the gas pipe that she has to turn off. Here again is a significant change in the original narrative. Ironically, given the criticism that Jordan has received with regard to gender politics, the bad or betraying women of Melville are absent, or are saved by Jordan. Just as questions of sexual or gender identity are problematised in *The Crying Game*, so, too, are they here through Philip/Philippa who holds on to an essential identity beyond the limits or visibility of her anatomy. This fact is explained by the various gang members to the immature Paulo, who, unsurprisingly, never understands Anne as anything more than an ideal of his own fantasy, or as someone to impress.

Meanwhile, the rest of the team, attempting to break through the art vault's floor, cut a gas pipe, causing a massive explosion. Miraculously, the paintings are undamaged. Having learnt of the plan, Roger arrives, only to dismiss the attempted break-in as amateurish and clearly not of Bob's making. Only the transsexual is captured as she remains shaking and crying in the sewer, a victim to her spider phobia.

Roger races to the casino to find, to his relief, that Bob is at the gambling table, having beaten the bank. Later, when Bob goes to collect his winnings, the manager of the casino is embarrassed as well as annoyed at not having the cash to pay him. Accepting a cheque, Bob, with Anne and Roger, leaves the casino, while Paulo is seen celebrating the theft of the money with one of the twins across the Italian border. Bob and Anne walk together on the Monte Carlo seafront which is coded as potentially the place of magical possibilities, even though elsewhere in Jordan, such as in *The Butcher Boy* and *Mona Lisa*, amongst others, it is discovered to be the place of ultimate loss and loneliness. In this instance, it is clear that they will live happily together on his winnings, for the film is nothing less than a fairytale where romance and optimism are rewarded. In such a world, Bob is allowed to become "the good thief" — whether figured as the biblical repentant sinner who is given salvation and heaven by Christ in the name of the Father and the Holy Ghost (the same Father who denied Bendrix Sarah in *End of the Affair*), or as the derring-do Robin Hood who steals from the rich to give to the worthy — and to enjoy his double booty of the money and the girl. He achieves a secular heaven, so to speak. Like at the end of *Mona Lisa* and *The Miracle*, in which the various characters attempt to translate or narrativise their adventures and dreams, the two lovers exchange stories.

In summary, Jordan considerably alters Melville's text so that everything is doubled, and fractured as if by a prism through which he views, and thereby alters, reality. So while *The Good Thief* carries the label of "remake", it is nonetheless a prime example of Jordan's filmmaking, and, as such, includes a number of elements that are central in his other work, namely an interest in the border between reality and fantasy, the relationship between rationality and irrationality, perception and appearance, the joy in the image and the visual, as well as performance and magic (such as in the detective's idle playacting), and the possibility of imagination, chance and love. Finally, it would not be a Jordan film without eclectic use of music, both diegetic and extra-diegetic (across the spectrum from Leonard Cohen to Jimi Hendrix to the crooning of "That's Life") as an expressive and poetic summary or embodiment of the film's narrative. For all its interest in the reality of the heist, the mundane reasons why one does certain things and the social world of Nice, it is, like so much of his work, a kind of simple and mythic fairytale. As Jordan comments, it is fundamentally "a story set in a place of the mind". Expanding on this, he explains, "We've built an imagined city, an imagined environment. There's a deeply romantic feel to this film."[26] For that reason alone, it is worthy of positive critical engagement.

Notes

¹ We would like to thank Neil Jordan for arranging a screening for us of *The Good Thief* prior to its cinema release. Interestingly, Conor McPherson, who has adapted and directed a Neil Jordan story as the feature film *The Actors* (2003), wrote a play in 1994 entitled *The Good Thief*, which features a criminal who goes on the run to Sligo.

² Besides copying the techniques and popular story ideas of European films, American producers and distributors simply duped or copied European films already in distribution. See Charles Musser (1990), *The Emergence of Cinema: The American Screen to 1907*, Berkeley/Los Angeles/London: University of California Press.

³ Quoted in Momentum Pictures Press Book for *The Good Thief* (hereafter referred to as Press Book), p. 8.

⁴ Press Book, p. 15.

⁵ Press Book, p. 12.

⁶ Jean Pierre Melville, quoted in Rui Nogueira (1971), *Melville*, London: Secker and Warburg, 53.

⁷ Ibid., pp. 53–4.

⁸ Press Book, p. 10. These views are very similar to those made by another Irishman, film director Rex Ingram, who, after a successful Hollywood career, including directing *The Four Horsemen of the Apocalypse* (1921), which made Rudolph Valentino a star, abandoned the American film industry for Europe. He began making films in the South of France and in the mid-1920s bought for $5 million the Victorine Studios in Nice, where he made a number of films under contract for MGM, including perhaps his greatest film, *Mare Nostrum* (1925–26), *The Magician* (1926) and *The Garden of Allah* (1927). Responding to criticism of his move to Europe, he argued as much on financial as artistic grounds, and believed that trans-European productions would challenge "bourgeois" Hollywood. See Liam O'Leary (1980), *Rex Ingram: Master of the Silent Cinema*, Dublin: The Academic Press, 145ff. Later productions based at the Victorine included Marcel Carné and Jacques Prévert's *Les Enfants du Paradis* (1944), Michael Powell's *Red Shoes* (1947), Alfred Hitchcock's *To Catch a Thief* (1954), Jean Cocteau's *Le Testament D'Orphée* (1959), Jacques Demy's *La Baie Des*

Anges (1962), *Chitty Chitty Bang Bang* (Ken Hughes, 1967), *Monte Carlo or Bust* (Ken Annakin, 1968), François Truffaut's *La Nuit Americaine* (1972), and *The Return of the Pink Panther* (Blake Edwards, 1974).

[9] See Jean Baudrillard, "Simulacra and Simulations", in *Jean Baudrillard: Selected Writings*, Mark Poster, ed. (1988), Cambridge: Polity Press. For Baudrillard, the line between reality/original/referent and the image/copy is complex in that, in the fourth phase of the image — the hyper-real or simulacrum — the real is no longer relevant. There *is* no original. "As simulacra, images precede the real to the extent that they invert the causal and logical order of the real and its reproduction" (Jean Baudrillard (1987), *The Evil Demon of Images*, Sydney: Power Institute Publications No. 3, 13). Despite Jordan's own challenging and fracturing of reality and play with meanings and multiple images, the link with Baudrillard is ultimately compromised by Jordan's modernist belief in a kind of reality. What he explores is the many ways reality can be perceived and understood. Images may for Jordan, like Baudrillard, hold a "primal pleasure unencumbered by aesthetic, moral, social or political judgements" (ibid., p. 28), but they are not "sites of the disappearance of meaning and representation" (ibid., p. 29). Instead, they are sites of challenge. Images, even while they enjoy a freedom, are in Jordan's work ultimately bound to narrative (and (sur)reality).

[10] Press Book, p. 11.

[11] Neil Jordan, quoted in Press Book, p. 9.

[12] The film conceivably could have been made in any casino city, but the location allows for greater social veracity (Press Book, p. 9).

[13] At a more personal level, both Jordan and Woolley have an intimate relationship with gambling. Jordan has described himself as an enthusiastic gambler who loves, in particular, cards (Press Book, p. 10), while Woolley's father was an addicted gambler (ibid., p. 22).

[14] Interestingly, this is the name given by Melville to Bob's crime partner, here named Raoul.

[15] While the horse's name may appear an ironic Irish reference to William, Prince of Orange, in fact, it is the name of the horse in Melville's film. Of course, William of Orange also let down the Irish . . .

16 The idea of the casino as art gallery in part came from one such establishment in Los Angeles called the Bellaggio, owned by the former managers of Studio 54. Their vulgar idea was to hang Picassos in order to attract customers (Press Book, p. 8). It is somewhat fitting that the building should house such paintings, considering the casino is actually the Regina Hotel designed by Marcel Biazini, where Queen Victoria stayed whenever she was in Nice and which was home to such artists as Matisse (Press Book, p. 9). Of course, Nice is steeped in artistic heritage, from painters (Picasso and Chagall) to writers (Maupassant, Apollinaire, Katherine Mansfield, Aldous Huxley, D.H. Lawrence, Ernest Hemingway, et al.) and filmmakers (Lumière Brothers, Jean Cocteau, Jean Marais).

17 This aspect of the film was highlighted in the earlier, non-biblical, title of the film, Double Down, which refers to "a gambling term in blackjack, where you place another bet on top of your initial bet" (Press Book, p. 10; see also Michael Dwyer, Irish Times Magazine, 7 July 2001: 20, and Irish Independent, 7 June 2001: 13).

18 The use of Jimi Hendrix's instrumental version of the American National Anthem, which closed the Woodstock Festival in 1969, and which is "copied" here by Vladimir, itself, of course, carries its own ironic comment, not least the Russian playing music interpreted, if not "composed" by an African-American. The association of Hendrix's powerful guitar solos and Vladimir's role as the "bug" in the "security" system allows for a metaphor for popular music/culture infiltrating art and technology.

19 In Thaddeus O'Sullivan's Ordinary Decent Criminal (2000), a similar device is used; in this case, an original Caravaggio is passed off as a fake.

20 It is some coincidence that the first James Bond book, Casino Royale, is also set in Monte Carlo.

21 This was the third of Jordan's films to be shot by cinematographer Chris Menges. Previously he had photographed Angel and Michael Collins.

22 While this dance may appear to fit the male gaze, which is argued as being entirely detrimental to women in which women are cast as mere actors in a male fantasy without any subjectivity, it is important

to understand that Anne is consciously playing with Bob and teasing him; he is all the time restrained. It is she who is clearly in control. In that sense, her dancing and deliberate playing with her own status as (sexual) image is akin to the notion of the masquerade whereby women put on masks of femininity. The adoption of such masks suggests that what is perceived as "natural" feminine identity is nothing more than a series of performances. Thereby it works to destabilise categories and challenge regressive gender politics. Her dance is somewhat reminiscent (at both a formal cinematographic level and thematic level) as that given by a club girl in *Leaving Las Vegas*. If that dance less self-consciously plays with notions around male gazing, the fact that the men seem trapped behind a brass bar and that Ben is in a disabling drunken state highlights male powerlessness. Interestingly, Sera in *Leaving Las Vegas* characterises her job as a prostitute as one of performance, and like Anne, though in a different context, she inserts herself into a mathematical discourse when she explains her work. Jordan had previously explored the masquerade and performance elsewhere, but particularly in *Mona Lisa* and *The Crying Game*, where it is a key feature.

[23] Wim Wenders's *The American Friend* (1977), based on Patricia Highsmith's *Ripley's Game*, perhaps more than any other film eloquently explores the relationship between "fake" American paintings and the European craft tradition, a film which, metaphorically, especially in the presence in it of American film directors Nicholas Ray and Samuel Fuller, serves as a meditation on the European/American cultural axis.

[24] Anne Crookshank and the Knight of Glin (1979; orig. 1978), *The Painters of Ireland c.1660–1920*, London: Barrie & Jenkins, second edition, 273.

[25] This coupling of criminal and detective, rehearsed rather pedantically in *Heat* (Michael Mann, 1995), and more imaginatively and complexly in *Face/Off* (John Woo, 1997) and *Insomnia* (Christopher Nolan, 2002), can be seen as yet another instance of the schizophrenic splitting of the contemporary subject, which is best expressed in *Fight Club* (David Fincher, 1999).

[26] Press Book, pp. 9–10. Put simply, "It's a Neil Jordan film, so it's no more a conventional heist movie than *The Crying Game* was a conventional thriller." (Stephen Woolley quoted by Michael Dwyer, *Irish Times* Magazine, 7 July 2001: 23).

Chapter Fifteen

Production and Exhibition Contexts

While Neil Jordan's films explore a range of themes which make him not just the most eclectic of Irish filmmakers and arguably the most interesting, as is discussed in previous chapters, the means of financing, crewing, casting and releasing of his films also places him apart from his Irish contemporaries. His mentor, as noted in the discussion of his early career, was British film director, John Boorman, an Irish resident since the early 1970s, who encouraged Jordan's interest in filmmaking by inviting him to become script consultant on *Excalibur* and by providing funds to make a promotional documentary about the film.[1] While Jordan and Boorman had already collaborated on a script (*Broken Dream*), and would do so again on another unproduced script (a historical tale, *The Rab*), it was the project which preceded this, Jordan's first feature film, *Angel*, which defined his relationship to Irish filmmaking throughout the 1980s and much of the 1990s.

Reference has been made in the *Angel* chapter to the tensions which its funding caused in Ireland, yet the allocation from the Film Board constituted less than twenty per cent of *Angel*'s budget, with the balance, £400,000, coming from Britain's newly established and innovative television station, Channel 4. Not only was *Angel* one of the first features to be funded by Channel 4, but it set a precedent for the channel's made-for-television films when it received a theatrical release at London's Scala cinema in autumn 1982. It was only after intensive lobbying that Channel 4 had agreed to allow the film to be shown theatrically, having initially rejected the proposal. As a result, as Ian Christie comments, without the screening, "Jordan's directorial career would have been damaged, if not aborted".[2]

Stephen (Steve) Woolley, programme manager at the Scala and co-founder with Nik Powell of a recently established film production and distribution company, Palace Pictures, had seen *Angel* at Cannes and liked it, and when it was screened at the Edinburgh Film Festival later in 1982, it was well received. It was the beginning of a relationship which has continued to the present, despite the collapse a decade later of Palace Pictures. Since *Angel*, Woolley has produced, co-produced or executive produced all except one (the American production *We're No Angels*) of Jordan's films, while Powell has been involved in all productions up to, but excluding, *Interview with the Vampire*. Although actor Robert de Niro (*We're No Angels*) and film and music billionaire David Geffen (*Interview with the Vampire, Michael Collins, The Butcher Boy*) have also received producer credits, it is Irishman Redmond Morris, besides Woolley and Powell, who most frequently shares the producer, co-producer or executive producer credit. These films include *The Miracle, The Crying Game, Interview with the Vampire, Michael Collins* and *The Butcher Boy*.[3]

Though much has been made of the Irish Film Board's support for *Angel*, it remains the only one of his thirteen feature films to have been funded by the Board. However, unlike in the 2000s, when the Board's annual production budget has been between €10 million and €13 million, in the 1980s it only had about €635,000 per annum to invest in films, while Irish tax-based incentives for private and corporate investors were not introduced until 1987, and then only after the Film Board had been closed down by the government. (It was not re-activated until 1993.) As a result, it is unsurprising that Jordan, who wished to make features for the commercial film market, should have developed a productive relationship with Woolley, Powell and Palace Pictures. Following the relative success of the modestly budgeted *Angel*, the next project, *Company of Wolves*, had no Irish finance, nor, indeed, Irish personnel, except, of course, for Jordan's regular actor Stephen Rea. It was the first film to be produced by Palace Pictures.

The sheer brashness of the anti-film establishment duo of Woolley and Powell led them not only to raise £2 million from the British company ITC for *Company of Wolves* after Channel 4 baulked at a budget which passed £1 million, but cheekily and cunningly succeeded in getting the film's premiere booked for the Rank flagship cinema, the Odeon Leicester Square, London, in September 1984. Rank thought that the most it would take in its first week was £40,000, but after a clever, teasing and relatively inexpensive publicity campaign, the film took £69,000 in its first seven days (Finney, 1997: 79), even though the film carried an Over-18s film censors' certificate, which excluded a major proportion of the hoped-for teenage audience. In America, the film was distributed by the sex-and-gore company Cannon, who marketed the film as a blood-and-guts product like *Friday the 13th* and released it, not in specialist arthouse cinemas, but in 800 mainstream cinemas in March 1985 (Finney, 1997: 81). While the film took a very respectable £1.4 million in the UK, its $4.3 million North American gross failed even to cover Cannon's print costs and advertising (Finney, 1997: 82).

After a period of hectic expansion, Palace Pictures needed a commercial success to give the company credibility and cash, having produced the artistically and commercially disappointing *Absolute Beginners* (1986) at a cost of £8.6 million, twice its 1984 budget, and with £500,000 of its own money invested. It was hoped *Mona Lisa* could be such a product. Although conceived before *Company of Wolves*, it only went into pre-production in October 1985, with a budget of just over £2 million. Filming began the following month with the backing of George Harrison's HandMade Films. It broke the house box office records at the Odeon Haymarket, taking £1.1 million during its first four weeks; it eventually rose to over £4 million at the UK box office (Finney, 1997: 129). With Bob Hoskins winning the Best Actor award at the 1986 Cannes Film Festival, and positive reviews of the film in the USA after its release there in June 1986, and where Hoskins was nominated for an Oscar as Best Actor, it took $10 million at the American box office. In the meantime, Jordan became one of the executive producers for the Irish crime film set in Dublin, *The Courier* (Joe Lee, Frank Deasy, 1988), with Woolley as co-

producer. The film's budget was about £1 million, of which
£820,000 came from Palace (Rockett, 1987: 258–9).

High Spirits, another Jordan-Woolley project, was also shot
in Ireland during the summer of 1987. Of all his films, Jordan
has reserved the most venom for Palace's American production
partners on this film. With the success of *Mona Lisa*, Woolley
and Jordan looked more to the USA for funding opportunities.
Woolley interested a senior Columbia Pictures executive,
Steve Sohmer, in the project in part because he took holidays
in Ireland each summer. The film was put into development as
an Irish "Ghost O'Busters", or as Woolley and Jordan had envisaged it, as a type of *Whiskey Galore!* American co-writer Michael McDowell (not credited on the film), who had worked on
Beetlejuice (Tim Burton, 1988), spent four days in Ireland with
Woolley and Jordan. However, as often happens in Hollywood,
Sohmer had moved jobs within Columbia by the time the script
was delivered, and the new head of the studio, David Puttnam,
had little interest in such a "vulgar comedy" (Finney, 1997:
142). This is not surprising, considering the approach being
taken by some of the American producers.

In a faxed seven-page memo from the USA dated 30 March
1987, seventy-plus amendments/revisions were sought not only
to re-orient the film towards an American audience, but to play
on some of the worst stereotypical excesses applied to the
Irish. "We now have an American focus that our audiences can
identify with," they wrote in response to Jordan's revised script,
but asked that Jack and Sharon, the newly-marrieds at the centre of the story, should be seen first in America: "It will make it
feel more like an American movie." By item three, stage-
Irishness (if not overt racism) was being sought: "The description that every house is a pub is extremely funny . . . Tell us that
the camera dollies down the single street past each of these
houses-pubs and give us the name of the pubs which can get
sillier as we move along."[4] While acceding to script changes to
satisfy the American producers, Jordan later recorded that "in a
way every script that one presents to the people who finance
films is a bit of a lie and every script that I present tells a kind of
a lie. It pretends to be one thing and my real intentions are

something quite different." To get the American backing, he had to write the second draft which enlarged the American aspect, something he didn't particularly want to do, and then shot quite a different script. "I don't think it is quite deceit, [because] I don't think anyone would be happy with the film that the consensus of backers seemed to be talking about at the start"; it was a way of ensuring that the "final product [could] be made with some kind of purity and some kind of integrity".[5]

Woolley gained the involvement of a wealthy financier, Wafic Said (or Sayeed), who offered to invest $12 million in the project, $5 million less than the Jordan/McDowell script required because of the high special effects budget. Eventually, Vision PDG became the principal investor in the film, but along with the other backers of the project, further rewrites were demanded, much to Jordan's irritation (Finney, 1997: 143). Though the film did very well for Palace at the UK box office, Woolley commented that it fell between "American *Airplane* style of humour and broad comedy, and wasn't really about the bunch of lovable Irish guys we'd envisioned at the start." For Jordan, another problem was that the American investors wanted to get the film into cinemas as quickly as possible. As a result, when previewed, "audiences were predictably confused, so it was recut". He added that the previews "were used by the investors as a pretext to make a different film to what I'd intended, and everybody's perspective got lost in the process" (Finney, 1997: 144). It was not the first time a producer had interfered in one of his films. During the making of *Mona Lisa*, HandMade's Denis O'Brien insisted that the Soho sex-shop and strip-joint montage be toned down and that music rather than dialogue and natural sound be used (as Jordan recalls in his commentary to the DVD edition of the film).

Jordan went straight from what he regarded as the disaster visited on him by the "scumbag" producers (Dwyer, 1997: 5), to his biggest budget yet, the $30 million *We're No Angels*. Though Jordan acknowledged that comedy is not his forte, this light comedy, which was received poorly by reviewers and the public alike, was, according to him, badly managed by the studio (Finney, 1997: 144). Perhaps the real problem with the film lies with de Niro's terrible performance which though inevitably reflects on Jordan's ability as a director to get the actor to deliver, may also have to do with a power struggle whereby de Niro is not simply a leading actor but was the film's executive producer.

After his disappointments with big-budget American projects, Jordan's career stabilised with *The Miracle*, modestly budgeted (if not in Irish terms at the time), at £2.7 million. With Woolley busy on other projects, line producer Redmond Morris was appointed the film's co-producer. While the film was critically well received, getting an award at the 1991 Berlin Film Festival and Best Original Screenplay from the London *Evening Standard*, Woolley later commented in the context of Palace's increasing financing difficulties that "on reflection, the sensible thing would have been to cancel" *The Miracle* and another Palace project, *The Pope Must Die* (Finney, 1997: 263). The film was released in America by Miramax but Jordan was disappointed at their lack of support for it and when it came to his next film, *The Crying Game*, he was "less than thrilled" that the company was going to release it. Aware that Miramax edited films as they saw fit, Jordan insisted that a clause be written into the contract that they could not change it (Finney, 1997: 275). In the end, it was Miramax's brilliant marketing of the film that made *The Crying Game* such a hit.

The Crying Game project, under the name *The Soldier's Wife*, was originally submitted in May 1982 to Channel 4's drama department, less than two months after *Angel's* controversial Irish premiere. Channel 4 was no more enthusiastic about the project a decade later when Jordan and the film's producer Steve Woolley pressed them to accept the script's unconventional "revelation" that the woman was really a man. Jordan and Woolley thought that the positive response to *The Miracle* at the Berlin Film Festival would make it relatively easy to fund *The Crying Game*, but *The Miracle* did not prove to be a commercial success and hence the script was treated with extreme caution by film financiers at Cannes a few months later, by which time Jordan had revised the script, placing the "revelation" scene at the centre of the narrative.

American investors such as Sony and Miramax were unimpressed by (or afraid of) the "taboo-breaking" script. Jordan recalled that "one executive said it was more than his career was worth even to be associated with it because it dealt with race, sexuality, [and] political violence".[6] Eventually, the film was funded from European sources with £1 million sterling being invested by Eurotrustees, a consortium of which Palace was the British member, along with Spanish, German, French and Italian film distributors, which had been established in 1990 to counter American dominance within the European film industry. A Japanese company, Nippon Film Development and Finance, invested a further £350,000, while British Screen, the UK's main source of public money for investment in feature films, put in £500,000 (Finney, 1997: 16–19).

The rest of the £2.3 million budget came from Channel 4, but not before brinkmanship negotiations over Dil's revelation scene. Channel 4's commissioning editors felt that Jordan's script was the best he had done up until the revelation of Dil's gender; thereafter, it was deemed an "anticlimax" (Finney, 1997: 20). Following intense pressure from Woolley and a meeting in Ireland between Jordan and Channel 4's Jack Lechner, a deal was agreed with Jordan writing what he later called a "fake ending" to satisfy Channel 4. He said that he shot it just to show Channel 4 that it didn't work. Afterwards, he got permission to shoot the original ending at an extra cost of £45,000. The unused footage "involved a somewhat incredible Hollywood-style snow scene and an escape to Barbados for certain leading characters" (Finney, 1997: 28).

Casting also caused problems for Channel 4, the actors' union Equity and the black press, who all objected to the American Forrest Whitaker playing the soldier. Additionally, Channel 4 had difficulty with English actress Miranda Richardson playing the IRA woman Jude on the basis of the ready availability of Irish actresses — an ironic reversal of British film industry practice where even minor British actors have been given lead roles in Irish subject films ahead of experienced Irish actors. Woolley and Jordan argued strongly in both cases that casting against nationality added to, rather than detracted from, the film's authenticity,

or, at least, helped create an estrangement effect. No such res-
ervations were made about Stephen Rea, who is seen by Jordan
in the tradition of the "unadorned style" of acting of Jean-Paul
Belmondo and Jean Gabin, and lauds his ability to project a character's inner meaning onto his almost blank face, a view shared
by the press which described his performance as "magnetic".[7]
Rea's own main acting reference points are Robert Mitchum,
Spencer Tracy and Humphrey Bogart, who were "incredibly
discreet, understated actors. They allowed the camera to
watch them thinking and that's enough, provided you are thinking."[8] It was, of course, the casting of Dil which proved to be
most problematic, but the film's casting director Susie Figgis
found cross-dresser Jaye Davidson, a fabric buyer for dress de-
signers who had once worked as a hairdresser. Following extensive screen tests, the reluctant actor was hired, with the
advantage that as an unknown, his gender was similarly a mystery
(Finney, 1997: 12–13).

With such a range of difficulties — from script content to
casting — all that was needed was a crisis at the production
company. Because of Channel 4's hesitancy, production was
postponed from July to 4 November 1991, by which time Palace
was in deep financial trouble. As a result, most of those working
on the film accepted payment deferrals and despite the crisis
which overcame Palace, all of those who worked on the film,
except producers Woolley and Powell, were paid in full by autumn 1993. The production was thrown into further disarray
during the first week of shooting when Director of Photography
Frederick Elmes left the set following technical difficulties and
disagreements with Jordan, who wanted to push the pace of
production faster than the more relaxed American wished (Finney, 1997: 27). In his place, Ian Wilson, a highly experienced British cameraman, was appointed immediately. In spite of the
problems, the film was in the can by Christmas and a rough-cut
was ready by January 1992. In April, it got its new title, *The Crying
Game*, but to the disappointment of all involved in the production, it was turned down for a screening at the Cannes Film Festival. April was also the month Palace was declared bankrupt,
with debts variously estimated at between £15 million and £30

million. Nevertheless, *The Crying Game* was released in the UK by Mayfair on 30 October 1992 as part of a pre-bankruptcy deal.

The film's release in Britain was hampered by a renewal of the IRA's bombing campaign in England the same week as the film was released, and it became embroiled in controversy over whether its was pro- or anti-IRA. Thus, the *Daily Telegraph* commented that "the recent plague of bombs in London will, no doubt, make it harder than usual for British cinemagoers to accept the notion of an IRA man with a conscience turned too delicate for the dirty work of terrorism".[9] The sterility of this debate (or right-wing British press comment) detracted from issues of race and gender which are at least as relevant to the film as its overt "political" terrorist aspects, and, undoubtedly, affected its relatively poor performance at the UK box office, where it took a mere £300,000 by Christmas 1992. Only when it was nominated for six Academy Awards and was a major hit in mainstream American cinemas was the hostility to the film slightly tempered in Britain and it proved, despite criticism of the poor distribution of the film by Mayfair, who rushed its country-wide distribution rather than wait for a slow build-up of interest in it, as had happened in America, to have continuing audience appeal, taking about £2 million in the UK. In Ireland, north and south, it took about €1 million at the box office, while in Europe, it had fared badly at the box office in those countries where it had been released prior to the Oscar nominations.

In the US, it was a very different story. Miramax's Bob Weinstein declared, having previously turned down the script, that it was "one of the greatest movies I've ever seen" (quoted Giles, 1997: 46). Also helpful was a rave review from *Variety* in which Todd McCarthy called it "an astonishingly good and daring film that richly develops several intertwined thematic lines, [taking] risks that are stunningly rewarded".[10] Vincent Canby also gave the film a positive review in the *New York Times*.[11] With a teasing publicity campaign aimed at keeping the "secret", Miramax enticed audiences into the cinema from its release in November 1992. The film was released shortly after Bill Clinton's election as President of the United States, in effect a changing of the guard after twelve years of Republican right-wing rule towards an apparently more open and liberal Democratic era. This change, allied with a vigorous debate on homosexuality in the American military which dominated Clinton's first month in the White House, January 1993, and the nomination of the film for six Academy Awards, including Best Picture and Jaye Davidson as Best Supporting Actor, gave the film renewed box office appeal.

During this time, the number of release prints increased from 239 to 1,000, with the film crossing over from arthouse to mainstream commercial cinemas (Giles, 1997: 49). Consequently, *The Crying Game* became the most profitable film in 1993 measured by the gap between total production costs, about $5 million, and gross US box office receipts, about $63 million. Miramax would have received about thirty per cent of this, or $19 million, but when the costs of film prints, advertising, and the Oscar campaign, estimated at $15 million, are taken into account, the company may have netted only $4 million. Since Miramax paid $1.5 million for the film rights, plus $1 million when it acquired North American copyright of the film, it had not made a significant profit by the end of its North American release. However, the company also retained video and Pay-TV rights and, on the back of *The Crying Game*, Miramax was sold by the Weinstein brothers to Disney for between $60 and $80 million (Finney, 1997: 283).

In the meantime, Jordan's Oscar success coincided with the push towards the rejuvenation of the Irish Film Board. Under the energetic and committed leadership of Michael D. Higgins, the first Minister for Arts and Culture with full Cabinet rank, an announcement was made on the day after Jordan's *Crying Game* win that the Film Board would be re-established, with film activist Lelia Doolan as Chairperson. Later, Jordan himself accepted an invitation to join the Board, and for four years he participated in the Board's deliberations, often as a script reader, as its budget increased exponentially during the 1990s and Irish filmmaking entered its most expansive period so far. It also put, as Jordan later commented, "all those issues and resentments of the old Film Board to rest" (Dwyer, 1997: 6–7).

The commercial success of *The Crying Game* paved the way for Jordan to return to big-budget American productions, this time a reworking of the vampire genre, with an adaptation of Anne Rice's novel *Interview with the Vampire*. Warner Bros. committed to it, and while Palace Pictures had folded, Woolley, who had set up the deal with Warners, was asked by Jordan to join the production team (Finney, 1997: 281). Worried that the Hollywood moguls would interfere with the project, David Geffen, a music billionaire, and head of Geffen Productions, who had been developing the 1976 novel for a decade, and Warners, both agreed to allow the film to be independently produced by Woolley with, of course, Geffen's approval, since he owned the project. Woolley's Lazarus-like rise from the ashes of Palace's collapse (with a production fee of circa $500,000) was in effect the pay-off for his decade-long collaboration with Jordan, for whom he had by now produced five films. Woolley and Powell's new film production vehicle was Scala Productions, named after their old cinema.

Casting for the $28 million project, which rose to $70 million by the end of the production, proved difficult. Daniel Day Lewis turned down the part of Lestat, the vampire. His replacement, Tom Cruise, was publicly criticised by author Anne Rice, saying that Cruise "is no more my vampire Lestat than Edward G. Robinson is Rhett Butler" and called on him to withdraw from the film (quoted in Finney, 1997: 291). (As noted in Chapter Nine, Rice changed her view after seeing the film.) Geffen, Warners and Jordan all supported Cruise, who was being paid $15 million to play Lestat, in the belief that the money would be recouped because of his star status. River Phoenix, who was to play the film's interviewer, died on 1 November 1995 just as production had begun in New Orleans, and was replaced by Christian Slater, who joined the cast of Cruise, Brad Pitt, Antonio Banderas, Stephen Rea and Kirsten Dunst. *Interview* was released at the end of 1994 and took $105 million in North America and a further $110 million in the rest of the world, before video, Pay-TV and television rights had been exploited (Finney, 1997: 292). While the film might have had a sequel, it was not until 2002 that such a film, *Queen of the Damned*, was released, with Irish actor Stuart Townsend playing Lestat, and Michael Rymer, not Jordan, directing. With the commercial success of *Interview* assured, Warners finally gave the go-ahead to the *Michael Collins* project.

It is impossible to separate *Michael Collins* as a film from its extraordinary production as an Irish national event and the subsequent response to the film, which saw many older people return to the cinema after a gap of forty years. The film touched a chord with a great many Irish people. Because of the production costs involved, historical reconstructions are rare in independent or marginal cinemas. Since the regeneration of Irish cinema from the mid-1970s, those few films set in the eighteenth or nineteenth centuries — *Caoineadh Airt Uí Laoire* (1975), *It's Handy When People Don't Die* (1982) and *The Outcasts* (1982), were shot as low-budget 16mm productions, while *Anne Devlin* (1984), even though shot on 35mm, cost only £500,000. In earlier periods, British and American films set during the 1916–22 period had largely concentrated on the military conflict during the War of Independence (1919–21) and shied away from the 1916 Rising (the notable exception is John Ford's *The Plough and the Stars*), because, of course, the building and destruction of a replica of the General Post Office, Dublin, headquarters of the Rising, would be expensive.

Those few British films of the 1980s and 1990s set during the War of Independence have tended to be "Big House" dramas set amongst the often neurotic Anglo-Irish, such as *Ascendancy* (Edward Bennett, 1982), *The Dawning* (Robert Knights, 1989), *Fools of Fortune* (Pat O'Connor, 1990), and *The Last September* (Deborah Warner, 1999).[12] In the 1990s, two Irish films set in the 1950s and concentrating on the legacy of the Irish civil war, *Korea* (Cathal Black, 1996), which cost a mere £500,000, and *Broken Harvest* (Maurice O'Sullivan, 1996), were the first films to explore such themes.

Jordan's version of the 1916–22 period opens with the final stages of the battle at the GPO and the subsequent surrender of the rebels. To make such a scene, and the other costly historical reconstructions, Jordan needed the support of a major American studio, Warner Bros. Nevertheless, about ten per cent of the film's $27 million budget came from the Section 35

Irish tax incentives, which had been introduced in the 1987 Finance Act.

Jordan's script for *Michael Collins* had been written as early as 1982, a productive and pivotal year for Jordan, which not only saw his first feature, *Angel*, released, but the genesis of his script for *The Crying Game*. At that time, British film producer David Puttnam had sought to interest Jordan in Bernard MacLaverty's novel *Cal*, but Jordan found it "too guilt-ridden" and, suggesting a more positive ending than in the novel, was not surprised when the offer was withdrawn. Nevertheless, Puttnam enquired of Jordan's interest in Michael Collins, leading to Jordan's first big studio contract, with Warner Bros.

Jordan wrote a script which was "dispassionate in its perspectives, fiercely accurate to the history and saw the central character heading towards the doom that was inevitable, given his beliefs and obsessions — nationalism and the use of violence for political ends" (Jordan, 1996: 40). Puttnam, though, felt the film lacked a villain, but, Jordan, wary of simply casting the British in such a role, noted that for Irish people "the divisions within the island are as fascinating as those across the Irish Sea". The wider world, Jordan ruefully recorded years later, "wants to see it in more simplistic terms" (Jordan, 1996: 4).

In the meantime, as noted, Puttnam took over at Columbia Pictures, but Warner Bros. wanted to keep the Collins project. Puttnam then came across another script on Collins, which he put into production with Michael Cimino as director. While the Cimino film collapsed, actor Kevin Costner wanted to make a Collins film, with himself in the title role, a project with which writer Eoghan Harris was associated. Happily for Jordan, this project also foundered.

Endlessly churning out drafts for the studio, Jordan got to make five films before the Collins project got underway. What had changed by the time the last of these films was made was not just that *The Crying Game* had proved to be a commercially successful film and winner of an Oscar, but that the Irish Peace Process was underway, and at the end of August 1994, the IRA called a ceasefire. While there had been a brief ceasefire in the 1970s, this one was regarded as being more stable as the warring factions had reached, in effect, a stalemate. Thus, with an optimistic, and relatively violence-free Ireland, American producers David Geffen and Warner Bros., with whom Jordan had worked on *Interview with the Vampire*, gave support to the project.

By now, too, Jordan's own characterisation of Collins had undergone change. Rather than being "the dispassionate, rather dry perspective" of the first draft, Collins began progressively to breathe with life. As a result, Jordan decided to show the three main protagonists — Collins, de Valera, Boland — "in all their confusions, divisions, hopes and delusions". He took the view that Collins simply turned the ambitions of Irish nationalism into "realistic aims" and showed how they could be "practically achieved". His "uniqueness" in Irish history, according to Jordan, was how he masterminded a brutal war and then tried to stop it. The fact that he was undone in the end, "makes him a genuinely tragic figure" (Jordan, 1996: 6–7). With the project approved by the financiers, Jordan "embarked on a process which was eerie in the way a whole series of contemporary events paralleled the ones in the past we were filming" (Jordan, 1996: 7).

In his diary and screenplay of the film, Jordan records the events from Christmas 1994, when *Interview with the Vampire* was released in Ireland, through to the *Michael Collins* pre-production, including negotiations for the film's $27 million budget (Jordan, 1996: 20). Over the following seven months, until production began on 2 July 1995, a hectic schedule of casting on both sides of the Atlantic, rewrites, and the logistics of a fourteen-week shoot over multiple locations in the greater Dublin area had to be put in place. The response to the project, not just from actors, but by the general public who were called to participate in the film as unpaid extras, was extraordinary, bringing thousands of people in their own period costumes to play in crowd scenes such as the Bloody Sunday massacre by the Black and Tans. Additionally, as Jordan records, "the level of co-operation from the authorities [was] really remarkable" (Jordan, 1996: 37), perhaps on both counts because the past and present-day events were somehow seen to be merging.

Principal shooting finished on 27 September, with a few additional days of filming on sets in New York in early 1995, ending on 9 February, the day the IRA ceasefire finished with the bombing of Canary Wharf, London. A film produced as part of an optimistic peaceful future was going to be released into a very different world of British/Irish politics. Unsurprisingly, Jordan records that everyone was depressed and subdued, while Stephen Rea reminded him that he had promised Warners that there would be "no more war if they made this movie" (Jordan, 1996: 64–5). Nevertheless, the film went on to become Ireland's top-grossing film, taking about €5 million at the box office, while the IRA's ceasefire was renewed in 1996. In America, though, Warners half-heartedly promoted the film and did not put the resources into trying to make it a national film release. Instead, they relied on video, DVD, and Pay-TV revenues. Thus, the discourses which surrounded the film were formed primarily in Ireland, north and south, and in Britain.

With a well-developed working relationship with Warner Bros. and David Geffen, Jordan's and writer Patrick McCabe's adaptation of *The Butcher Boy* went into production relatively quickly. Commenting that after doing a "big Hollywood film", he felt "the need to do a small film again very quickly", he said that Warners had been good about *The Butcher Boy*, since it was not "the kind of thing they usually do".[13] It was well-received both in Ireland, where film critic Ciaran Carty called it Jordan's "masterpiece",[14] and elsewhere (especially in the USA, where both novel and film were reviewed positively, making many film critics' top ten list of films for 1998), but it failed to make a major impact at the box office. In Ireland, north and south, it took €1.4 million, making it a mid-ranking film for the year.

With this relative success, once more a big-budget film loomed, this time the $40 million *In Dreams*. As *In Dreams* was nearing completion in 1998, it was reported from the Cannes Film Festival that Jordan had entered into a three-year £35 million deal with DreamWorks SKG, the multi-billion dollar studio controlled by David Geffen, Steven Spielberg and Jerry Katzenberg. Regarded as one of the most attractive ever negotiated by a European director, it was envisaged that DreamWorks

SKG would provide the finance for three or four features a year produced by Jordan and his business partner Stephen Woolley.[15] The new Jordan/Woolley company was called after their first collaboration, The Company of Wolves, based in London, but with a Dublin office. By then, Geffen Pictures had backed four of Jordan's films.

The second of Jordan's releases in 1999, *The End of the Affair*, was a relatively expensive period film. It was generally well-received by critics and trade publications, and was nominated for four Golden Globe awards, while Julianne Moore was nominated in the Best Actress category for the Academy Awards. An area of controversy surrounding the film was the decision by the British Board of Film Classification to give the film an Over-18s certificate. This prompted Stephen Woolley to publicly harangue the censors,[16] not least because in Ireland it received an Over-15s certificate from the Film Censor.

Following her Oscar-nominated performance for *The End of the Affair*, Jordan cast Julianne Moore as the sole actor in his 14-minute adaptation of Samuel Beckett's *Not I* (1972), a role made famous by Billie Whitelaw. The filming on 35mm of all of Beckett's plays inevitably threw into relief (or disarray) the very precise instructions (stage directions) Beckett attached to every aspect of his plays' productions. Thus, in the shift from the theatre to the cinema (or more correctly, since the Beckett films were shown on television and released on video and DVD, into the living room), the more fluid and subjective experience in the theatre is transformed by the precise cinematic decisions which lock the viewer into the director's point-of-view who, nevertheless, remains a distracted uncentred viewer.

Thus, in *Not I*, the lit mouth is the only part of the anatomy which is visible to the audience, and, in Whitelaw's mesmeric version, the viewer (in the theatre or its televisual version) was glued to it. Jordan chose to film the mouth from five camera angles and these are intercut, often quite rapidly, to produce a different effect. Jordan in the documentary about the series dismisses criticism from Beckettians whom he says privilege only one interpretation of the work. However, it is clear that the cutting from one angle to the next serves as a distracting

(even distancing) from Beckett's intense text. That text presents the viewpoint of the subject in the third person as if the
themes being discussed — conception, birth, death, defecation,
sexual intercourse, words/speech, listening and weeping — are
too painful to be spoken about in the first person. It is no
longer "pure Beckett" but a creative reinterpretation which
arguably works to emphasise television's aesthetic.

In interviews, Jordan has told how Beckett (along with Bob
Dylan and The Rolling Stones) were early influences on him.
Jordan had wished to adapt for the series other plays by
Beckett, but his ideas were at variance with the protective
Beckett estate, which insisted on fidelity to the text. "There is
something about the way Beckett confines actors which is very
interesting," Jordan told an interviewer before shooting *Not I*.
He added that he was going to explore "the whole process of
confinement" and while he declared he would be "absolutely
faithful" to the text, he regarded Beckett as "a jailer". While he
loves his work, he was "not fully convinced by it". Perhaps then
the use of the five camera angles and editing is Jordan's way of
trying to free the actor from the "tyranny" of Beckett's textual
confinement, while still following his stage directions.[17]

Less than two years later, when Jordan had written his first
piece for the theatre since the early 1970s, he was shocked to
realise the difference between the two media. His short play,
White Horses, which he also directed, was performed at the Gate
Theatre Dublin in October 2001 as part of the Dublin Theatre
Festival. In it, George (Peter McDonald) and Paula (Catherine
McCormack) who have been living together in a routine relationship, taking each other for granted, find their relationship
coming under strain. While dividing their music collection,
George discovers a tape recording of Paula's visit to a psychic
(played by Stephen Rea) in which their break-up is foretold.
George and Paula find that they can only speak to each other
through a tape recorder. He listens to her sessions with the psychic, and misreads the man's intentions, whereupon he becomes
jealous of her (platonic) relationship with the psychic. Later,
George replays the tape of his own visit to the psychic. During a
visit to the sea she decides not to swim to her death to avoid

the break-up, but returns to tell George she doesn't love him. George saves her life, but he is devastated as a consequence.

The use of the tape recorder inevitably resonates with theatre's most famous use of the tape recorder in performance in Samuel Beckett's *Krapp's Last Tape* (1958), directed by Atom Egoyan and performed by John Hurt, for the filmed series. In that play, and in Egoyan's filmed version of it, human interaction with technology, a major feature of twentieth-century cultural explorations, is brought to the forefront. Jordan, though, seems to have been as interested in his play with themes and images familiar from his earlier work. As he put it in 2000, "I can never end a story until I get it to the sea" (O'Mahony, 2000: 6).

Perhaps encouraged by the award (along with Van Morrison) in 1998 by the French government of the Distinction of Les Arts et Lettres, as Officer in the Order, Jordan has shown a strong commitment to European mainland projects.[18] While his 2002 feature, *The Good Thief*, which cost $25 million, was funded by the Canadian production and distribution company, Alliance Atlantis, his decision to make the film in France was a conscious rejection of American corporate filmmaking, as noted in the discussion of the film (see Chapter Fourteen).

This commitment to European filmmaking is continuing with one of his next films, ironically his most expensive film so far, the proposed $55–$70 million Italian Renaissance epic about the Borgia family, who dominated Italy during the fifteenth and sixteenth centuries. Initially the script centred on Lucrezia Borgia (1480–1519), who was the daughter of a corrupt pope, Alexander VI, married three times, was accused of incest, and hosted an orgy at the Vatican, with Christina Ricci to play Lucrezia and her brother Cesare to be played by Ewan McGregor. Broadening the scope of the project to encompass the whole family, Jordan commented that it "is about power and treachery and how a family is torn apart by getting what they want. [The papacy] really tears them to shreds".[19]

Notwithstanding Jordan's desire to develop European big budget productions, this project, like many of Jordan's since the mid-1990s, was developed for the Hollywood studio Dream-Works SKG by Imagemovers, and produced by Jack Rapke,

Steve Sharkey and Robert Zemeckis, along with Jordan and Woolley's Company of Wolves. However, its backers, firstly, Myriad Pictures, and then Initial Entertainment Group, which part-funded Martin Scorsese's *Gangs of New York* (2002), balked at the size of the budget, so its scale may need to be pared back before it goes into production.

At another level, Jordan showed his commitment to European ventures when in 1999 he teamed up with film director Jim Sheridan in support of the Amsterdam-based United Pan-Europe Communications (UPC), a joint venture to develop television programming for distribution over television networks in Ireland and elsewhere. Their plan to produce programmes for a new television concept called CityONE was intended to introduce a new type of "vox pop" style interactive programme to television viewers in Dublin.[20] However, the company was linked to Tara Television, which provided Irish programmes on British cable television, and has since collapsed.

Among the other projects Woolley and Jordan have originated through Company of Wolves is *The Actors*, from a short story by Jordan and developed into a screenplay by the playwright Conor McPherson in the expectation that Jordan would direct it. However, perhaps recalling Jordan's own disappointments with film comedies, it was decided that McPherson, whose work is more imbued with comedy than Jordan's, would direct the film. Initially, it was a DreamWorks SKG project, but when they wanted to have a major American star play the lead, it was decided by McPherson and Jordan that it wouldn't work. Consequently, the film was re-financed by Miramax, Film Four and the Irish Film Board.[21] *The Actors* (2003) is a comedy caper which concerns two struggling actors who become involved with Dublin criminals. While researching his role as Richard III in a local production, O'Malley (Michael Caine) befriends a gangster, Barreller (Michael Gambon). O'Malley and his raw young acolyte Tom (Dylan Moran) are forced to disguise themselves in order to pull off a money-making scam.

Other Company of Wolves projects in development are *Breakfast on Pluto*, an adaptation of the Booker-nominated novel from *The Butcher Boy* writer Patrick McCabe; *True History of the*

Kelly Gang from the best-selling novel by Peter Carey; and an original screenplay called *No Man's Land* which is due to be Stephen Rea's directorial debut. By the time these projects are realised, Neil Jordan's next novel may be published . . . Indeed, even before then we may have seen a new Neil Jordan film, another attempt at a big-budget European project, this time from producer Uberto Pasolini (*The Full Monty*) with Michael Kuhn's London-based production company. *The Return*, from a script by playwright and screenwriter Edward Bond (Nicolas Roeg's 1971 *Walkabout*), which has been extensively re-worked by Jordan, seems to explore themes familiar from the director's previous films, such as confusion of identity and the nature of the family. In a reprise of *The Return of Martin Guerre*, this return features Odysseus, disguised as a beggar, who, following the fall of Troy, returns to his island kingdom of Ithaca after ten years away. He finds his faithful wife Penelope besieged by predatory suitors, who believe he is dead. Maintaining his disguise, he goes through a period of tortured self-doubt before revealing his true identity, and killing the usurpers with the aid of his son Telemachus.

Notes

[1] *Excalibur* was based at Ardmore Studios, Bray, County Wicklow, Ireland's only three-sound-stage studios which had opened in 1958 and where Boorman was the chairman of the nationalised company's board during 1975–82, then known as the National Film Studios of Ireland.

[2] Ian Christie (2000), "As Others See Us: British Film-making and Europe in the 90s", in *British Cinema of the 90s*, Robert Murphy, ed., London: British Film Institute, 70.

[3] Redmond Morris's father Lord Killanin was John Ford's Irish contact since they became friends in the 1930s; he worked on *The Quiet Man*, where he is credited under his "secular" name Michael Morris. Killanin and Ford, along with actor Tyrone Power, established an Irish production company, Four Provinces Films Ltd, which made *The Rising of the Moon* (1957) and a couple of other films before becoming dormant.

[4] Neil Jordan Papers, Manuscripts Accessions 4761, Box 5, National Library of Ireland.

[5] Neil Jordan, *South Bank Show*, 1988.

[6] *Sunday Telegraph*, 19 February 1993.

[7] *Sunday Times*, 1 November 1992.

[8] Stephen Rea in conversation with Luke Gibbons and Kevin Whelan, *The Yale Journal of Criticism*, vol. 15, no. 1, spring 2002: 15–16. Rea went on to comment that he aspired to be "a narrative actor of the old American style — experiencing emotion rather than displaying it. . . . Acting should aspire to being pure thought" (p. 16), and that Robert Altman was his favourite film director. Commenting on his relationship with Neil Jordan, he regards him as being "brilliant with narrative" and that "he tells a great story, which makes the acting easier" (p. 15). On a personal level, he said that while they are friendly, "we don't see each other very often. He doesn't have to tell me too much . . . I believe that acting is about getting out of the way of the material, not imposing yourself between the material and the people receiving it" (p. 13).

[9] *Daily Telegraph*, 29 October 1992.

[10] *Variety*, 14 September 1992.

[11] *New York Times*, 26 September 1992.

[12] Incidentally, Jordan is executive producer of *The Last September*, a result, in part, no doubt, of the fact that its producer, Yvonne Thunder, was once his assistant.

[13] *Sunday Business Post*, 22 February 1998.

[14] Ciaran Carty, *Sunday Tribune* Magazine, 20 July 1997: 26.

[15] *Financial Times*, 22 May 1998.

[16] *The Guardian,* 5 February 2000: 18.

[17] Gerry McCarthy, *Sunday Times* Culture, 30 January 2000: 19.

[18] *Irish Times*, 1 July 1998: 8.

[19] John Burns, *The Sunday Times*, 13 October 2002: 8.

[20] *Irish Times*, 3 May 1999: 4.

[21] *Irish Times* magazine, 18 May 2002: 10–14.

Neil Jordan Filmography

Abbreviations key: pc: production company; d: director; sc: scriptwriter/ written by; p: producer; co-p: co-producer; exec. p: executive producer, DoP: Director of Photography/Cameraman; prod. dsgn: production design; m: music composer/conductor; ed: editor.

Films directed and/or written by Neil Jordan

The Making of Excalibur: Myth into Film (USA, 1981)

p/d: Neil Jordan, DoP: Seamus Deasy, graphic dsgn: Hilliard Hayden, ed: Rory O'Farrell, 16mm, 46 mins, colour.

Includes interviews with Excalibur's director John Boorman, designer Tony Pratt, Director of Photography Alex Thomson, actors Paul Gregory (Perceval), Nicol Williamson (Merlin), Cherie Lunghi (Guinevere), Nicholas Clay (Lancelot), Helen Mirren (Morgana).

Angel (Ireland, 1982)

pc: A Motion Picture Company of Ireland Production. In association with Bord Scannán na hÉireann/Irish Film Board. For Channel 4. d/sc: Neil Jordan, p: Barry Blackmore; exec. p: John Boorman; DoP: Chris Menges, ed: J Patrick Duffner; prod dsgn: John Lucas, 92 mins, colour.

Veronica Quilligan (Annie), Stephen Rea (Danny), Alan Devlin (Bill), Peter Caffrey (Ray), Honor Heffernan (Deirdre), Lise-Ann McLoughlin (Bride), Ian McElhinney (Bridegroom), Derek Lord (Best Man), Ray McAnally (Bloom), Donal McCann (Bonner), Marie Kean (Aunt Mae), Don Foley

(Bouncer), Gerald McSorley (Assistant), Liz Bono (Girl Assistant), Tom Collins (Photographer), Tony Rohr (George), Anita Reeves (Beth), Sorcha Cusack (Mary), Michael Lally (Uncle), Macrea Clarke (Francie).

Premiered at Celtic Film Festival, Wexford, 31 March 1982. Neil Jordan won the London *Evening Standard* Award for Most Promising Newcomer for this film, while Chris Menges won the *Evening Standard* Award for Best Technical Achievement.

Company of Wolves (GB, 1984)

pc: ITC Entertainment present A Palace Pictures Production. A Neil Jordan Film. d: Neil Jordan, sc: Angela Carter and Neil Jordan, adapted from her own story by Angela Carter, p: Chris Brown and Stephen Woolley, exec. p: Stephen Woolley and Nik Powell, DoP: Bryan Loftus, prod. dsgn: Anton Furst, art d: Stuart Rose, m: George Fenton, ed: Rodney Holland. 95 mins, colour.

Angela Lansbury (Granny), David Warner (Father), Graham Crowden (Old Priest), Brian Glover (Amorous Boy's Father), Kathryn Pogson (Young Bride), Stephen Rea (Young Groom), Tusse Silberg (Mother), Micha Bergese (Huntsman), Sarah Patterson (Rosaleen), Georgia Slowe (Alice), Susan Porrett (Amorous Boy's Mother), Shane Johnstone (Amorous Boy), Dawn Archibald (Witch Woman), Richard Morant (Wealthy Groom), Danielle Dax (Wolfgirl), Vincent McClaren (Devil Boy), Ruby Buchanan (Dowager), Jimmy Gardner (Ancient), Roy Evans (Eyepatch), Edward Marksen (Lame Fiddler), Jimmy Brown (Blind Fiddler), Terence Stamp (Prince of Darkness), Terry Cade, Gareth Milne, Graeme Crowther, Nick Hobbs, Dinny Powell, Bill Weston, Tex Fuller (Stuntmen).

Winner of best film and Best Director's Award by the London Critics' Circle and a Golden Scroll for Outstanding Achievement from the Academy of Science Fiction and Horror Films.

Mona Lisa (GB, 1986)

pc: Handmade Films, A Palace Pictures Production, d: Neil Jordan, sc: Neil Jordan, David Leland, p: Stephen Woolley, Patrick Cassavetti, co-p: Chris Brown, Ray Cooper, Nik Powell, exec. p: George Harrison, Denis O'Brien, DoP: Roger Pratt, prod. dsgn: Jamie Leonard, m: Michael Kamen, ed: Lesley Walker, 104 mins, colour.

Bob Hoskins (George), Cathy Tyson (Simone), Michael Caine (Mortwell), Robbie Coltrane (Thomas), Clarke Peters (Anderson), Kate Hardie (Cathy), Zoe Nathenson (Jeannie), Sami Davis (May), Rod Bedall (Terry), Joe Brown (Dudley), Pauline Melville (George's wife), Hossein Karimbeik (Raschid).

Bob Hoskins won the Best Actor Award at the Cannes Film Festival, the Golden Globe Award for Best Actor, and an Academy Award nomination for Best Actor. The film itself was nominated for a Golden Globe Award, a Los Angeles Film Critics' Award and a Best Screenplay nomination from the Writers' Guild of America. It was also nominated in the categories of Best Film, Best Director and Best Original Screenplay in the 1986 BAFTAs.

High Spirits (USA, 1988)

pc: Vision P.D.G. A Palace Pictures production, A Neil Jordan Film, d/sc: Neil Jordan, p: Stephen Woolley, David Saunders, co-p: Nik Powell, Selwyn Roberts, exec. p: Mark Damon, Moshe Diamant, Eduard Sarlui, assoc. p: Jon Turtle, DoP: Alex Thomson, prod. dsgn: Anton Furst, ed: Michael Bradsell, 96 mins, colour.

The Irish: Peter O'Toole (Peter Plunkett), Donal McCann (Eamon), Mary Coughlan (Katie), Liz Smith (Mrs Plunkett), Tom Hickey (Sampson), Tony Rohr (Christy), Hilary Reynolds (Patricia), Isolde Cazelet (Julia), Little John (gateman); The Americans: Steve Guttenberg (Jack), Beverly D'Angelo (Sharon), Jennifer Tilly (Miranda), Peter Gallagher (Brother Tony), Martin Ferrero (Malcolm), Connie Booth (Marge), Krista Hornish (Wendy), Matthew Wright (Woody), Paul O'Sullivan (Graham); The Ghosts: Daryl Hannah (Mary Plunkett), Liam Neeson (Martin Brogan), Ray McAnally (Plunkett Senior), Aimee Delamain (Great Granny Plunkett), Ruby Buchanan (Great Aunt Nan), Preston Lockwood (Great Uncle Peter).

We're No Angels (USA, 1989)

pc: Paramount, d: Neil Jordan, sc: David Mamet, based on the play La Cuisine des Anges by Albert Husson, p: Art Linson, exec. p: Robert De Niro, co-p: Fred Caruso, p. assoc: Patti Roberts, DoP: Phillipe Rousselot, prod. dsgn: Wolf Kroeger, 106 mins, colour.

Robert De Niro (Ned), Sean Penn (Jim), Demi Moore (Molly), Hoyt Axton (Father Levesque), Bruno Kirby (Deputy), Ray McAnally (Warden), James Russo (Bobby), Wallace Shawn (Translator), John C. Reilly (Young Monk), Jay Brazeau (Sheriff), Ken Buhay (Bishop Nogulich), Elizabeth Lawrence (Mrs Blair), Bill Murdoch (Deputy), Jessica Jickels (Rosie),

Frank C. Turner (Shopkeeper), Matthew Walker (Blacksmith), Sheelah Newman (Townswoman).

Red Hot & Blue: A Tribute to Cole Porter to Benefit Aids Research (GB, 1990)

pc: Palace Film Company, p: Leigh Blake, Joanne Sellar, "Miss Otis Regrets" and "One of Those Things", part of 17 contemporary performances of Cole Porter's songs in film, d: Neil Jordan, 90 mins, colour. Neil Jordan contribution circa 5 mins.

The Miracle (GB, 1991)

pc: Promenade Film Productions, For Palace Pictures. In association with Film Four International and British Screen. A Palace/ Promenade production. A Neil Jordan Film, d/sc: Neil Jordan, p: Stephen Woolley, Redmond Morris, exec. p: Nik Powell, Bob Weinstein, Harvey Weinstein, DoP: Philippe Rousselot, art d: David Wilson, ed: Joke Van Wijk, m: Anne Dudley, 97 mins, colour.

Beverly D'Angelo (Renée Baker), Donal McCann (Sam Coleman), Niall Byrne (Jimmy Coleman), Lorraine Pilkington (Rose), J.G. Devlin (Beausang), Cathleen Delany (Miss Strange), Tom Hickey (Tommy), Shane Connaughton (Rose's father), Mikkel Gaup (Jonner), Sylvia Teron (Muscular Lady), Anita Reeves (Ballroom Singer), Ruth McCabe (Wardrobe Mistress), Ger O'Leary (Barman); Sam's Band: Earl Gill (trumpet), Johnny Devlin (saxophone), Chris Kenevey (piano), Tommy Donoghue (drums); Destry Rides Again: Stephen Brennan (Johnny/Destry), Martin Dunne (Kent), Stanley Townsend (Washington), Dermod Moore (Brunowski), Mary Coughlan (Mrs Brunowski), Mal Whyte (Mayor), Darragh Kelly (First Cowboy), Alan Archibold (Second Cowboy), The Clane Musical Society (Chorus).

Premiered at the Berlin Film Festival, February 1991, when it was awarded the Prize of the German Art Film Theatre Association. Irish release, 19 April 1991.

The Crying Game (GB, 1992)

pc: Palace Pictures/Channel 4 Films. In Assocation with Eurotrustees and Nippon Film Development Finance Inc (NDF). With the participation of British Screen. A Neil Jordan Film, d/sc: Neil Jordan, p: Stephen Woolley, co-p: Elizabeth Karlsen, exec. p: Diana

Dill, DoP: Ian Wilson, art d: Chris Seagers, m: Anne Dudley, ed: Kant Pan, 112 mins, colour.

Forest Whitaker (Jody), Miranda Richardson (Jude), Stephen Rea (Fergus Hennessy), Adrian Dunbar (Peter Maguire), Breffini McKenna (Tinker), Joe Savino (Eddie), Birdie Sweeney (Tommy), Jaye Davidson (Dil), Andrée Bernard (Jane), Jim Broadbent (Col), Ralph Brown (Dave), Tony Slattery (Deveroux), Jack Carr (Franknum), Josephine White, Shar Campbell (Bar Performers), Brian Coleman (Judge), Ray De-Haan, David Crionnelly (Security Men).

Irish release, 29 October 1992. Nominated for six Academy Awards — Best Picture, Best Director, Best Actor, Best Supporting Actor, Best Achievement in Film Editing, and Best Original Screenplay, for which Neil Jordan won an Oscar. In addition, it was voted Best Foreign Film by the Los Angeles Film Critics' Association and Best Screenplay by the New York Film Critics' Circle and the Writers' Guild of America. It also received the Best Foreign Film Independent Spirit Award and was nominated for a Golden Globe Award for Best Drama and the Mystery of America's Edgar Allan Poe Award for Best Film. In the UK, the film won the BAFTA for Best British Film and was nominated for five other BAFTA Awards including Best Screenplay, Best Actor, Best Supporting Actress and Best Editing. Jordan was selected Best Director by the Guild of Regional Film Writers and nominated for Best Screenplay by the Writers' Guild of Great Britain. The film also received Norway's award for Best Foreign Film. In 1993, Stephen Woolley won the Producer of the Year Award from the Producers' Guild of America and an Academy Award nomination for *The Crying Game.*

Interview with the Vampire: The Vampire Chronicles (USA, 1994)

pc: Geffen Pictures, d: Neil Jordan, sc: Anne Rice, based on her novel *Interview With the Vampire*, p: David Geffen, Stephen Woolley, co-p: Redmond Morris, DoP: Phillipe Rousselot, Rob Legato (Paris), prod. dsgn: Dante Ferretti, m: Elliot Goldenthal, ed: Mick Audsley, Joke van Wijk, 122 mins, colour.

Brad Pitt (Louis), Christian Slater (Malloy), Tom Cruise (Lestat), Stephen Rea (Santiago), Antonio Banderas (Armand), Kirsten Dunst (Claudia), Virginia McCollam (Whore on Waterfront), John McConnell (Gambler),

Mike Seelig (Pimp), Bellina Logan (Tavern Girl), Thandie Newton (Yvette), Lyla Hay Owen (Widow St Clair), Lee Emery (Widow's Lover), Indra Ove, Helen McCrory (New Orleans Whores), Monte Montague (Plague Victim Bearer), Nathalie Bloch (Maid), Jeanette Kontomitras (Woman in Square), Roger Lloyd Pack (Piano Teacher), George Kelly (Dollmaker), Nicole Dubois (Creole Woman), Micha Bergese, Rory Edwards, Marcel Lures, Susan Lynch, Louise Slater, Matthew Sim, François Testory, Andrew Tiernan, Simon Tyrrell, George Yiasoumi (Paris Vampires), Sara Stockridge (Estelle), Laure Marsac (Mortal Woman on Stage), Katia Caballero (Woman in Audience), Louis Lewis-Smith (Mortal Boy), Domiziana Giordano (Madeleine).

Nominated for Best Original Score and Best Art Direction, Academy Awards, 1995.

Michael Collins (USA, 1996)

pc: Warner Bros. Pictures Inc, d/sc: Neil Jordan, p: Stephen Woolley, co-p: Redmond Morris, DoP: Chris Menges, prod. dsgn: Tony Pratt, m: Elliot Goldenthal, ed: Patrick Duffner, 132 mins, colour.

Liam Neeson (Michael Collins), Julia Roberts (Kitty Kiernan), Aidan Quinn (Harry Boland), Alan Rickman (Eamon De Valera), Stephen Rea (Ned Broy), Ian Hart (Joe O'Reilly), Charles Dance (Soames), Brendan Gleeson (Tobin), Stuart Graham (Seamus Cullen), Gerard McSorley (Cathal Brugha), Jim Sheridan (Jameson), Frank Laverty (Sean McKeoin), David Gorry (Charlie Dalton), Tom Murphy (Vinny Byrne), Sean McGinley (Smith), Gary Whelan (Hoey), Frank O'Sullivan (Kavanagh), Jonathan Rhys Myers (the Smiling Youth), Gary Lydon, David Wilmot (Squad Youths), Joe Hanly (Squad Man), Paul Hickey (Dublin Castle Soldier), Tony Clarkin (Soldier), Ian McElhinney (MacBride), Luke Hayden (McCrae), Michael Ford (Black and Tan), Alan Stanford (Vice-Consul MacCready).

Michael Collins won the Golden Lion for Best Film, and Liam Neeson the Best Actor award, the Volpi Cup, at the 1996 Venice Film Festival. Chris Menges was joint winner of the Best Cinematography award of the 1996 Los Angeles Film Critics Association. Elliot Goldenthal (Best Original Score — Motion Picture) and Liam Neeson (Best Performance by an Actor in a Motion Picture Drama), were nominated for the 1997 Golden Globe awards. Nominated for the 1997 Academy Awards in Best Cinematography (Chris Menges) and Best Original Dramatic Score (Elliot Goldenthal). Chris Menges was nominated for the 1997 award for Outstanding Achievement in Cinematography in Theatrical Releases by the American Society of Cinematographers. He was also nominated for Best Cinematography, and Alan Rickman for Best Performance in a Supporting Role, at the 1997 BAFTA awards. Liam Neeson won the 1997 *Evening Standard* British Film Award for Best Actor.

The Butcher Boy (USA, 1997)

pc: Geffen Pictures presents A Neil Jordan Film. Produced with the support and investment incentives for the Irish film industry. d: Neil Jordan, sc: Neil Jordan and Patrick McCabe from the novel *The Butcher Boy* by Patrick McCabe, p: Redmond Morris, Stephen Woolley, exec. p: Neil Jordan, DoP: Adrian Biddle, prod. dsgn: Anthony Pratt, m: Elliot Goldenthal, ed: Tony Lawson, 110 mins, colour.

Stephen Rea (Da Brady), Fiona Shaw (Mrs Nugent), Eamonn Owens (Francie Brady), Alan Boyle (Joe Purcell), Niall Buggy (Father Dom), Brendan Gleeson (Father Bubbles), Peter Gowen (Leddy), Stuart Graham (Priest at College), Ian Hart (Uncle Alo), Tom Hickey (Gardener), Sean Hughes (Psychiatrist 1), John Kavanagh (Dr Boyd), Rosaleen Linehan (Mrs Canning), Pat McGrath (Farmer on Tractor), Sean McGinley (Sergeant), Gerard McSorley (Psychiatrist 2), Gina Moxley (Mary), Sinéad O'Connor (Our Lady/Colleen), Ardal O'Hanlon (Mr Purcell), Milo O'Shea (Father Sullivan), Aisling O'Sullivan (Ma Brady), Anita Reeves (Mrs Coyle), Andrew Fullerton (Philip Nugent), Anne O'Neill (Mrs McGlone), Joe Pilkington (Charlie McGlone), Jer O'Leary (Dublin Man), Pat Leavy (Dublin Café Woman), Janet Moran (Dublin Shopkeeper), Padraic Breathnach (Man on Lorry), John Olohan (Mr Nugent), Mikel Murphy (Buttsy), Brendan Conroy (Devlin), Gregg Fitzgerald, John Finnegan, Gavin Kelty, Eoin Chaney (Bogmen), Ciarán Owens, Shane O'Connor (Boys at Fountain), Paolo Tullio (Mr Caffola), Siobhan McElvaney, Aine McEneaney (Girls in Shooting Gallery), Pat McCabe (Jimmy the Skite), Tony Rohr (Bogman in Mental Hospital), Birdy Sweeney (Man in Well), Marie Mullen (Mrs Thompson), Macdara O'Fatharta (Alien Priest), Ronan Wilmot (Policeman), Vinnie McCabe (Detective), Dermot Healy (Bogman in Hospital).

Premiered at Galway Film Fleadh, July 1997. The film won a Silver Bear Award for Best Director at the Berlin Film Festival, and Eamonn Owens received a special mention for his performance. Neil Jordan was awarded the Crystal Iris Award at the 1998 Brussels International Film Festival.

In Dreams (USA, 1999)

pc: A DreamWorks Picture presentation, d: Neil Jordan, sc: Bruce Robinson and Neil Jordan, based on the novel *Doll's Eyes* by Bari Wood, p: Stephen Woolley, co-p: Redmond Morris, DoP: Darius Khondji, prod. dsgn: Nigel Phelps, m: Elliot Goldenthal, ed: Tony Lawson,100 mins, colour.

Annette Bening (Claire Cooper), Katie Sagona (Rebecca Cooper), Aidan Quinn (Paul Cooper), Robert Downey, Jr (Vivian Thompson), Stephen Rea (Doctor Silverman), Paul Gilfoyle (Detective Jack Kay), Prudence Wright Holmes (Mary), Krystal Benn (Ruby), Pamela Payton-Wright (Ethel), Margo Martindale (Nurse Floyd), Kathleen Langlois (Snow White), Jennifer Berry (Hunter), Emma J Brown, Jennifer Dragon, Samantha Kelly, Jennifer Caine Natenshon, Bethany M Paquin, Erica Sullivan (Dwarves), Amelia Claire Novotny (Prince), Kristin Sroka (Wicked Stepmother), Robert Walsh, Denise Cormier (Couple at School Play), John Flore (Policeman), Ken Cheeseman (Paramedic), Dennis Boutsikaris (Doctor Stevens), Devon Cole Borisoff (Vivian Thompson, as a Boy), Lonnie Farmer (Nurse Rosco), June Lewin (Kindly Nurse), Dorothy Dwyer (Foster Mother), Geoff Wigdor (Vivian Thompson, as a Teenager), Wally Dunn (Walter), Eric Roemele (Security Man, 1970s), Dossy Peabody (Vivian's Mother), John Michael Vaughan (Helicopter Pilot), Brian Goodman (Policeman in Squad Car), Michael Cavanagh (Voice of Judge).

The End of the Affair (USA/Germany, 1999)

pc: Columbia Pictures, A Stephen Woolley production, d: Neil Jordan, sc: Neil Jordan, based on the novel *The End of the Affair* by Graham Greene, p: Stephen Woolley, Neil Jordan, co-p: Kathy Sykes, Neil Jordan, DoP: Roger Pratt, prod. dsgn: Anthony Pratt, m: Michael Nyman, ed: Tony Lawson, 102 mins, colour.

Ralph Fiennes (Maurice Bendrix), Julianne Moore (Sarah Miles), Stephen Rea (Henry Miles), Ian Hart (Mr Parkis), Jason Isaacs (Father Richard Smythe), James Bolam (Mr Savage), Samuel Bould (Lance Parkis), Heather Jay Jones (Henry's Maid), Cyril Shaps (Waiter), Penny Morrell (Bendrix's Landlady), Dr Simon Turner (Dr Gilbert), Deborah Findlay (Miss Smythe), Jack McKenzie (Chief Engineer), Nicholas Hewetson (Chief Warden).

The film was nominated for four Golden Globe Awards, two Academy Awards, including Julianne Moore for Best Actress, and ten BAFTA Awards. Neil Jordan received the BAFTA award for Best Adapted Screenplay.

Not I (Ireland, 2001)

pc: Blue Angel Films and Tyrone Productions for RTE and Channel 4 in association with Bord Scannán na hÉireann/Irish Film Board, Julianne Moore in Samuel Beckett's *Not I* (1972), d: Neil Jordan, p: Stephen Woolley, exec. p: Michael Colgan, Alan Moloney, Joe Mullholland, assoc. p: Edward Beckett, DoP: Roger Pratt, ed: Tony Lawson, 14 mins, colour.

The Good Thief (Canada, 2002)

pc: A Stephen Woolley/Alliance Atlantis/John Wells production, sc/d: Neil Jordan, p: Stephen Woolley, Seaton McLean, DoP: Chris Menges, prod. dsgn: Anthony Pratt, cost. dsgn: Penny Rose, 108 mins, colour.

Nick Nolte (Bob), Tcheky Karyo (Roger), Said Taghmaoui (Paulo), Nutsa Kukhianidze (Anne), Gerard Darmon (Raoul), Marc Lavoine (Remi), Patricia Kell (Yvonne), Warren Zavatta (Petit Louis), Nicolas Dromard (Luigi), Sarah Bridges (Philippa), Ouassini Embarek (Said), Emir Kusturica (Vladimir), Sergio Candiota (Fernandez), Julien Maurel (Philippe), Theo Trifard (Bill), Frederico Scotto (Chief Security Man), Laurent Grevill (Casino Manager), Roland Munter (Spanish Night Club Heavy), Damien Arnone (Security Guard), Mark Polish (Albert), Mike Polish (Bertram), Jean M'bale (Monitor Security Guard), Ralph Fiennes (Tony Angel).

Adaptations of Neil Jordan Work by Other Directors

Miracles and Miss Langan (Ireland, 1979)

A radio play (1972) broadcast by RTE and BBC, adapted by Neil Jordan for television, pc: RTE, d: Pat O'Connor. Transmission, RTE, 1 November 1979, 58 mins.

Deirdre Donnelly (Susan Langan), Malcolm Douglas (Ben d'Arcy), Godfrey Quigley (Headmaster), Jimmy Caffrey, Eithne Lydon, Aine Ni Mhuiri, Michael Duffy, Lise-Ann McLaughlin.

Sean (Ireland, 1980)

Neil Jordan wrote four (of thirteen) episodes in RTE-produced adaptation of Sean O'Casey's *Autobiographies*.

Traveller (Ireland, 1981)

pc: A Joe Comerford Film, British Film Institute Production Board. In association with The Arts Council of Ireland and RTE, d/ed: Joe Comerford, sc: Neil Jordan, p: Margaret Williams, DoP: Thaddeus O'Sullivan, 16mm, 80 mins, colour.

Judy Donovan (Angela Devine), Davy Spillane (Michael Connors), Alan Devlin (Clicky), Marian Richardson (Angela's voice), Johnny Choil Mhadhc (Devine), Paddy Donovan (Connors).

Night in Tunisia (Ireland, 1983)

pc: RTE in association with Channel Four, d/p: Pat O'Connor, sc: Neil Jordan from his short story "Night in Tunisia" from collection *Night in Tunisia and other stories*, DoP: Peter Dorney, cost. dsgn: Inez Nordell, dsgn: Quentin Mitchell, m. dir: Johnny Devlin, ed: Myles Merriman, 1983. Transmission, 9 November 1983, 53 mins. Locations: Bettystown, Laytown, Butlins, County Meath.

Michael ("Mick") Lally (Bill), Ciaran Burns (Luke), Jill Boyle (Rene), Jim Culleton (Nick), Grainne O'Reilly (Rita), Rodney Chichignoud (Jamie).

The Actors (Ireland, 2003)

pc: Company of Wolves with the support of Miramax, Film Four International, and the Irish Film Board, d: Conor McPherson, sc: Conor McPherson from a story by Neil Jordan, p: Stephen Woolley, Redmond Morris, Neil Jordan, DoP: Seamus McGarvey, ed: Emer Reynolds, m: Michael Nyman, 92 mins, colour.

Michael Caine (O'Malley), Michael Gambon (Barreller), Dylan Moran (Tom), Miranda Richardson, Lena Headey, Michael McElhatton, Aisling O'Sullivan, and cameo appearances from film director Damien O'Donnell, Gate Theatre director Michael Colgan, actress Alison Doody and television presenter Marty Whelan.

Other Production Credits — Executive Producer:

The Courier (Joe Lee/Frank Deasy, GB, 1988)

The Last September (Deborah Warner, Ireland/GB/France, 1999)

Selected documentaries/television magazine items about Neil Jordan

Visual Eyes, pc: RTE, Neil Jordan interviewed by Dave Fanning on release of *Mona Lisa*, with extracts from *Angel*, *Company of Wolves* and *Mona Lisa*. Transmission, 13 August 1986, ca. 15 mins.

Freeze Frame, pc: Yellow Asylum for RTE, d: Alan Gilsenan, p: Martin Mahon, location report, interviews with Neil Jordan, producer Steve Woolley, actors and technicians on set of *High Spirits*, and extracts from various Jordan films. Transmission, 15 February 1988, 26 mins.

Neil Jordan: A Profile (Ireland, 1988), pc: Faybury Films, d/sc: Michael Sheridan, p: Paddy Breathnach, DoP; Seamus Deasy, ed: Amanda Sutton, narration: Stanley Townsend, 53 mins, colour. Includes dramatised extracts from the short stories "Skin" and "Night in Tunisia", and from the novel *The Past*. Includes interviews with Ronan Sheehan, Angela Carter, John Boorman, and Beverly D'Angelo.

Neil Jordan (GB, South Bank Show, 1988), pc: Thames Television, presenter: Melvyn Bragg. Retrospective of Neil Jordan's film career as *High Spirits* was being released. Includes interviews with Neil Jordan, *High Spirits* producer David Saunders, actor Peter O'Toole, and designer Anton Furst; and extracts from *Angel*, *Company of Wolves*, *Mona Lisa*, *High Spirits*, *La Strada* (Federico Fellini, 1954) and *The Quiet Man* (John Ford, 1952).

Freeze Frame, pc: RTE, location report on set of *The Miracle* with Neil Jordan interviewed by Michael Dwyer, and with extracts from *Mona Lisa*, *We're No Angels*, and *High Spirits*. Transmission, 28 March 1991, 26 mins.

Kenny Live, pc: RTE, Neil Jordan interviewed by Pat Kenny on release of *The Crying Game*. Transmission, 31 October 1992, 15 mins.

Neil Jordan (GB, Late Show, BBC2 TV, 17 January 1995), Upon release of *Interview with the Vampire* and publication of *Sunrise with Sea Monster*, review of career. Interviews with Neil Jordan, Patrick McCabe, Jim Sheridan, Stephen Woolley, John Banville and Stephen Rea, who also reads from *Night in Tunisia* and *Sunrise with Sea Monster*, 17 mins.

The Late Late Show, pc: RTE, Neil Jordan interviewed by Gay Byrne on release of *Interview with the Vampire* with two extracts from film, and the publication of *Sunrise with Sea Monster*. Transmission, 20 January 1995.

Irish Cinema: Ourselves Alone? (Ireland, 1995), pc: Poolbeg Productions for RTE and Bord Scannan na hÉireann/ Irish Film Board, p/d: Donald Taylor Black, sc: Kevin Rockett, ed: Maurice Healy, 50 mins, colour. Includes an interview with Neil Jordan and extracts from *Angel* and *High Spirits*.

Neil Jordan (GB, South Bank Show, 1996), pc: Thames Television, presenter: Melvyn Bragg. Neil Jordan interviewed on release of *Michael Collins* by Melvyn Bragg. Others interviewed are Michael Collins's biographer Tim Pat Coogan; historian John Regan; counter-insurgency expert Col. Michael Dewar; politician and Michael Collins's niece, Mary Banotti; unionist politician David Ervine; poet Tom Paulin; film producer Stephen Woolley; actor Liam Neeson; and journalist Ed Moloney. Includes extracts from *Michael Collins*, 51 mins.

Neil Jordan Bibliography

"On Coming Home" (first short story by Neil Jordan to be published), *Irish Press*, 14 September 1974: 6.

"Song of the Retired Madame" (poem), in *St Stephen's*, vol. 3, no. 2, 1975: 38.

"Skin" (short story), *Irish Press*, 1 February 1975: 6.

"Mr Solomon" and "Outpatient" (short stories), *Irish Press*, 19 July 1975: 6.

"The Bird Imitator" (short story), *Icarus*, no. 68, 1975: 39–40.

"Last Rite" (short story), *Stand*, vol. 16, no. 4, 1975: 10 - 14.

Night in Tunisia and other stories (1976), Dublin: The Irish Writers' Co-Operative, Dublin; reprinted, 1977; Readers' and Writers' Co-Operative, London, 1979; Brandon Books, Dingle, Co. Kerry, 1982; New York: Vintage, 1993.

"The House" (short story), *Icarus*, no. 69, 1976: 18–22.

"Her Soul" and "Café" (short stories), *Journal of Irish Literature*, vol. 2, May 1976: 13–17.

"Sand" (short story), *Irish Press*, 20 November 1976: 6.

"Skin" (short story), *Best Irish Short Stories*, David Marcus, ed., London: Paul Elek, 1976: 57–63.

"A Bus, A Bridge, A Beach" and "The Old Fashioned Lift" (short stories) in *Paddy No More: Modern Irish Short Stories*, William Vorm, ed., Dublin: Wolfhound Press, 1977: 99–118.

"Watching Sea from Balearics" (poem), in *Broadsheet*, no. 19, 1978: 26–30.

"Word and Image" (film review), *Film Directions*, vol. 1, no. 2, 1978: 10–11.

The Past (novel, 1980), London: Jonathan Cape; London: Vintage, 1993.

The Dream of A Beast (novella, 1983), London: Chatto & Windus; The Hogarth Press, 1989.

Mona Lisa (screenplay with David Leland, 1986), London: Faber and Faber.

"Lines Written in Dejection", *Producer* (London), May 1987. Also included in *High Spirits* (1989b).

"The Woman Who Did" (short story), *Irish Times,* 29 August 1985: 11.

Angel (screenplay, 1989a), London: Faber and Faber.

High Spirits (screenplay, 1989b), London: Faber and Faber.

"Neil Jordan's Guilty Pleasures" (favourite films), *Film Comment*, vol. 28, no. 6, Nov–Dec 1992: 36–9.

A Neil Jordan Reader (1993a): *Night in Tunisia and other stories* (1976); *The Dream of A* Beast (1983), and *The Crying Game* (1993), New York: Vintage.

The Crying Game (screenplay, 1993b), London: Vintage.

Sunrise with Sea Monster (novel, 1994), London: Chatto & Windus.

Michael Collins: Film Diary and Screenplay (1996), London: Vintage.

"Tally Ho! Mr Harris" (1996b) (reply to Eoghan Harris's attack on *Michael Collins*), *Irish Times*, 23 October 1996: 13.

<u>Note</u>: *Source material references for Neil Jordan's films by Angela Carter (1977; 1995), Graham Greene (2001), Patrick McCabe (1992), Anne Rice (1976), and Bari Wood (1993) may be found in the General Bibliography.*

Neil Jordan Papers, Manuscripts Accessions 4761, National Library of Ireland

Box 1 contains *Mona Lisa* script dated January 1985 (3 copies), script, 8 February 1985; script, March 1985; script, 3 April 1985, script, 2 May 1985; undated script outline, partial drafts, typed and handwritten, and book proofs (3 copies) of *Mona Lisa* screenplay.

Box 2 contains "Travellers" outline, undated; typed and handwritten drafts of *The Soldier's Wife*, including "Final Outline", undated; *The Soldier's Wife* script, 9 June 1991; script, 11 June 1991; rewrites, 12 August 1991; 2nd draft dated 24 September 1991 (3 copies); outline production schedule, 2 October 1991; and two-page outline *Rikki's Hands*.

Box 3 contains *High Spirits* storyboard, 6 November 1987; *The Miracle*, 1st draft, incomplete, n.d; 2nd draft, n.d; 3rd draft, 5 February 1990 (2 copies); rewrites, including *Destry* rewrites from *The Miracle*, ca. 7 May 1990.

Box 4 contains *The Miracle*, final script, 5 February 1990; rewrites and amendments; *We're no Angels*, David Mamet script, 1st draft, December 1987 (3 copies); storyboard of Ned and Rosie falling into river; *We're No Angels* handwritten notepad, n.d.; other drafts.

Box 5 contains *Ghost Tours*, original script, n.d; *Hotel d'Esprit* — A Treatment; *High Spirits* script, 9 September 1987; undated drafts, rewrites, scene outline; storyboard of bus crash scene, handwritten amendments and rewrites; memo on script from Warner Bros., 30 March 1987; rewrite by Neil Jordan of Kampmann/Porter version, 2 April 1987.

Box 6 contains *Ghost Tours* by Neil Jordan and Michael McDonnell, 13 August 1986; *High Spirits* 1st draft, 17 September 1986; 2nd draft, 21 October 1986; script, 31 October 1986; notes on script outline, Neil Jordan, 15 March 1987; script, 1987; rewrite, 1 April 1987; script, 9 April 1987; script, 19 October 1987; storyboards, set plans; script, 10 August 1987; notebook.

Box 7 contains *Brute Music*, A Film, 1st treatment, June 1980; *Brute Music* and *Angel* outlines, undated; *The Miracle*, 3rd draft, 5 February 1990 (3 copies); Outline, "Stardust. Lost Sex. Story."; storyboard, *The Miracle*; handwritten scene, n.d.

General Bibliography

Anwell, Maggie (1988), "Lolita Meets the Werewolf" in *The Female Gaze*, Lorraine Gamman and Margaret Marshment, eds., London: The Women's Press, pp. 76–85.

Barra, Allen (1990), "Here Comes Mr Jordan" (interview), *American Film*, vol. 15, no. 4, pp. 36–41, 55.

Barry, Kevin (1982), "Discarded Images: Theories of Narrative in Cinema", *The Crane Bag*, vol. 6, no. 1, pp. 45–51.

Behan, Brendan (1959), *The Hostage*, London: Methuen.

Bettelheim, Bruno (1978), *The Uses of Enchantment*, London: Penguin; orig. London: Thames and Hudson, 1976.

Brophy, Philip (1986) "Horrorality: The Textuality of Contemporary Horror Films" in *The Horror Reader*, Ken Gelder, ed. (2000), London: Routledge, pp. 276–84; orig. in *Screen*, vol. 27, no. 1.

Brown, Terence (1981), *Ireland: A Social and Cultural History 1922–79*, London: Fontana.

Burke, Marina (1993), *Film Ireland*, No. 34, April/May, pp. 16–21.

Butler Cullingford, Elizabeth (2001), *Ireland's Others: Gender and Ethnicity in Irish Literature and Popular Culture*, Cork: Cork University Press.

Byrne, Paul (1999), "The Dream Maker" (interview), *The Big Ticket*, vol. 2, no. 4, pp. 22–3.

Byrne, Terry (1997), *Power in the Eye: An Introduction to Irish Film*, Lanham, Maryland: Scarecrow Press.

Carter, Angela (1977), "The Company of Wolves", in *Bananas*, no. 3, Emma Tennant, ed., London/Melbourne/New York: Quarter Books. Reprinted in Angela Carter (1979), *The Bloody Chamber*.

Carter, Angela (1995), *The Bloody Chamber*, London: Vintage; orig., London: Victor Gollancz, 1979.

Carty, Ciaran (2000), "Jordan's Journey", *Sunday Tribune*, 30 January 2000: 10–11.

Christie, Ian (1985), *Arrows of Desire: The Films of Michael Powell and Emeric Pressburger*, London: Waterstone.

Comiskey, Ray (1986), "Neil Jordan: Future Intense Perfect", *Irish Times*, 6 September 1986.

Cullen, Fintan (1997), *Visual Politics: The Representation of Ireland 1750–1930*, Cork: Cork University Press.

Curtis, L.P. (1971), *Apes and Angels*, Newton Abbot: David and Charles.

Curtis, Liz (1984), *Nothing But the Same Old Story: The Roots of Anti-Irish Racism*, London: Information on Ireland.

Dick, Leslie (1998), "*The Butcher Boy*" (review), *Sight and Sound*, vol. 8, no. 3, pp. 44.

Dwyer, Michael (1997), *Neil Jordan in Conversation with Michael Dwyer at the Galway Film Fleadh, July 13 1997*, The Fleadh Papers, vol. 2, Galway: A *Film West* Publication (booklet).

Edge, Sarah (1995), "'Women are trouble, did you know that Fergus?': Neil Jordan's *Crying Game*", *Feminist Review*, no. 50, summer.

Finney, Angus (1997) *The Egos have Landed: The Rise and Fall of Palace Pictures*, London: Mandarin; orig. 1996.

Foster, R.F. (1993), *Paddy & Mr Punch*, London: Penguin.

Gallagher Winarski, Kathleen (1999), "Neil Jordan's *Miracle*: From Fiction to Film", in *Contemporary Irish Cinema: From* The Quiet Man *to* Dancing at Lughnasa, James MacKillop, ed., Syracuse: Syracuse University Press.

Gibbons, Luke (1992), "On the Beach", *Artform*, October, p. 13.

Gibbons, Luke (1996a), *Transformations in Irish Culture*, Cork: Cork University Press.

Gibbons, Luke (1996b), "Engendering the State: Narrative, Allegory and *Michael Collins*", *Eire/Ireland*, nos. 3/4, fall/winter: 261–9.

Gibbons, Luke (1997a), "Demisting the Screen: Neil Jordan's *Michael Collins*", *The Irish Literary Supplement*, vol. 16, no. 1, spring.

Gibbons, Luke (1997b), "Framing History: Neil Jordan's *Michael Collins*", *History Ireland*, vol. 5, no. 1, pp. 47–51.

Gibbons, Luke (2002), *The Quiet Man*, Cork: Cork University Press.

Giles, Jane (1997), *The Crying Game*, London: British Film Institute.

Glicksman, Marlaine (1990), "Irish Eyes" (interview), *Film Comment*, vol. 26, no. 1, pp. 9–11, 68–71.

Greene, Graham (2001), *The End of the Affair*, London: Vintage; orig. 1951.

Grene, Nicholas (2000), "Black Pastoral: 1990s Images of Ireland", in *Litteraria Pragensia*, vol. 10, no. 20.

Grimm, Jacob and Wilhelm (1982), *Selected Tales*, trans., Introduction and notes, David Luke, London: Penguin.

Hill, John (1999), "Allegorising the Nation: British Gangster Films of the 1980s", in *British Crime Cinema*, Steve Chibnall and Robert Murphy, eds., London/New York: Routledge.

Hill, John (1987), "Images of Violence", in Rockett *et al.*

Hopper, Keith (2001), "'A Gallous Story and a Dirty Deed': Word and Image in Neil Jordan and Joe Comerford's *Traveller* (1981)", *Irish Studies Review*, vol. 9, no. 2, August 2001: 179–91.

Hopper, Keith (1997), "'Cat Calls from the Cheap Seats': The Third Meaning of Neil Jordan's *Michael Collins*", *The Irish Review*, no. 21, autumn/winter 1997: 1–28.

James, Joy (1995), "Black *Femmes Fatales* and Sexual Abuse in Progressive 'White' Cinema: Neil Jordan's *Mona Lisa* and *The Crying Game*," *Camera Obscura*, no. 36, September: 33–47.

Kearney, Richard (1982), "Avenging Angel: An Analysis of Neil Jordan's First Irish Feature Film", *Studies*, autumn: 297–302.

Kelly, Richard (1999), "*In Dreams*" (review), *Sight and Sound*, vol. 9, no. 5, pp. 50–1.

Kuznets, Lois Rostow (1994), *When Toys Come Alive*, New Haven and London: Yale University Press.

Linehan, Hugh (2000), "Green Giant", *Irish Times*, 27 January 2000.

Lloyd, David (1999), *Ireland after History*, Cork: Cork University Press.

McCabe, Patrick (1992), *The Butcher Boy*, London: Picador.

McCarthy, Gerry (2000a), "Jordan's Affair of the Head", *Sunday Times* (Culture section), 16 January 2000: 8.

McCarthy, Gerry (2000b), "*The End of the Affair*", *Film West*, no. 39: 12–15.

McLoone, Martin (1998), "The Abused Child of History: Neil Jordan's *The Butcher Boy*", Cineaste, vol. XXIII, no. 4, pp. 32–6.

McLoone, Martin (2000), *Irish Film: The Emergence of a Contemporary Cinema*, London: British Film Institute.

McSwiney, Seamus (1996), "Treaty Makers and Filmmakers", *Film West*, no. 26, autumn: 10–16.

Marx, Leo, (1964), *The Machine in the Garden*, New York: Oxford University Press.

Miller, William Ian (1997), *The Anatomy of Disgust*, Cambridge, MA/London: Harvard University Press.

Moretti, Franco (1995) "Dialectic of Fear" (extract) in *The Horror Reader*, Ken Gelder, ed. (2000), London: Routledge: 148–160.

Murphy, Kathleen (1999) "A Study in Scarlet", *Film West*, no. 36, pp. 12–15. Extract from article of same title, orig. in *Film Comment*, vol. xxxv, no. 2: 12–15.

O'Connor, Frank (1931), *Guests of the Nation and Other Stories*, London: Macmillan.

O'Mahony, John (2000), "Big-Screen Visionary", *The Guardian*, 29 January 2000: review 6–7.

O'Toole, Fintan (1996), "The Man Who Shot Michael Collins", *Independent on Sunday*, 3 November 1996, magazine section.

Peachment, Chris (1982), "Bad Day Near Black Rock", *Times*, 27 October.

Pramaggiore, Maria (1998), "The Celtic Blue Note: Jazz in Neil Jordan's 'Night in Tunisia', *Angel* and *The Miracle*", Screen, Vol. 39, no. 3, autumn.

Pramaggiore, Maria (1999), "'I Kinda Like You as a Girl': Masculinity, Postcolonial Queens, and the 'Nature' of Terrorism in Neil Jordan's *The Crying Game*", in *Contemporary Irish Cinema: From* The Quiet Man *to* Dancing at Lughnasa, James MacKillop, ed., Syracuse: Syracuse University Press.

Rafferty, Terrence (1994), "*Interview with the Vampire*", New Yorker, 21 November; reprinted in *Flesh and Blood*, Peter Keough, ed., San Francisco: Mercury House, 1995.

Raftery, Mary and Eoin O'Sullivan (1999), *Suffer the Little Children*, Dublin: New Island Books.

Rice, Anne (1976), *Interview with the Vampire*, London: Warner.

Rockett, Kevin, Luke Gibbons, John Hill (1987), *Cinema and Ireland*, London: Croom Helm; (1988), London: Routledge.

Rogers, Lori (1997) "'In Dreams Uncover'd': Neil Jordan, *The Dream of a Beast* and the Body-Secret" *Studies in Contemporary Fiction*, vol 39, no. 1, pp. 48–54.

Seltzer, Mark (1998) "The Serial Killer as a Type of Person", in *The Horror Reader*, Ken Gelder, ed. (2000), London: Routledge, 97–107; orig. in *Serial Killers*, New York: Routledge.

Sheehy, Ted (1998), "*The Butcher Boy*" (interview), *Film Ireland*, no. 63, February/March: 14–15.

Taubin, Amy (1995a), "Bloody Tales", *Sight and Sound*, vol. 5, no. 1, pp. 8–11.

Taubin, Amy (1995b), "The Dispossessed", *The Village Voice*, 26 January 1999, pp. 64.

Toibin, Colm (1982), "The *In Dublin* Interview: Neil Jordan Talks with Colm Toibin", *In Dublin*, no. 152, 29 April.

Wood, Bari (1993), *Doll's Eyes*, London: Harper Collins.

Young, Lola (1990), "A Nasty Piece of Work: A Psychoanalytical Study of Sexual and Racial Difference in *Mona Lisa*", in *Community, Culture, Difference*, J. Rutherford, ed., London: Lawrence & Wishart.

Zilliax, Amy (1995), "'The Scorpion and the Frog': Agency and Identity in Neil Jordan's *The Crying Game*", *Camera Obscura*, no. 35, May.

Zipes, Jack (1993), *The Trials and Tribulations of Little Red Riding Hood*, 2nd edition, New York and London: Routledge.

Zizek, S. (1993), "From Courtly Love to *The Crying Game*", *New Left Review*, no. 202, November/December, pp. 95–108.

Index